LONDON'S
SECRET PLACES

Graeme Chesters & David Hampshire

Survival Books • Bath • England

First published 2013

Survival Books Limited
Office 169, 3 Edgar Buildings
George Street, Bath BA1 2FJ, United Kingdom
☎ +44 (0)1935-700060, ✉ info@survivalbooks.net
🖥 www.survivalbooks.net

British Library Cataloguing in Publication Data
A CIP record for this book is available
from the British Library.

ISBN: 978-1-907339-92-9

Printed in Singapore by International Press Softcom Limited

Acknowledgements

We've been the fortunate recipients of much help, support and enthusiasm in researching and writing this book. In addition to the many photographers who provided images, we would like to heartily thank the following people, in no particular order: David Perkins (Roots & Shoots), Helen Idle (Rivington Place), Penny Fussell (Drapers' Company), Mick Taylor (Wandle Industrial Museum), Ginette Kentish (Musical Museum), Rachel Bairsto (BDA Museum), Julie Ryan & Douglas Lee (Capel Manor), Imbal Mizrahi (Photographers' Gallery), Susan Bowler (Queen's Larder), Gary Brailsford-Hart (City of London Police), Matthew Jones (College of Arms), Susan Fenwick (Company of Watermen & Lightermen), Liberty Rowley (Mall Galleries), Clare Sexton (Valence House), Anna Evans (Royal Court Theatre), Natacha Antolini (Institut français), Catherine Parry-Wingfield (Sandycombe Lodge), Heather Jones (London Wildlife Trust), Doug Daniels (Hampstead Observatory), Varind Ramful (Serpentine Gallery), Sarah Eicker (Fitzroy House), Liz McAllister (Freightliners Farm), Tim Webb (RSPB), Hardip Sohal (Valentines Mansion), Adam (Fullers Brewery), Paul Williams (Honeywood Museum), Ann Vincent (House Mill), Alison Wright (Camden Arts Centre), New Collier & Michael Sherry (Brunei Gallery), Claire (de Morgan Centre), Brenda Martin (Dorich House Museum), Amy Rolph (RFU), Marina (Wimbledon Lawn Tennis Museum) and Sue Bradburn (Royal College of Art).

Finally, special thanks are due to Peter Read, who commissioned and edited this book, Alex Browning for proof-reading, Di Bruce-Kidman for the DTP and cover design, Jim Watson for the superb maps and our partners (Louise and Grania), for continuing with the pretence that writing is a proper job. Last, but not least, a special thank you to the many photographers who provided images (listed on page 318) – the unsung heroes – whose beautiful images add colour and bring London to life.

London's Hidden Secrets

A Guide to the City's Quirky & Unusual Sights

ISBN: 978-1-907339-44-0

Graeme Chesters

A unique and unusual guide to London's hidden and lesser-known sights not found in standard guidebooks. London is a city with a cornucopia of secret places, being ancient, vast and in a constant state of flux. London's Hidden Secrets takes you off the beaten path to seek out the more unusual places that often fail to register on the radar of both visitors and residents alike, and aims to sidestep the chaos and queues of London's tourist-clogged attractions and visit its quirkier, more mysterious side.

£10.95

London's Hidden Secrets Volume 2

Discover More of the City's Amazing Secret Places

ISBN: 978-1-907339-79-0

Graeme Chesters
& David Hampshire

Hot on the heels of London's Hidden Secrets comes another volume of the city's largely undiscovered sights, many of which we were unable to include in the original book. In fact, the more research the authors did, the more treasures they found, until eventually a second volume was inevitable. Inside you'll discover a wealth of historic churches and other ancient buildings; secret gardens and 'lost' cemeteries; fascinating small museums and galleries; atmospheric pubs and stunning hotels; cutting-edge art and design, and much more: 140 destinations in all corners of the city. Written by two experienced London writers, LHS 2 is for both those who already know the metropolis and newcomers wishing to learn more about its hidden and unusual charms.

£10.95

Contents

3. KENSINGTON & CHELSEA 99

4. CAMDEN & ISLINGTON 119

NOTE

Before visiting anywhere mentioned in this book, it's advisable to check the opening times, which are liable to change without notice.

Introduction

L ondon is one of the world's leading tourist destinations with a wealth of world-class attractions – more than any other city in the world – that draw millions of visitors a year; amazing museums and galleries, beautiful parks and gardens, stunning palaces and grand houses, and much, much more. These are covered in numerous excellent tourist guides and online, and need no introduction here. What aren't so well known are London's numerous smaller attractions, most of which are neglected by the throngs who descend upon the tourist-clogged major sights. What *London's Secret Places* does is seek out the city's lesser-known, but no less worthy, 'hidden' attractions.

When we set out to research and write this book's sister title *London's Hidden Secrets*, we had no idea just how many treasures we would find – and the more research we did, the more 'secrets' we discovered – until a second volume and this third book became inevitable. We have both lived and worked throughout the city and, like most long-term London residents, we thought we knew the city pretty well. However, we were surprised to find just how many little-known delights London has to offer – not only had we previously not visited many of the places featured in this book, we hadn't even heard of many of them!

Inside you'll discover a wealth of fascinating small museums and galleries; historic churches and other ancient buildings; captivating parks and gardens and historic 'lost' cemeteries; atmospheric pubs; cutting-edge art and design; and much more. A total of almost 140 destinations in all corners of the city and its suburbs. Of course, not all are secrets, but many are hidden and largely unknown except to a small band of insiders and locals.

London's Secret Places isn't intended as a walking guide, although many of the places covered are close to one another – particularly in the hubs of Westminster and the City in central London – where you can easily stroll between them. Almost all are, however, close to public transport links and relatively easy to get to. What's more, the vast majority are free, so there's no excuse for not getting out and exploring!

With a copy of *London's Secret Places* to hand to inspire you, you need never be bored of London (or life). Researching and writing this book has been a pleasure and a labour of love – we hope you enjoy discovering the city's secret places as much as we did.

Happy Hunting!   **Graeme Chesters & David Hampshire**
December 2012

Regent's Park

Baker Street

MARYLEBONE

GLOUCESTER PLACE

BAKER

Lancaster Gate

BAYSWATER ROAD

Kensington Gardens

Hyde Park

The Serpentine

25

Royal Albert Hall

KENSINGTON ROAD

KNIGHTSBRIDGE

High Street Kensington

26

27

Victoria & Albert Museum

BROMPTON ROAD

Natural History Museum

South Kensington

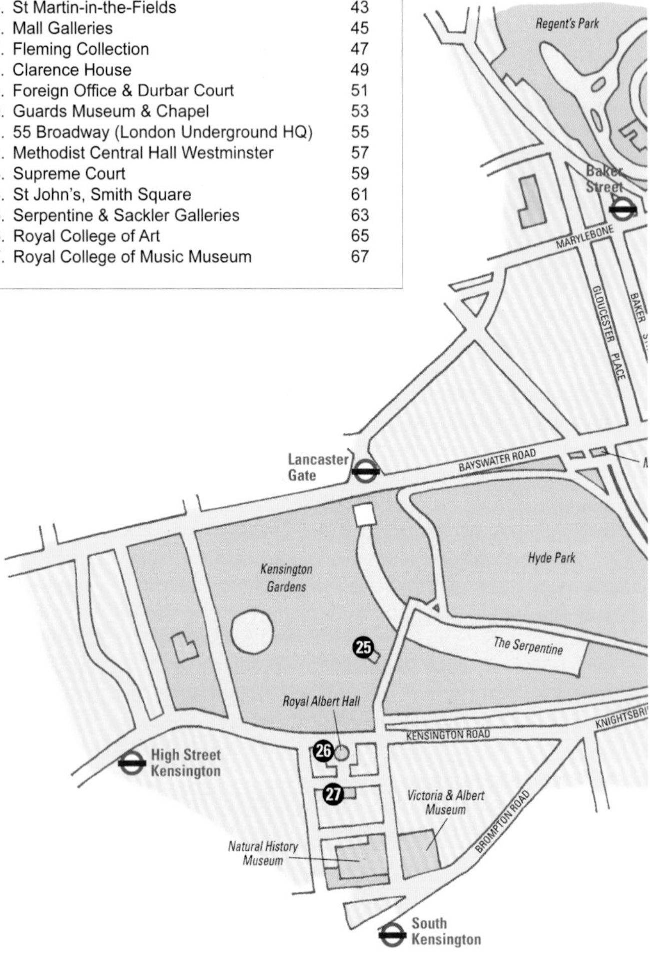

CHAPTER 1

CITY OF WESTMINSTER

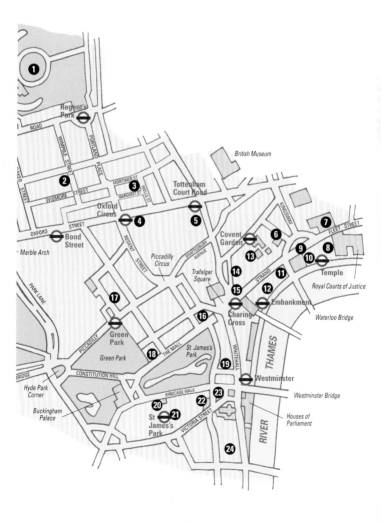

Address: Inner Circle, Regent's Park, NW1 (☎ 020-7486 7905, 🖳 www.londongardensonline.org.uk and www.openairtheatre.org).

Opening hours: Daily, 5am to dusk; garden café, 10am to 4pm (winter), 10am to 9pm (summer).

Cost: Free. Theatre tickets from around £20 to £50 (see website).

Transport: Baker St or Regent's Park tube station.

QUEEN MARY'S GARDENS & OPEN AIR THEATRE

Queen Mary's Gardens – tucked away in the Inner Circle of Regent's Park – contain London's largest and best formal rose garden, and are a honey-pot for garden lovers (and bees) in spring and summer, when tens of thousands of plants are in bloom. The gardens – named after the wife of George V – were laid out in 1932 on a site that had originally been used as a plant nursery and was later leased to the Royal Botanic Society. There are still some of the original pear trees in the gardens, which supplied fruit to the London Market in the early 1800s. Queen Mary's Gardens are most famous for their beautiful rose garden, containing almost every species in existence.

The rose garden contains 400 different varieties of roses in separate and mixed beds, and a total of some 30,000 rose plants, plus around 30,000 other plants including the national collection of delphiniums and 9,000 begonias – a total of over 60,000 plants in landscaped beds surrounded by a ring of pillars covered in climbers and ramblers. The planting was renewed by landscape architects, Colvin and Moggridge, in the '90s and is arranged in a design which is in harmony with the circular site and adds a 'sense of mystery'. Within the rose garden is a small lake filled with ornamental ducks and carp, in the centre of which is an island rockery.

Queen Mary's Gardens plays host to the Open Air Theatre, a permanent venue (now in its 80th season) with a three- to four-month summer season. Each season typically consists of a production of *A Midsummer Night's Dream*, a second Shakespeare play, a musical and a children's show, performed in rotation. The theatre boasts one of the longest 'bars' in any theatre in London, stretching the entire length of the seating, which also serves full meals from an hour and a half before performances begin, as well as during the interval. A BBQ is also provided plus a picnic lawn with tables where the audience can enjoy their own food.

> **The Inner Circle contains the beautiful Triton Fountain – at the northern end of the central walk – designed by William McMillan RA (1887-1977) and donated in 1950 in memory of Sigismund Goetze (1866-1939) by his wife.**

The park also contains the Garden Café, serving teas, coffees, lunch and summer suppers. The perfect spot to round off the perfect day.

❝ *A fragrant theatrical experience…* **❞**

Address: 64 Wimpole Street, W1G 8YS (☎ 020-7563 4549, 🖥 www.bda.org/museum).

Opening hours: Tue and Thu, 1-4pm.

Cost: Free.

Transport: Oxford Circus or Bond Street tube station.

BRITISH DENTAL ASSOCIATION MUSEUM

*T*he British Dental Association (BDA) Museum tells the absorbing – and often painful – history of dental care in the UK. From 19th-century dental floss to toothache cures, clockwork drills to toothpaste adverts, there's more to discover than you may imagine. With over 30,000 items, the museum has the largest collection of material relating to the history of dentistry in the UK, dating from its time as a gruesome public spectacle to the complex procedures and treatment of today.

The BDA Museum began life in 1919, when Lilian Lindsay (the first woman to qualify as a dentist in the UK and the BDA's first female president in 1946), donated several old dental instruments to the association that she had been storing in a box under her bed! The museum was developed primarily for the education of BDA members, but in 1967 (when it moved to its present home) it opened its doors to the general public. In autumn 2005 the museum was redesigned with the aim of making it more accessible to the public, as well as dentists. The collection includes dental instruments and equipment, furniture, photographs, archives, and fine and decorative art.

> **The 18th century saw the first modern, commercially manufactured toothbrush, when in 1780 William Addis began selling brushes made with cow bone handles, with horse or pig hair for bristles.**

The torment of toothache is something we have in common with our ancestors, although those living in Ancient Egypt, Greece and Rome may not have had as many cavities as we have today due to the lack of sugar and processed food in their diet. However, their teeth were worn down by the coarse food they ate, which required much more chewing.

Until the 17th century, the drawing of teeth was done by barber-surgeons, tooth drawers and 'tooth operators'. The term 'dentist' didn't appear until the 18th century, when the French dentist Pierre Fauchard published his treatise *Le Chirurgien Dentiste* in 1728. This set out for the first time everything that was known about dental disease, with full case histories and illustrations of how to deal with them.

We have come a long way since then – as the museum illustrates – and the last century has seen an explosion of new materials, techniques and technology, along with a better understanding of dental disease and its prevention.

An absorbing museum (with a small shop) that – hopefully – won't give you nightmares.

❝ *A pain-free visit to the dentist* **❞**

AT A GLANCE

Address: **7 Margaret Street, W1W 8JG** (☎ **020-7636 1788,**
🖥 **www.allsaintsmargaretstreet.org.uk).**

Opening hours: **Daily, 7am to 7pm. See website for services times.**

Cost: **Free (but donations are welcome).**

Transport: **Oxford Circus tube station.**

ALL SAINTS MARGARET STREET

*A*ll Saints Margaret Street is a stupendous (Grade I listed) Anglican church built in the High Victorian Gothic Revival style, celebrated for its architecture, style of worship and musical tradition. It was designed by prolific church architect William Butterfield (1814-1900) and built between 1849 and 1859 at a cost of £70,000.

Butterfield departed considerably from medieval Gothic practice, using red brick for the church – long out of fashion in London – with the walls banded and patterned in black brick, and the spire banded with stone. The interior is richly patterned, with inlays of marble and tile. The east wall of the chancel is covered by a series of paintings on gilded boards, the work of Ninian Comper (1864-1960) in 1909, and a restoration of earlier work by William Dyce. The Lady Chapel is also by Comper.

The church's style of worship is Anglo-Catholic, that is 'the Catholic faith as taught by the Church of England', offering members and visitors a traditional style of liturgy as advocated by the Oxford Movement of the mid-19th century, including ritual, choir and organ music, vestments and incense.

> "It is the first piece of architecture I have seen, built in modern days, which is free from all signs of timidity or incapacity... it challenges fearless comparison with the noblest work of any time. Having done this, we may do anything: there need be no limits to our hope or our confidence."
>
> **John Ruskin (1819-1900)**

All Saints is also noted for its musical tradition. The organ, built in 1910, is a four-manual Harrison and Harrison instrument with 65 speaking stops. Until 1968, the music was provided by a choir of men and boys, who were honoured to sing at the coronations of Edward VII, George V and VI, and Elizabeth II. (William Lloyd Webber, father of composer Andrew and cellist Julian, was the Director of Music from 1939-1948.) When the choir school (which counted Laurence Olivier as an alumnus) closed in 1968, a professional adult choir was introduced. The repertoire for choir and organ stretches from the Renaissance to the 21st century, and includes several pieces commissioned for the church.

All Saints has been described as a 'savage masterpiece' (attributed to K Theodore Hoppen) and an 'orgasm' (Ian Nairn), who said that 'the building could only be understood in terms of compelling, overwhelming passion'. One of the great monuments of Victorian art.

❝ *Butterfield's masterpiece will amaze and delight you* **❞**

PHOTOGRAPHERS' GALLERY

*T*he Photographers' Gallery is the largest public gallery in London dedicated to photography. From the latest emerging talent, to historical archives and established artists, it's *the* place to see photography in all its forms. It was the first independent gallery in Britain devoted to photography, founded by Sue Davies in 1971 at 8 Great Newport Street in a converted Lyon's Tea Bar. Nine years later the gallery expanded to include an additional gallery space at 5 Great Newport Street, thus occupying two separate sites on the same street. In December 2008, the gallery moved to a nearby building on Ramillies Street, a former warehouse built in 1910, where a major redevelopment was begun in 2010.

Designed by award-winning Irish architects O'Donnell+Tuomey, the galley features three dedicated floors of gallery spaces. Situated at the heart of the building, between two of the exhibition floors, is the studio floor, which hosts a range of talks, events, workshops and courses, as well as a *camera obscura*, the study room, and Touchstone – a changing display of a single photographic work. Complementing the exhibition and education floors are a new bookshop, a print sales room and a café/bar, all at street level.

The Photographers' Gallery has been instrumental in establishing photography's important role in culture and society. It has provided a focus for the medium in London and was the first public gallery in the country to exhibit key names in international photography such as Juergen Teller (fashion), Robert Capa (photojournalism), Sebastião Salgado (documentary) and Taryn Simon (contemporary art), while also promoting the work of UK-based photographers such as Martin Parr, Zineb Sedira and Corinne Day.

One of Europe's foremost galleries dedicated to photography, The Photographers' Gallery awards the high-profile annual Deutsche Börse Photography Prize, worth £30,000 in 2012. Past prize winners include Andreas Gursky (1998), Shirana Shahbazi (2002), Robert Adams (2006), and Sophie Ristelhueber (2010). There's also an annual graduates' exhibition – FreshFacedandWildEyed (FFWE) – which celebrates the breadth and dynamism of photographic work produced by recent graduates across the UK.

The Photographers' Gallery occasionally displays work from unexpected sources, for example its exhibition of photographs from The London Fire Brigade archives and a presentation of studio portrait photography by Harry Jacobs, a high street studio photographer who worked for over 40 years in south London.

A wealth of inspiration for everyone from phone snappers to professionals.

 A picture perfect gallery for the 21st century

Address: House of St Barnabas, 1 Greek Street, Soho Square, W1D 4NQ (☎ 020-7437 1894, 🖥 www.hosb.org.uk).

Opening hours: Tours – between 9am and 11am on Tue and Thu – contact HOSB for information. The house can also be hired for events.

Cost: Contact HOSB.

Transport: Tottenham Court Road tube station.

THE HOUSE OF ST BARNABAS-IN-SOHO

*T*he House of St Barnabas in Soho (Grade I listed) is a Georgian building with one of the finest Rococo plasterwork interiors in London. The house was completed as a shell in 1746 and sold to the Beckford family, wealthy plantation owners and politicians in Jamaica and England. It was Richard Beckford who commissioned the interior design, completed in 1754. As Soho became less fashionable at the end of the Georgian era, the house became the offices of the Metropolitan Board of Works in 1811 and the famous civil engineer Sir Joseph Bazalgette worked here.

> Outside the house attached to the railings is the 'Penny Chute' – still in use today – where coins fall down a pipe to the alms box in the kitchen below.

In 1862 the House of Charity – founded to help homeless people in Victorian Society – moved into the house. The charity was founded in 1846 by Dr Henry Monro, a physician from Bethlem Hospital (see page 309) in Southwark, and Mr Roundell Palmer, a barrister who became Lord Chancellor of England. One of the first tasks of the charity was to build the magnificent Chapel of St Barnabas (designed by Joseph Clarke), built on the site of the Georgian stable yard. Daily church attendance was expected of hostel occupants, hence the chapel, which is still in use today.

The house boasts an array of stunning 18th-century period features; chandeliers, silk-lined walls and delicate Rococo plasterwork, plus a lovely, secluded private garden – one of only two in Soho – surrounded by ivy-covered walls. The house has been restored to its original glory by designer Russell Sage, creating a distinctive and stylish environment, with a perfect mix of faded grandeur and witty English eccentric details.

Between the house and the chapel lies the courtyard, also known as the 'secret garden', with an association with Charles Dickens. Research published in 'The Dickensian' in 1963 suggests that the historic rooms and gardens of the house were the fictitious lodgings of Dr Manette and Lucy in *A Tale of Two Cities*.

The House of Charity was renamed the House of St Barnabas-in-Soho in 1961, and provided refuge and accommodation for homeless people in and around Soho for 160 years, until closing as a residence in 2006, and being re-launched as a venue and Life Skills Centre.

❝ *The most beautiful (ex) hostel in the world* **❞**

Address: **Catherine Street, WC2B 5JF** (☎ **020-7850 8790, tours 0844-412 2705,** ⌨ **www.royaldrurylanetheatrelondon.com and www. reallyuseful.com/theatres/theatre-tours).**

Opening hours: **Tours (1 hr) Mon-Wed and Fri, 2.15 and 4.15pm, Thu and Sat, 10.15 and 11.45am.**

Cost: **Tours – adults £9, Children £7, groups (min. 10) £6.50 per person. For shows see website.**

Transport: **Covent Garden tube station.**

THEATRE ROYAL DRURY LANE

*T*he Theatre Royal Drury Lane (Grade I listed) is one of London's most historic and splendid theatres. The building you see today is the most recent in a line of four theatres at the same location dating back to 1663, the first of which was built at the behest of Thomas Killigrew in the early years of the English Restoration. Actors who appeared at the 'Theatre Royal in Bridges Street' included Nell Gwyn (who met Charles II here) and Charles Hart. It was destroyed by fire in 1672 and replaced by a larger theatre designed by Sir Christopher Wren. Renamed the 'Theatre Royal in Drury Lane', it opened in 1674 and survived for almost 120 years, during which its management included Colley Cibber, David Garrick (for 29 years) and Richard Brinsley Sheridan (whose play, *The School for Scandal*, received its first performance here in 1777).

In 1791, under Sheridan's management, the building was demolished to make way for a much larger theatre (seating 3,600) which opened in 1794, but survived for just 15 years before burning down in 1809. The building that stands today was designed by Benjamin Wyatt and opened in 1812. It was renowned for its spectacular Victorian melodramas and pantomimes, but since the 1920s its history has mirrored the development of the modern musical. From the original London productions of American musicals *Rose Marie*, *The Desert Song* and *Show Boat*, through Ivor Novello's romantic operettas and Rodgers and Hammerstein's groundbreaking post-war shows, to *The Producers* and *The Lord of the Rings*. *My Fair Lady* held the record as the theatre's longest run for many years, though Cameron Mackintosh's record-breaking production of *Miss Saigon* – ten years and 4,263 performances – is the current record holder.

> The theatre has two royal boxes – built for George III and the Prince Regent (who loathed each other) – and both the National Anthem and Rule Britannia were first performed here.

The theatre has been graced by actors as diverse as Shakespearean Edmund Kean, child actress Clara Fisher, comedian Dan Leno, Noël Coward and the comedy troupe Monty Python (who recorded an album here). Today, it's owned by composer Andrew Lloyd Webber's Really Useful Group and mostly stages popular musical theatre.

Visitors can take a 'Through The Stage Door' tour hosted by professional actors, who take you on a memorable journey through the theatre's history, meeting famous characters such as Garrick, Sheridan, Grimaldi and Nell Gwyne along the way.

❝ *The theatre that refused to die* **❯❯**

AT A GLANCE

Address: The Strand, WC2A 2LL (☎ 020-7947 6000, tours 020-7947 7684, 🖥 www.justice.gov.uk/guidance/courts-and-tribunals/courts/rcj/index.htm, ✉ rcjtours@talktalk.net).

Opening hours: Tours (2 hrs), first and third Tuesday of each month, 11am and 2pm, plus other dates for groups.

Cost: Tours – Adults £12, concessions £10 (aged 60 and over), children £5 (under 14), groups £10 per person (minimum 10 people).

Transport: Temple tube station.

ROYAL COURTS OF JUSTICE

*T*he Grade 1 listed Royal Courts of Justice (RCJ), commonly called the Law Courts, is a vast, imposing building housing the Courts of Appeal and the High Court of Justice of England and Wales. It's one of the last great wonders of Victorian neo-Gothic revival architecture, designed by George Edmund Street RA (1824-1881), a solicitor turned architect. Built in the 1870s, it was officially opened in December 1882 by Queen Victoria. The finished building contained 35 million Portland stone bricks, over 3.5mi (5.6km) of corridors and some 1,000 clocks, many of which had to be wound by hand.

> The RCJ took over eight years to complete, due in part to a stonemasons strike during which masons were brought from Germany to keep work going, and housed within the building to protect them from the wrath of their striking English counterparts. Supplies came in through a secret underground tunnel.

Entering through the main gates in the Strand, you pass under two elaborately carved porches fitted with iron gates. The carvings over the outer porch consist of heads of the country's most eminent judges and lawyers. Over the highest point of the upper arch is a figure of Jesus, lower down (to the left and right) are figures of Solomon and Alfred the Great, while Moses is at the northern front of the building. Also at the northern front, over the Judges entrance, are a stone cat and dog representing litigants fighting in court.

The building is a Victorian interpretation of 13th-century Gothic architecture, with imposing Portland stonework, beautiful mosaic marble floors, stunning stained glass windows, elaborate carvings and oak wood panelling. The walls of the magnificent Great Hall – reminiscent of a cathedral – are lined with portraits of past Lord Chancellors and keepers of the Great Seal. The building also houses the Costume Display Gallery which celebrates the evolution of legal costumes throughout history, as well as the Painted Room and Bear Garden, which Queen Victoria allegedly named as such because the crowds of litigants and lawyers here reminded her of a bear pit.

Public tours of the Royal Courts are available (see opposite) and visitors are also invited to watch civil trials (criminal trials take place at the Old Bailey down the road), although there may be restrictions depending on the actual cases being tried.

❝ *A marvel of Victorian Gothic architecture* **❞**

Address: **Two Temple Place, WC2R 3BD** (☎ **020-7836 3715,**
🖥 **www.twotempleplace.co.uk and www.twotempleplace.org).**

Opening hours: **Periodic exhibitions, Mon-Sat (except Tue), 10am to
4.30pm, Sun noon to 5pm (hours may vary – check website).**

Cost: **Free.**

Transport: **Temple tube station.**

TWO TEMPLE PLACE

*T*wo Temple Place, known for many years as 'Astor House', is a masterpiece of irreverent excess and fun – built in 1895 for William Waldorf Astor (1848-1919), later first Viscount Astor. It was built on reclaimed land following completion of the Victoria Embankment in 1870 and designed by John Loughborough Pearson (1817-1897) and his son Frank (1864-1947). Temple Place is both an architectural gem and a treasure house of exquisite works by the likes of William Silver Frith (1850-1924), Sir George Frampton RA (1860-1928), Nathaniel Hitch (1845-1938) and Thomas Nicholls (1825-1900).

The building has just two floors and a lower ground floor, and is broadly of Tudor design, built of Portland stone. It has splendid carvings on the exterior stonework by Nathaniel Hitch (1845-1938) and above the parapets is a superb gilded weathervane in beaten copper depicting Columbus' caravel *Santa Maria* by J. Starkie Gardner (1844-1930). The enchanting bronze lamp standards flanking the base of the balustraded entrance steps are a foretaste of the riches within.

Palatial outside, inside it's a showcase for Britain's finest 19th-century craftsmen. Unfettered by the consideration of finance (it cost £250,000 to build in 1895, equivalent to £25m today), emboldened by the freedom of expression granted to him, and with materials and craftsmen of the highest quality, Pearson

> **Two Temple Place is postmodernism before its time, a Disney Gothic that's a thrill to visit – it's not to be missed!**

was able to create a building worthy of its distinguished owner. From the splendid marble floor and imposing staircase in the grand hall and gallery (with its glorious stained glass and coved and panelled ceiling), to the great hall with its hammer beam ceiling, gilded carvings, silver gilt panels and huge stained glass windows, Temple Place is a masterpiece.

A widower, Lord Astor used it as his London home and as the Astor Estate Office until his death in 1919, when it was sold by the Astor family. Since then it has been owned by various companies and is now owned by the Bulldog (charitable) Trust, whose HQ it is. The Trust hosts periodic exhibitions, such as *William Morris: Story, Memory, Myth* (Oct 2011 to Jan 2012) and *Amongst Heroes: the artist in working Cornwall* (Jan-Apr 2013).

However, most exhibits pale against the backdrop of this long-hidden architectural gem, which for the splendour of its ornamentation and conception is difficult to beat. Keep an eye on the website for upcoming exhibitions.

66 *A Gothic Revival extravaganza and treasure house* **99**

Address: Strand, WC2R 1ES (☎ 020-7836 3126, 🖥 www.stmarylestrand.org).

Opening hours: Visitors, Tue-Thu, 11am to 4pm and Sun, 10am to 1pm. See website for service times.

Cost: Free (but donations are welcome).

Transport: Temple tube station.

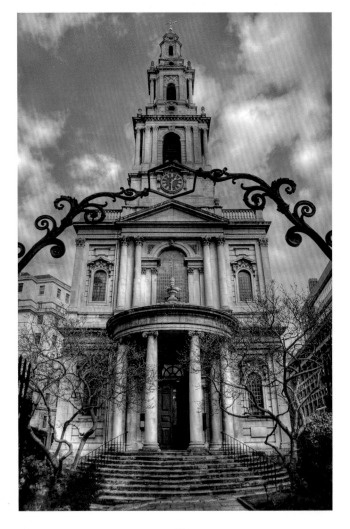

ST MARY LE STRAND

*S*t Mary le Strand (Church of England) is a tiny, elegant 18th-century Baroque church – one of only two London churches standing on a traffic island (the other being St Clement Danes) – situated on the Strand, one of the city's principal and most ancient thoroughfares. It was the second London church called St Mary le Strand – the first was thought to date to the 12th century. It was demolished in 1549 by Edward Seymour, 1st Duke of Somerset (and eldest brother of Jane Seymour) when Lord Protector of England – beheaded for his sins in 1552 – the rubble was recycled to build Somerset House.

> **Bonnie Prince Charlie is alleged to have renounced his Roman Catholic faith in the church to become an Anglican during a secret visit to London in 1750, and the parents of Charles Dickens, John Dickens and Elizabeth Barrow, were married here in 1809.**

St Mary was the first of the 50 new churches built in London under the Commission for Building Fifty New Churches – the so-called 'Queen Ann Churches'. Designed by architect James Gibbs (a Roman Catholic who trained in Rome) and begun in 1714, it was completed in September 1717, although it wasn't consecrated until 1st January 1723. It was designed as an Italianate structure with a small campanile over the west end and no steeple, but was later altered against Gibbs' wishes. The extravagant Baroque ornamentation of the exterior was criticised at the time, and matters weren't helped when one of the decorative urns surmounting the exterior of the church fell and killed a passer-by in 1802.

The interior is richly decorated with a plastered ceiling in white and gold, inspired by the churches Gibbs had seen in Rome. The walls were influenced by Michelangelo, while the steeple shows the influence of Sir Christopher Wren. The church is built to an extremely lavish standard and faced with carved stone inside and out. The woodcarving is by John Simmonds; note the excellent carving on the panelling in the chancel, the door cases to the eastern vestries and the altar rails.

The church narrowly escaped destruction twice during the 20th century: it was almost demolished at the start of the century to widen the Strand (the graveyard was sacrificed instead), and was badly damaged during the Blitz. Since 1982, St Mary le Strand has been the official church of the Women's Royal Naval Service (WRNS or Wrens).

 Where Bonnie Prince Charlie became an Anglican?

KING'S COLLEGE CHAPEL

*T*he King's College Chapel (Grade I listed) is a magnificent example of Victorian architecture, designed by the eminent architect George Gilbert Scott (1811-1878) and completed in 1864. A century and a half later, the Chapel continues to provide a spiritual focus for King's community and a peaceful space at the heart of the college.

King's College was founded by King George IV and the Duke of Wellington in 1829 as a university college in the tradition of the Church of England, and became one of the two founding colleges of the University of London in 1836. Today, King's is a multi-faculty, research-led, teaching institution with over 16,000 students and 5,000 staff, catering for all faiths and beliefs.

When the original college building (Grade I listed) by Robert Smirke was completed in 1831 it included a chapel. However, it was considered too low church and plain, and in 1859 the council asked Sir Gilbert Scott to design a more impressive chapel, and his scheme – on the lines of an ancient Christian basilica – was accepted.

The beautiful Scott chapel is situated on the first floor directly above the Great Hall, reached by an impressive double staircase from the main entrance. Scott had to overcome a number of structural difficulties and used a lightweight construction system for the arcade and upper nave walls that concentrated the loading above the iron columns on the floor below. The wall is fabricated in iron with paired ornamental cast iron columns and an applied timber frame facing above.

Among the many highlights are the organ by Henry Willis, dating from the 1860s, reconstructed by his grandson in the 1930s; the lovely angel designs on the largest pipes were only revealed during restoration. The lower walls of the chapel have a rich composition using a painted tile motif, also discovered during restoration work and faithfully recreated, while the west wall contains the original tile design. The chapel also houses a wealth of poignant memorials.

Regular services are held in the chapel representing many different traditions, all of which are open to the public. The chapel choir sing at the Wednesday communion service and choral evensong on Tuesdays at 5.30pm.

A wonderful, spiritual building, reflecting the college's motto: *Sancte et Sapienter* (with holiness and wisdom).

> **The chapel was restored in 2000-01, when Scott's original decorative scheme was substantially reinstated, despite significant changes made in the 1930s and the post-war period.**

 A 'secret' Gilbert Scott masterpiece

AT A GLANCE

Address: **Savoy Hill, WC2R 0DA** (☎ **020-7836 7221**,
🖥 **www.duchyoflancaster.co.uk/duties-of-the-duchy/the-queens-chapel-of-the-savoy**).

Opening hours: Daily, except Monday – but check it isn't closed for renovation work. Public services are held on Sundays and Wednesday lunchtimes, except in August and September (see website for times).

Cost: **Free.**

Transport: **Temple tube station.**

SAVOY CHAPEL

*T*he Savoy Chapel (or the Queen's Chapel of the Savoy) is a charming 15th-century chapel, dedicated to St John the Baptist, with a delightful garden. The chapel has always been royal property as part of the Savoy Hospital complex, and is owned by the monarch as part of the Duchy of Lancaster, as a peculiar (not falling within a bishop's jurisdiction) with its chaplain appointed by the Duchy. It was made the chapel of the Royal Victorian Order in 1937.

The original chapel was within Peter of Savoy's palace, and was destroyed along with it in the Peasant's Revolt in 1381. The current chapel building was constructed in the 1490s (completed in 1512) by Henry VII as a side chapel off the Savoy Hospital's (for homeless people) nave, which was secular rather than sacred, and housed 100 beds. The hospital was in ruins by the 19th century and the chapel was the only part to survive demolition.

The chapel has been the host to various congregations, notably that of St Mary-le-Strand when it had no church building of its own from 1549-1714. Also the German Lutheran congregation of Westminster (now at Sandwich Street and Thanet Street, near St Pancras) was granted royal permission to worship here, when it split from Holy Trinity (the City of London Lutheran congregation, now at St Anne and St Agnes). The new congregation's first pastor, Irenaeus Crusius (previously an associate at Holy Trinity), dedicated the chapel as the Marienkirche or the German Church of St Mary-le-Savoy on the 19th Sunday after Trinity in 1694.

As an Anglican church, the chapel was known in the 18th century as a place where marriages without banns might illegally occur, and was referred to in Evelyn Waugh's book *Brideshead Revisited* as 'the place where divorced couples got married in those days – a poky little place'. Most of the stained glass windows in the chapel were destroyed in the London Blitz during WWII, although a triptych stained glass memorial window survives. Depicting a procession of angelic musicians. It's dedicated to the memory of Richard D'Oyly Carte (who was married in the chapel in 1888) and was unveiled by Sir Henry Irving in 1902.

> **Being the property of the Queen, any expenses incurred by the chapel are borne by the monarchy.**

The chapel ceiling was restored to its former splendour in 1999 in honour of HM the Queen's Golden Jubilee.

❝ *A glorious, hidden 15th-century chapel* **❞**

Address: 8 John Adam Street, WC2N 6EZ (☎ 020-7930 5115,
💻 www.thersa.org).

Opening hours: Weekday tours by appointment.

Cost: Free.

Transport: Embankment tube station.

ROYAL SOCIETY OF ARTS

*T*he Royal Society of Arts (RSA) is the intellectual and social home of some of the greatest thinkers and social activists of the past 250 years. The RSA – or to give it its full name 'The Royal Society for the encouragement of Arts, Manufacturers and Commerce' is a British multi-disciplinary institution. Founded in 1754 and granted a royal charter in 1847, its patron is HM Elizabeth II and HRH The Princess Royal is president.

Among its eclectic roll of famous (past and present) members are Charles Dickens, Adam Smith, Benjamin Franklin, Karl Marx and William Hogarth, while RSA Medal winners – the 'Albert Medal', the 'Benjamin Franklin Medal' and the 'Bicentenary Medal' (all still awarded today) – include Nelson Mandela, Sir Frank Whittle and Professor Stephen Hawking. Today, the RSA has over 27,000 fellows in 70 countries worldwide – fellowship is bestowed upon those who have achieved (or demonstrated the potential to achieve) a contribution to society in a cultural or arts-related sphere.

> **The RSA was also responsible for devising the 'blue plaques' scheme in 1866 to commemorate the links between famous people and buildings by placing plaques on their walls, which since 1986 has been operated by English Heritage.**

The RSA's ambitious mission expressed in its founding charter was to 'embolden enterprise, enlarge science, refine art, improve our manufacturers and extend our commerce', but also encompassed a desire to alleviate poverty and secure full employment.

The Royal Academy of Arts was formed as the RSA's spin-off organisation in 1768 by Sir Thomas Gainsborough and Sir Joshua Reynolds, two early members of the RSA, as a result of its first exhibition of contemporary art. The RSA's launching of the modern world's first public examinations in 1882 led to the RSA Examinations Board (now part of the Oxford, Cambridge and RSA Examinations Board).

The home of the RSA was designed by the Adam Brothers in 1774 as part of their innovative Adelphi scheme, and expanded into adjacent buildings in later years (2-6 John Adam Street and 18 Adam Street). The original building includes the Great Room, featuring a magnificent sequence of paintings by Irish artist James Barry, titled *The Progress of Human Knowledge and Culture*. The first occupant of 18 Adam Street was the Adelphi Tavern – mentioned in Dickens's *The Pickwick Papers* – where the former private dining room contains a magnificent Adam ceiling.

The RSA arranges weekday public tours of the splendid RSA House by appointment.

 The spiritual home of Britain's greatest artists and thinkers 🙵

Address: 31 Bedford Street, Covent Garden, WC2E 9ED (☎ 020-7836 5221, 💻 www.actorschurch.org).

Opening hours: Mon-Fri, 8.30am to 5pm, Sat, varies depending on events, Sun, 9am to 1pm (5pm when there's evensong). See website for service times.

Cost: Free (but donations are welcome).

Transport: Covent Garden tube station.

ST PAUL'S CHURCH, COVENT GARDEN

*S*t Paul's Church, commonly known as 'The Actors' Church', is a beautiful parish church with an impressive Tuscan portico. It was designed by Inigo Jones in 1631 as part of a commission by Francis Russell, 4th Earl of Bedford, to create a square with 'houses and buildings fit for the habitations of gentlemen and men of ability'. The church was completed in 1633 but wasn't consecrated until 1638 due to a dispute.

The first known victims of the 1665-1666 outbreak of the plague in England were buried in the churchyard on 12th April 1665: the start of the worst plague in London's history. In 1788, Thomas Hardwick began a major restoration, but the church was badly damaged by fire in 1795. Although much was destroyed, the parish records were saved, as was the pulpit by Grinling Gibbons. The church was restored again under the supervision of Thomas Hardwick and reconsecrated on 1st August 1798.

St Paul's connection with the theatre began as early as 1663 with the establishment of the Theatre Royal Drury Lane (see page 25), and was further assured in 1723 with the opening of Covent Garden Theatre, now the Royal Opera House. On 9th May 1662, Samuel Pepys noted in his diary the performance of an 'Italian puppet play' under the portico – the first recorded 'Punch and Judy' show, now commemorated by the annual MayFayre service.

> Among those buried at St Paul's are poet and satirist Samuel Butler, woodcarver Grinling Gibbons, painter Sir Peter Lely, Thomas Arne (composer of 'Rule Britannia') and the Australian conductor Sir Charles Mackerras. The ashes of Dame Ellen Terry and Dame Edith Evans also rest in St Paul's.

The church contains a wealth of memorials dedicated to famous personalities, including Charlie Chaplin, Noel Coward, Gracie Fields, Stanley Holloway, Boris Karloff, Vivien Leigh and Ivor Novello. The artist JMW Turner and dramatist WS Gilbert (of Gilbert and Sullivan fame) were both baptised at St Paul's.

St Paul's is famous for its concerts and has it own professional chamber orchestra, the Orchestra of St Paul's (OSP). In addition to a concert series in Covent Garden, the OSP gives regular performances throughout the UK. The church is also famous for its summer repertory season, when performances are given in the church's award-winning 'Inigo Jones Garden', which (when not being used as a theatre) provides a haven of calm amidst the bustle of central London.

66 *The other St Paul's, aka 'The Actors' Church'* **99**

AT A GLANCE

Address: 47 Chandos Place, Covent Garden, WC2N 4HS (☎ 020-7836 0291, 🖥 www.harpcoventgarden.com).

Opening hours: Mon, 10.30am to 11pm, Tue-Sat, 10.30am to 11.30pm, Sun, noon to 10.30pm.

Cost: Free (but you should buy a drink).

Transport: Charing Cross tube and rail station.

THE HARP

*T*he Harp in Covent Garden is a tiny gem of a pub, famous for its superb ales and traditional atmosphere, *sans* TV, music or games machines. In 2010 it was crowned CAMRA's – 'Campaign for Real Ale' for the uninitiated – National Pub of the Year, the first London boozer to be awarded the accolade. However, don't let this put you off. The Harp may be situated in the midst of tourist London, but it retains the feel of a friendly neighbourhood local.

Situated just a few short steps away from Charing Cross and close to Theatreland, the Harp is a pretty little pub with stained glass Welsh harps decorating its windows, adorned with hanging flower baskets in summer. It's a narrow building with a downstairs main bar and an upstairs parlour that retains the intimate feel of a Victorian snug. It's furnished in traditional wood panelling and mirrors, many etched with images of harps (so you won't forget its name).

> If you fancy a bit of peace and quiet, you can retire to the more relaxed 'gentlemen's club' bar upstairs, with its comfortable chairs and more intimate atmosphere (but get in early).

The main bar – a single long room with one side dominated by the bar – is decorated with numerous hand-pump beer labels, while the walls are covered with old Victorian paintings and '60s prints, including theatre memorabilia and portraits of thespians such as James Mason and Elizabeth Taylor.

Despite being modest – in size and character – and serving the most basic of food (sausages in baguettes), the Harp is famous for is the quality and variety of its real ales and ciders, its agreeable ambience and friendly staff. It's a real ale paradise, with eight hand pumps offering a frequently changing variety of beers, though there are always two each from the celebrated micro breweries, Sambrook's of Battersea and Sussex's Dark Star. And always available among the eight are two dark beers – mild, porter or stout – which aren't easy to find nowadays. Equally rare is the choice of real ciders and perries from artisan producers. There's also the usual range of lagers, Guinness and wines, but real ale is the overwhelming choice of regulars.

Although not a place for a quiet drink – it's always heaving at lunchtimes and early evenings and remains busy at other times – the Harp is a real pub for real beer drinkers and highly recommended.

66 *Heavenly music for beer-lovers* **99**

Address: Trafalgar Square, WC2N 4JJ (☎ 020-7766 1100,
🖥 www.smitf.org).

Opening hours: Preferred visiting times: Mon, Tue and Fri, 8.30am to
1pm and 2-6pm; Wed, 8.30am to 1.15pm and 2-5pm; Thu, 8.30am to
1.15pm and 2-6pm; Sat 9.30am to 6pm; and Sun 3.30-5pm. Tours (max.
25) are usually offered twice a month, on Thursday mornings, and must
be booked well in advance. See website for service times.

Cost: Free (but donations are welcome). Audio tours £3.50. Tours £5
per person.

Transport: Charing Cross or Embankment tube station.

ST MARTIN-IN-THE-FIELDS

*S*t Martin-in-the-Fields (Grade I listed) is one of London's most beloved non-cathedral churches – noted for its fine architecture, work with the poor and musical tradition, and not least its historic place at the heart of the nation. It's an Anglican church dedicated to St Martin of Tours (316-397), a Bishop whose shrine became a famous stop-over for pilgrims on the road to Santiago de Compostela. The earliest known reference to a church here is in 1222, though excavations have shown the land was used as a burial spot as early the 5th century AD.

The church was rebuilt by Henry VIII in 1542 to keep plague victims from being taken through his Palace of Whitehall; at this time it was literally located 'in the fields', isolated between the cities of Westminster and (the City of) London. In 1606, James I granted land for a new churchyard and the church was enlarged. A number of famous people were buried here during the 17th century, including chemist and physicist Robert Boyle (1627-1691) and Nell Gwynne (1650-1687), mistress of Charles II.

Various 18th-century notables were buried in the new church, including the émigré sculptor Roubiliac (1702-1762), who had settled locally, and the furniture-maker Thomas Chippendale (1718-1779), whose workshop was in the same street (St Martin's Lane) as the church. The church has a close relationship with the Royal Family, whose parish church it is, as well as with 10 Downing Street and the Admiralty.

Its ethos as the 'Church of the Ever Open Door' – coined in the early 20th century, when its work with homeless people began – continues today, although it isn't literally always open. The church is also famous for its regular lunchtime and evening concerts: many ensembles perform here, not least the Academy of St Martin-in-the-Fields, which was co-founded by Sir Neville Marriner (b 1924) and John Churchill, a former

> **In 1710, St Martin's was found to be in a state of decay and it was decided to build a new church, which you see today, designed by James Gibbs and completed in 1726. The design was widely criticised at the time, but subsequently became famous and was copied widely (particularly in the US).**

Master of Music at St Martin's. The crypt houses a popular award-winning café, where jazz concerts are held, and is also home to the London Brass Rubbing Centre, an art gallery, and a book and gift shop.

66 *A splendid 18th century church but, alas, no fields* **99**

Address: 7 Carlton House Terrace, The Mall, SW1Y 5BD (☎ 020-7930 6844, 🖥 www.mallgalleries.org.uk).

Opening hours: Daily, 10am to 5pm during exhibitions (unless otherwise stated), **including Bank Holidays.**

Cost: Free except for Federation of British Artists (FBA) exhibitions – adults £2.50, concessions and groups (min. 10 people) £1.50.

Transport: Charing Cross tube station.

MALL GALLERIES

*T*he Mall Galleries (on the Mall, next door to the Institute of Contemporary Arts – occupying a Grade 1 listed building) is one of the coolest art venues in London, following a major refurbishment in 2007. It's one of London's major contemporary art showcases, with three main galleries, a bookshop and a café, and is also home to the Federation of British Artists (FBA). The FBA consists of eight of the UK's leading art societies (all of which hold their Annual Exhibition at the Mall Galleries) – including the Royal Society of British Artists, the Royal Institute of Painters in Water Colours and the Royal Institute of Oil Painters – with over 500 member artists. The Galleries serve as a national focal point for contemporary figurative art by living artists working in the UK, and aim to 'promote, inspire and educate audiences about the visual arts'.

The Mall Galleries host several of the UK's premier open art competitions, including The Threadneedle Prize and the ING Discerning Eye, as well as the popular BITE: Artists Making Prints show. In addition to the member societies, other societies and individual artists also stage shows at the Mall Galleries. Over 100 prizes and awards are administered each year by the societies, including the £30,000 Threadneedle Prize (🖳 www.threadneedleprize. com), the UK's leading showcase for paintings and sculptures. FBA members regularly exhibit their work and also accept open submissions from the public.

The Galleries' education department runs a schools' programme, including gallery based workshops, which introduces students to the work of member artists and diverse art practices. The Galleries also offer a wide-ranging programme of activities for adults, including gallery talks and tours, art workshops, debates and artist demonstrations. Gallery projects include a drawing school and summer courses run by the New English Art Club, as well as The Hesketh Hubbard Art Society, the largest life drawing society in London. In March 2012, the Galleries unveiled a radical re-development of the former East Gallery, which has been transformed into a distinctive and highly contemporary space, renamed 'The Threadneedle Space' (after its sponsors).

The Mall Galleries' bookshop specialises in tickets for events and books relating to British figurative art, ranging from artist monographs and reference guides to specialist art magazines and tutorial DVDs.

One of London's foremost galleries with an exciting programme of exhibitions and workshops.

 Showcase for Britain's leading contemporary artists

AT A GLANCE

Address: 13 Berkeley Street, W1J 8DU (☎ **020-7042 5730,**
🖥 **www.flemingcollection.co.uk**).

Opening hours: **Tue-Sat, 10am to 5.30pm. Art tours (1½ hrs) available on Mon (10am and 6pm).**

Cost: **Adults £3.50, children (6-16 years) and students free. Art tours £12 (morning, min. 15 people) and £21.60 (evening, min. 40 people).**

Transport: **Green Park tube station.**

FLEMING COLLECTION

*T*he Fleming Collection is the finest assembly of Scottish art in private hands and the only dedicated museum granting public access to Scottish art all year round. The Collection was begun in 1968 by the Scottish banking firm Robert Fleming & Co, founded in Dundee. In 1968 the bank moved to a new building in Crosby Square in the City of London and it was decided to create a collection for the purpose of decorating the space.

This task was given to one of the bank's directors, David Donald. The only guideline was that the paintings should be by Scottish artists or Scottish scenes by any artists, to emphasise the bank's proud Scottish origins. Scottish art was largely unknown outside of Scotland until the '80s, making prices relatively low, enabling a large collection to be amassed in a short period.

The Collection comprises over 750 oils and watercolours from 1770 to the present day, including works by Raeburn, Ramsay, Wilkie, and the iconic paintings of the Highland Clearances, *The Last of the Clan* by Thomas Faed and *Lochaber No More* by John Watson Nicol. It's particularly noted for its works by William McTaggart, the Glasgow Boys, D. Y. Cameron, Anne Redpath and a superb group of paintings by the Colourists. It remains a living and growing collection through further acquisitions.

> In March 2000, Flemings bank was sold to Chase Manhattan Bank, New York. To avoid the Collection being lost, the Fleming family funded a new charitable foundation, The Fleming-Wyfold Foundation, to purchase the Collection before the sale.

The Collection was moved to its current premises on Berkeley Street in 2002 as a revolving exhibition based on works from the Collection and as a showcase for contemporary Scottish art in London. This meant that the exhibition programme has had to juggle between showing works from the permanent collection as well as loan exhibitions. However, in 2010 the opportunity arose to rent the floor directly above the gallery and create additional space. This opened in June 2011 as Gallery Two, showing selected works from the permanent collection, while temporary exhibitions, drawn from both private and national collections, are held in the original 'Gallery One'.

The Fleming Collection continues to grow, the main thrust being directed towards buying the work of young Scottish artists, while opportunities are also taken to fill historical gaps.

A unique collection well worth a visit.

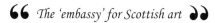

66 *The 'embassy' for Scottish art* **99**

Address: Stable Yard Road, SW1 1BA (☎ 020-7766 7300, 🖥 www. princeofwales.gov.uk/personalprofiles/residences/clarencehouse).

Opening hours: Open in August for guided tours only (¾hr), Mon-Fri 10am to 4pm, Sat-Sun 10am to 5.30pm. Check website or phone for details and tickets.

Cost: **£9 adults, £5 under-17s, under-5s free.**

Transport: **Green Park or St James's Park tube station.**

HRH The Prince of Wales

CLARENCE HOUSE

*C*larence House is the official residence of the Prince of Wales (since 2003), the Duchess of Cornwall and Prince Harry, where the Prince and Duchess receive several thousand official guests annually from the UK and overseas, bringing together people from all walks of life through official seminars, lunches, receptions and dinners. It's a working residence and provides office accommodation for their Royal Highnesses' official staff, who support them in undertaking their public and charitable duties.

The House, situated beside St James's Palace and sharing its garden, was built between 1825 and 1827 to the designs of John Nash for Prince William Henry, Duke of Clarence, who lived here as William IV from 1830 until 1837. It was once the London home of Her Majesty The Queen (then Princess Elizabeth) and The Duke of Edinburgh following their marriage in 1947, and was also the home of Queen Elizabeth, the Queen Mother, from 1953 until her death in 2002. The Prince of Wales took over Clarence House on 4th August 2003, the anniversary of the Queen Mother's birth.

The House has been much altered, reflecting the changes in occupancy and use over almost two centuries; it was extensively refurbished and redecorated for the Prince of Wales, while maintaining the familiar atmosphere of a much-loved family house.

Visitors are given a guided tour of the five rooms and adjoining spaces on the ground floor. You can also view items from the Royal Collection and from the collection of Queen Elizabeth the Queen Mother, which is particularly strong in 20th-century British art, including important works by John Piper, Graham Sutherland, Walter Sickert and Augustus John. Superb examples of Fabergé, English porcelain and silver, particularly pieces relating to the Bowes-Lyon family, are also on display.

Clarence House is the last remaining great London house to be maintained for the purpose for which it was built; as the official London residence of the Prince of Wales and the Duchess of Cornwall, it continues to play a part in the life of the Royal Family and the nation. The gardens were opened in full to the public for the first time in 2011.

The decoration of the rooms retains the ambience created by The Queen Mother, and much of her collection of works of art and furniture has been retained.

Clarence House shop sells a range of souvenirs, many designed exclusively for the Royal Collection.

" *A house fit for a (future) king* "

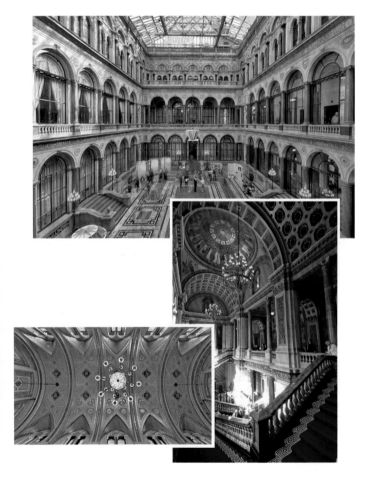

FOREIGN OFFICE & DURBAR COURT

*T*he Foreign and Commonwealth Office (FCO) occupies a magnificent building which originally provided premises for four separate government departments: the Foreign Office, the India Office, the Colonial Office and the Home Office. Construction of the building began in 1861 and was completed in 1868. George Gilbert Scott (1811-1878), the unsung hero of British architecture, was responsible for the overall classical design of the building, while Matthew Digby Wyatt (1820-1877 – the India Office's surveyor) designed and decorated the magnificent interior of the India Office, which is acknowledged as his masterpiece.

Scott designed the new Foreign Office as 'a kind of national palace or drawing room for the nation', with the use of rich decoration to impress foreign visitors, which was also true of Wyatt's India Office. The Locarno Suite consists of three rooms originally designed by Scott for diplomatic dinners, conferences and receptions. The largest room, looking out on to the Main Quadrangle, was originally designated the Cabinet Room, but seems not to have been used as such in the 19th century.

Durbar Court (the name dates only from 1902, when some of the coronation celebrations of Edward VII were held here), lies at the heart of the India Office. Originally open to the sky, the four sides of the court are surrounded by three storeys of columns and piers supporting arches. Completed in 1868 as part of the new block of Government Offices, it included the India Office and later (1875) the Colonial and Home Offices.

> **The FCO is open to the public only during Open House London Weekend (unless you have friends in the FCO…), which is in September (see opposite). It's well worth making a special trip to view this magnificent building.**

During the 20th century, the impact of two world wars and the growing complexity of public business and international affairs led to severe overcrowding, and the shortage of money during post-1945 austerity Britain and distaste for anything Victorian led to the building's deterioration. In the '60s, the decision was made to demolish Scott's creation and erect new offices, but a public outcry led to the offices being designated a Grade I listed building. This resulted in a £100m restoration between 1984 and 1997, which not only brought the building and fine rooms back to life, but increased the available space for much less than the cost of demolition and rebuilding.

 An eclectic Italian-Indian masterpiece

Address: Wellington Barracks, Birdcage Walk, SW1E 6HQ (☎ 020-7414 3428/3271, chapel ☎ 020-7414 3228, 🖥 www.theguardsmuseum.com).

Opening hours: Museum, daily, 10am to 4pm. For chapel services, see website.

Cost: Adults £5, senior citizens and students £2.50, children (16 and under) free.

Transport: St James's Park tube station.

GUARDS MUSEUM & CHAPEL

*T*he Guards Museum is a captivating collection (housed in Wellington Barracks) that traces the history of the five regiments of Foot Guards – Grenadier, Coldstream, Scots, Irish and Welsh Guards – which together with the two regiments of Household Cavalry (the Life Guards and the Blues and Royals – who have their own museum: 🖳 www.householdcavalrymuseum.co.uk) make up Her Majesty's Household Division. Together they enjoy the privilege of guarding The Sovereign and the Royal Palaces.

The museum opened in 1988 and tells the story of the Guards' regiments from the 17th century to the present day. Displays include examples of different Guards' uniforms chronicling the evolving dress over 350 years, paintings, weapons, models, sculptures and artefacts such as mess silver, which paint a vivid portrait of the regiments' history and what being a soldier in the Guards is all about. The collection is primarily intended as an educational aid to help young Guardsmen learn about their regimental heritage and to show a wider audience the multi-faceted nature of the Guards' operational lives, both in combat and on ceremonial duties.

The Foot Guards are first and foremost professional soldiers, who perform a dual role of combat soldier and ceremonial. Many people are surprised to learn that the soldiers in the Household Division are primarily fighting soldiers at the forefront of Britain's commitment to the UN, NATO and the country's security. Over the centuries they have fought in most major British Army campaigns, which remains so to this day. For example, in 2012 all five regiments of Foot Guards were either in, had just retuned from, or were training for operations in Afghanistan. Their high standard of training is recognised worldwide and their NCOs and Warrant Officers are called upon by numerous countries to train their own forces.

The Guards (or 'Royal Military') Chapel – situated a few hundred yards from the museum – is the religious home of the Household Division. Normal Sunday services are open to the public and are accompanied by a professional choir and the band of one of the regiments of the Household Division.

> **Built in 1838, the chapel was damaged during the Blitz and in 1944 was totally destroyed by a V1 flying bomb during the morning service, which claimed 121 lives and injured 140. The chapel was rebuilt in the '60s in a modern style.**

The engrossing Guards Museum also has a delightful shop, known as 'The Guards Toy Soldier Centre'.

 The Queen's Guards in all their glory

Address: **55 Broadway, SW1H 0BD** (🖥 www.tfl.gov.uk/corporate/historicalarchives/17335.aspx).

Opening hours: **Unrestricted access to exterior sculptures and arcades during business hours. The interior can also be visited during the annual Open House London weekend** (see 🖥 www.openhouselondon.org.uk).

Cost: **Free.**

Transport: **St James's Park tube station.**

55 BROADWAY
(LONDON UNDERGROUND HQ)

*N*umber 55 Broadway – also know as the London Underground Headquarters – is a dramatic Art Deco building overlooking St James's Park and straddling St James's Park tube station. It was designed by Charles Holden and built in 1927-1929 as the HQ for the Underground Electric Railways Company of London (UERL), the main forerunner of London Underground. The modern and assertive design was considered an architectural masterpiece and Holden was awarded the RIBA London Architecture Medal in 1931. The building was Grade II listed in 1970 and upgraded to Grade I in 2011.

The building – faced with Portland stone – has two storeys covering the whole site, over the centre of which rises the 175ft (53.3m) tower, with four spur wings carried out to the perimeter. The upper office floors are on a cruciform design – which afforded the optimum level of natural light – stepping back towards the central clock tower at the top. The ground floor – previously London Transport offices – now contains a shopping arcade and many original Art Deco details. When completed, it was the tallest steel-framed office building in London, until being overtaken by Holden's (University of London) Senate House.

The building displays ten sculptures. Halfway along the north and east façades are a matched pair of graphic naked figures, *Day* and *Night*, by Jacob Epstein (see box), while on each elevation the pediment above the sixth floor is decorated with a relief representing 'the four winds'; each sculpture is repeated twice, making a total of eight. The eight reliefs are carved by leading avant-garde sculptors of the day, who included Eric Aumonier, A H Gerrard, Eric Gill (who did three sculptures), Henry Moore, Samuel Rabinovitch and Allan Wyon.

The ground floor is traversed by three travertine marble-clad and paved arcades, which retain their ornamental ventilation grilles in a geometric design, wall clocks set into a low-relief sunburst in Travertine marble, polygonal travertine-clad columns, and coffered ceilings. If you get an opportunity to see the whole building (see opposite), don't hesitate, as some of the Art Deco interiors are stunning.

> The *Day* and *Night* sculptures created public outrage on their unveiling. Newspapers started a campaign to have the statues removed and one company director, Lord Colwyn, even offered to pay the cost. In the end, Epstein agreed to remove 1.5in from the penis of the smaller figure, *Day*, and ultimately the furore died down.

 A carbuncle that became an iconic landmark

Address: Storey's Gate, SW1H 9NH (☎ church, 020-7654 3809, events 020-7222 8010, 🖳 www.methodist-central-hall.org.uk and www.c-h-w.com).

Opening hours: **Daily, free guided tours between 9.30am and 5pm. Note that the Great Hall may be in private use, so it's wise to check in advance. See website for services.**

Cost: **Free.**

Transport: **Westminster or St James's Park tube station.**

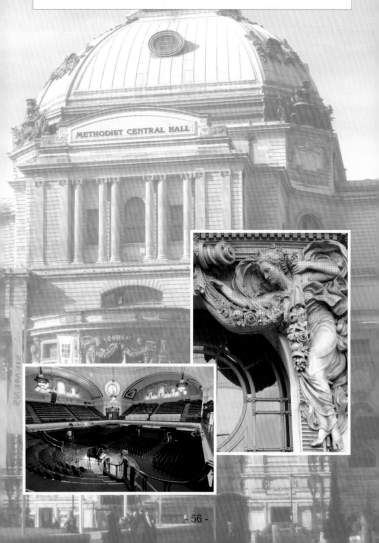

METHODIST CENTRAL HALL WESTMINSTER

*M*ethodist Central Hall – also called Westminster Central Hall – is a magnificent, richly-decorated Methodist church. It's a multi-purpose Edwardian building – Methodist church, conference and exhibition centre, concert hall, art gallery, office building, events venue and tourist attraction. The Hall was built in 1905-11 to mark the centenary of the death of John Wesley (the founder of Methodism) in 1791. It was funded by the 'Wesleyan Methodist Twentieth Century Fund' – or the 'Million Guinea Fund' as it became known – which raised one million guineas from one million Methodists.

> **The Football World Cup 'Jules Rimet trophy' was stolen from the Hall on 20th March 1966, but was recovered seven days later.**

Central Hall was designed by Edwin Alfred Rickards (1872-1920) of the firm Lanchester, Stewart and Rickards, in Viennese Baroque style with Romanesque decoration. It's an early example of the use of a reinforced concrete frame for a building in Britain – the domed ceiling of the Great Hall is a pioneering achievement in architectural engineering and the second-largest of its type in the world. The vast scale of the self-supporting ferro-concrete structure reflects the original objective that Central Hall was intended to be 'an open-air meeting place with a roof on it'. The angels in the exterior spandrels were designed by Henry Poole RA.

The beautiful Great Hall – with its impressive domed ceiling – seats up to 2,160 people and houses a splendid organ, containing 4,731 pipes. There's a long tradition of great music within the Central Hall, which is maintained though Church services and regular free public organ recitals. In 1968 it hosted the first public performance of Andrew Lloyd Webber's, *Joseph and the Amazing Technicolor Dreamcoat*, in a concert that also included his father, organist William Lloyd Webber (who was Musical Director at Central Hall), his brother, cellist Julian Lloyd Webber, and pianist John Lill.

The Hall hosted the first meeting of the United Nations General Assembly in 1946. In return for the use of the Hall, the Assembly voted to fund the repainting of the walls of the church in light blue – which still remains. It has been regularly used for political rallies – speakers have included Winston Churchill and has also welcomed members of the Royal Family and ambassadors from many countries – Mahatma Ghandi spoke in the Lecture Hall in autumn 1931 and General de Gaulle founded the Free French here in the early 1940s.

A unique and uplifting building with a fascinating history.

66 *A grand Edwardian building designed to inspire* **99**

Address: **Middlesex Guildhall, Parliament Square, SW1P 3BD**
(☎ 020-7960 1900/1500, 🖥 www.supremecourt.gov.uk).

Opening hours: **Mon-Fri, 9.30am to 4.30pm. Courts are usually in session Mon, 11am to 4pm and Tue-Thu, 10.30am to 4pm. Guided tours (50 mins) most Fridays, 11.30am, 1.30 and 3pm, and during the summer recess (see website for details).**

Cost: **Free. Guided tours (maximum 25) – adults £5, concessions £3.50, children under 16 free.**

Transport: **Westminster tube station.**

SUPREME COURT

*T*he Supreme Court of the United Kingdom is housed in the splendid Gothic extravaganza that is Middlesex Guildhall (Grade II* listed) in Westminster, which it shares with the Judicial Committee of the Privy Council. The Supreme Court is the highest court in all matters under English (includes Wales) and Northern Ireland law and Scottish civil law, and court of last resort and the highest appellate court in the UK. (The High Court of Justiciary remains the supreme court for criminal cases in Scotland.) The Supreme Court was established on 1st October 2009 and assumed the judicial functions of the House of Lords, which were exercised by the 'Law Lords'.

> **The Guildhall incorporates a doorway at the rear dating from the 17th century, which was a part of the Tothill Fields Bridewell prison.**

Middlesex Guildhall was built as the HQ for Middlesex County Council, abolished in 1965, after which it was used by the Greater London Quarter Sessions and later as a Crown Court centre. It was converted – not without controversy – for use by the Supreme Court in 2007-09. The building was designed by the Scottish architect James S. Gibson (1861-1951) and constructed in 1912-13, in what architectural expert Nikolaus Pevsner termed 'Art Nouveau Gothic', and decorated with fantastic medieval-looking gargoyles and other architectural sculptures by Henry Charles Fehr (1867-1940).

The building has a Portland stone exterior (load bearing with an internal steel frame) and a slate roof. It consists of three storeys, a basement and a dormered attic storey, with a steep hipped roof nine bays wide. The entrance is a segmental arched deep set portal with great segmental arched window above, framed by canted bay towers. A tower with large arched windows and lofty stone chimney stacks rises above the building to the same height as the nearby parish church of St Margaret. The exterior is decorated with fine stone carvings, and parapets and dormers, designed to mirror the nearby Palace of Westminster. Most impressive of all is the relief frieze above and to the sides of the entrance, extending over the canted bay towers.

On the lower ground floor a permanent exhibition provides an insight into the work and history of the Court, as well as that of the building. Members of the public are welcome to watch the Justices at work and can also book a guided tour (see opposite). There's a café on the lower ground floor.

❝ *A supreme Gothic delight* **❞**

Address: **Smith Square, SW1P 3HA (☎ 020-7222 106, 🖥 www.sjss.org.uk).**

Opening hours: **Mon-Fri, 10am to 5pm (until 6pm on concert days); Restaurant: Mon-Fri, 10.30am-2.45pm – on concert nights it re-opens two hours before performances. Thursday (1pm, £10) lunchtime concert series (see website).**

Cost: **See website for details of concerts and prices.**

Transport: **Westminster or St James's Park tube station.**

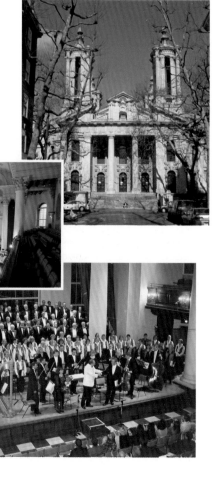

ST JOHN'S, SMITH SQUARE

*S*t John's, Smith Square (Grade 1 listed) is a former church that's regarded, not only as a masterpiece of English Baroque architecture, but as one of London's finest concert venues, attracting internationally renowned artists and performers.

Like so many of London's best and most beloved churches, St John's was planned under the Commission for Building Fifty New Churches in 1711, and was designed by Thomas Archer (1668-1743) and completed in 1728. The architectural style usually provokes a reaction in viewers – and comments aren't always complimentary! While his contemporaries included Vanbrugh and Hawksmoor, Archer's style owes more to the Italian influences he experienced on his Grand Tour, particularly that of Borromini.

For over 200 years St John's served the surrounding parish, though it appeared somewhat accident-prone. In 1742 its interior was damaged by fire, requiring extensive restoration; in 1773 it was struck by lightning and in 1815 the towers and roof had to be shored up. Finally on 10th May 1941, it was gutted by fire during the Blitz, leaving only a shell for over 20 years. The building was saved by the determination and dedication of Lady Parker of Waddington, who formed the Friends of St John's in 1962 to raise funds and restore the church to its former splendour for use as a concert hall. Work began in 1965 and the inaugural recital was given on 6th October 1969 by Dame Joan Sutherland and Richard Bonynge.

Since its resurrection as a concert venue, St John's has been regarded internationally as one of London's major concert halls, particularly for classical concerts. Its superb acoustic is suitable for most forms of music and its versatility enables it to accommodate a wide range of music without losing its special atmosphere of elegant intimacy. The atmospheric, brick-vaulted crypt houses the Smith Square Bar & Restaurant, and also contains an exhibition of photographs of historical St John's and the Concert Hall Box Office.

A concert at St John's is a pleasure not to be missed.

> St John's is often referred to as 'Queen Anne's Footstool' because when Archer was designing the church he asked the Queen what she wanted it to look like, whereupon she allegedly kicked over her footstool and said 'Like that!', giving rise to the building's four corner towers. The towers were, in fact, added to stabilise the building against subsidence.

 A splendid Baroque church resurrected as a concert hall

Address: Kensington Gardens, W2 3XA (☎ 020-7402 6075, 🖥 www.serpentinegallery.org).

Opening hours: Daily, 10am to 6pm. See website for information about exhibitions.

Cost: Free.

Transport: Lancaster Gate or South Kensington tube station.

Serpentine Gallery

SERPENTINE & SACKLER GALLERIES

*E*stablished in 1970 and housed in a classical (but unprepossessing) 1934 tea pavilion, the Serpentine Gallery is one of London's most important contemporary art galleries, yet unknown to many. The Gallery's world-renowned, temporary exhibition programme showcases work by the finest contemporary artists working across a huge variety of media. The secluded location to the west of the Long Water in Kensington Gardens makes this small and airy gallery an attractive destination, while its huge windows beam natural light onto the pieces, making the space perfect for sculpture and interactive displays.

Notable artists who have been exhibited here include Man Ray, Henry Moore, Andy Warhol, Bridget Riley, Anish Kapoor, Andreas Gursky, Christian Boltanski, Gabriel Orozco, Tomoko Takahashi, Philippe Parreno, Louise Bourgeois, Richard Prince, Wolfgang Tilmans, Gerhard Richter, Gustav Metzger, Damien Hirst and Jeff Koons. In Summer 2012, the Gallery presented a major exhibition of the work of artist Yoko Ono (John Lennon's widow).

In the grounds of the Gallery is a permanent work by artist and poet Ian Hamilton Finlay, dedicated to the Serpentine's former patron, Diana, Princess of Wales. The work comprises eight benches, a tree-plaque, and a carved stone circle at the Gallery's entrance.

The Serpentine Gallery Pavilion commission (begun in 2000) is an annual programme of temporary structures by internationally acclaimed architects and designers, which has become an important site for architectural experimentation. The series is unique and showcases the work of an international architect (or design team) who hasn't completed a building in England at the time of the Gallery's invitation. Each pavilion is sited on the Gallery's lawn for three months and the immediacy of the commission – a maximum of six months from invitation to completion – provides a unique model.

In summer 2012, the Serpentine Gallery opened its new space, the Serpentine Sackler Gallery (named after Dr Mortimer and Theresa Sackler), designed by the celebrated, award-winning architect Zaha Hadid. It's an innovative arts venue for the 21st century housed in an early 19th-century (1805), Grade II-listed building, The Magazine (a former powder store), in Kensington Gardens. The Serpentine Sackler aims to present the stars of tomorrow in art, architecture, dance, design, fashion, film, literature, music, performance and technology.

The Serpentine also has an excellent bookshop, which remains open in between exhibitions when the Gallery itself is closed. Why not finish your visit with lunch or tea in the Sackler or Orangery restaurant – bon appétit!

66 *Two world-class galleries for the price of one* **99**

Address: **Kensington Gore, SW7 2EU** (☎ **020-7590 4444,**
🖳 **www.rca.ac.uk**).

Opening hours: **Most exhibitions are open daily from 10am to 5.30pm
(see website for details).**

Cost: **Free.**

Transport: **High Street Kensington or South Kensington tube station.**

ROYAL COLLEGE OF ART

*T*he Royal College of Art (RCA) is a public research university specialising in art and design, and the world's only wholly postgraduate university of art and design. The RCA's galleries and lecture theatres are home to a lively programme of exhibitions, events and talks, most of which are free. There are also regular exhibitions of work by postgraduate students, lectures by leading art and design figures, and academic symposia.

The RCA was founded in 1837 as the Government School of Design and in 1853 became the National Art Training School with the Female School of Art in separate buildings. In 1896 it was renamed the Royal College of Art and in 1967 was granted a Royal Charter, endowing it with university status and the power to grant its own degrees. The RCA building, designed by staff from the RCA, is Grade II listed and dates from the '60s.

In its early days the RCA was dominated by a distinctive version of the Arts and Crafts philosophy. However, by the early 1900s that atmosphere had changed and it was the birthplace of 'The New Sculpture' movement, when students included such luminaries as Barbara Hepworth and Henry Moore. In the '30s and '40s, new courses were introduced such as graphic design and fashion, with students including the likes of Robin and Lucienne Day.

The '60s saw an industrial design course established, along with vehicle design in 1967, early graduates of which went on to design cars such as the Audi Quattro (Martin Smith), the Aston Martin DB7 (Ian Callum, now Head of Design at Jaguar) and the Porsche 911 (Tony Hatter). In recent decades, the fashion department has produced a new type of art student, including Gavin Turk, Tracey Emin, and Jake and Dinos Chapman, who were part of the movement that became known as the 'Young British Artists'.

Today, the RCA is the world's most influential art college with an unrivalled creative environment – one of the most concentrated and exciting communities of artists and designers to be found anywhere.

> **In the '50s and '60s the RCA was at the centre of the explosion of pop art culture, a vibrant, invigorating movement, whose alumni included Peter Blake, David Hockney and RB Kitaj, while the fashion and textiles department was leading its own design revolution with soon-to-be household names Ossie Clark and Zandra Rhodes.**

 An inspiration for artists and designers everywhere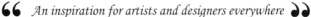

Address: Prince Consort Road, SW7 2BS (☎ 020-7591 4300, 🖥 www.rcm.ac.uk).

Opening hours: Tue-Fri, 11.30am to 4.30pm. Tours (1 hr) are held regularly during term time on Tue (2-3pm) and Thu (noon-1pm); to book ☎ 020-7591 4310/4867.

Cost: Free. Guided museum tours (maximum 25 people) £5 per head, concessions £4.

Transport: South Kensington tube station.

ROYAL COLLEGE OF MUSIC MUSEUM

*T*he Royal College of Music (RCM) is a conservatoire established by royal charter in 1882, housed in a beautiful red brick Victorian building. It was founded in 1882 to provide systematic training for professional musicians, and establish a school of music to rank alongside the conservatoires of Berlin, Brussels, Leipzig, Milan, Paris and Vienna.

The college building was designed by Sir Arthur Blomfield (1829-1899) in Flemish Mannerist style – using red brick dressed with buff-coloured stone. Construction began in 1892 and the building opened in May 1894. It was largely financed by donations from Yorkshire industrialist Samson Fox, whose statue stands in the entrance hall, along with that of the Prince of Wales (later Edward VII).

Students in its early days included Samuel Coleridge-Taylor, Gustav Holst, Ralph Vaughan Williams and John Ireland, while its later alumni include Benjamin Britten, Colin Davis, Gwyneth Jones, Neville Mariner, Rick Wakeman, Andrew and Julian Lloyd Webber, and John Williams. Today it trains some 650 students from over 50 countries.

The RCM's main concert venue is the Amaryllis Fleming (a cello player and teacher) concert hall, a 468-seat, barrel-vaulted concert hall, also designed by Blomfield; built in 1901 it was extensively restored in 2008-09. The Britten theatre, which seats 400, was opened by Queen Elizabeth II in 1986 and is used for opera, ballet, music and theatre. There's also a 150-seat recital hall dating from 1965, as well as several smaller recital rooms, including the three organ-equipped Parry Rooms.

Since opening in 1882, the College has had a distinguished list of teachers and alumni, including most of the composers who brought about the 'English musical renaissance' of the 19th and 20th centuries.

The College's museum houses a collection of over 1,000 instruments and accessories from the 15th century to the present day. Among them is the anonymous clavicytherium (c1480), believed to be the earliest surviving stringed keyboard instrument, and remarkable and unfamiliar instruments such as the contrabassophon, division viol, serpent and glass armonica, plus trombones owned and played by Elgar and Holst. The RCM also holds significant collections of research material dating from the 15th century onwards, including autographs (musical scores in the composer's own handwriting) such as Haydn's String Quartet Op. 64/1, Mozart's Piano Concerto K491 and Elgar's Cello Concerto.

Members of the public can attend a wide range of events, including lecture tours with live demonstrations, seminars, lecture recitals, concerts and special exhibitions.

66 *A college fit for budding master musicians* **99**

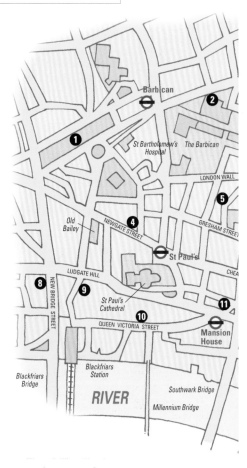

CHAPTER 2

CITY OF LONDON

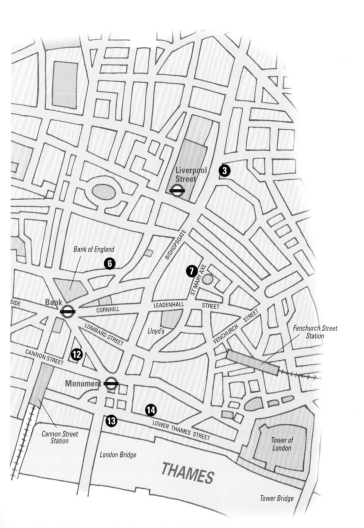

Address: **East Market Building, EC1A 9PQ (☎ 020-7332 3092, 🖳 www.smithfieldmarket.com).**

Opening hours: **Mon-Fri, 3am until mid-morning; to see the market at its best, visitors should arrive by 7am. Tours (1½ hrs) by City Guides (🖳 www.cityoflondontouristguides.com) once a month commencing at 7am (min. age 16, max. number 12 – booking necessary).**

Cost: **Free. Tours – adults £8, concessions £6.**

Transport: **Barbican tube station.**

SMITHFIELD MARKET

S mithfield (meat) Market is one of London's oldest markets – dating back over 800 years – housed in an imposing Victorian (Grade II* listed) building in one of the City's most historic areas. Smithfield is a meat market and the last surviving historical wholesale market in central London. In the 12th century, Smithfield was a vast recreational area where jousts and tournaments took place, but from the 13th century it was used as a place of execution for criminals, heretics and political opponents, including major historical figures such as Scottish patriot William Wallace and Wat Tyler, the leader of the Peasant's Revolt.

A livestock market occupied the site as early as the 10th century, which grew in size and significance over the centuries. Live animals were brought to the market on the hoof (later by rail) and slaughtered on site; by the end of the 18th century the number of animals being transported to London was causing mayhem and encroaching on nearby streets and houses. And conditions were appalling – both for the animals and workers – which raised major health concerns. This led to a new cattle-market being opened outside the City in Copenhagen Fields (Islington) in 1855.

> Smithfield was also the location of the Bartholomew Fair for almost 700 years – three days of merrymaking, dancing, selling and music – until being banned in 1855 due to violence, drunkenness and debauchery (its *raison d'être!*).

The current Italian-inspired covered market was designed by Sir Horace Jones (1819-1887) – whose masterpiece was Tower Bridge – and opened in 1868. The main wings (known as the East and West Market) are separated by the Grand Avenue, a wide roadway roofed by an elliptical arch – a vast cathedral-like structure of ornamental cast iron, stone, Welsh slate and glass. At the two ends of the arcade, four huge statues represent London, Edinburgh, Liverpool and Dublin, and bronze dragons hold the City's coat of arms. At the corners of the market, four octagonal pavilion towers were built, each with a dome and carved stone griffins. The market has been extended, modified and rebuilt (e.g. due to fire and WWII damage) over the past 140 years, but is still dominated by its original Victorian buildings.

Before you leave, visit one of Smithfield's excellent pubs or restaurants, such as the celebrated St John's, Café du Marché or 26 Smithfield – if you arrive early enough you can even have breakfast in one of the local pubs.

❝ *A carnivore's delight!* **❞**

AT A GLANCE

Address: Silk Street, London Wall, EC2Y 8DS (☎ 020-7638 4141, 🖥 www.barbican.org.uk).

Opening hours: Centre – Mon-Sat, 9am to 11pm; Sun and Bank Holidays, noon to 11pm; Art Gallery – daily, 11am to 8pm, except for Weds, 11 to 6pm and Thurs, 11am to 10pm; Conservatory – 11am to 5.30pm on most Sundays. See website for information about tours.

Cost: Free. Tours – adults £8, concessions £6.

Transport: Barbican tube station.

BARBICAN ARTS CENTRE

*T*he Barbican Arts Centre (Grade II listed) is a prominent example of British Brutalist concrete architecture and Europe's largest arts and conference venue, staging a comprehensive range of art, music, theatre, dance, film and creative learning events. The Centre hosts classical and contemporary music concerts, theatre performances, film screenings and art exhibitions. It's owned, funded, and managed by the City of London Corporation, the third-largest funder of arts in the UK, and was built as the city's gift to the nation at a cost of £161m. It was opened by Queen Elizabeth II on 3rd March 1982.

The Centre comprises the 1,949 seat Barbican Hall, the 1,166-seat Barbican Theatre, the 200-seat Pit theatre, a 286-seat cinema, the Barbican Art Gallery, 'The Curve' gallery, plus a library, Lakeside Terrace, roof-top tropical conservatory, gardens and three restaurants. It's home to the London Symphony Orchestra, while the BBC Symphony Orchestra is also based in the Barbican Centre's concert hall.

The Arts Centre is part of the vast 40-acre (16ha) Barbican Estate, which includes three residential tower blocks. It was built between 1965 and 1976 and designed by architects Chamberlin, Powell and Bon.

> **Designated a site of special architectural interest for its scale, cohesion and ambition, the Arts Centre's design – a concrete ziggurat – is controversial and divides opinion: it was voted 'London's ugliest building' in an unofficial poll in 2003.**

The second-floor library is one of the largest public libraries in London and contains a separate arts library, a large music library and a children's library. The library houses the 'London Collection' of historical books and resources, some of which date back 300 years, all available on loan. The library presents regular literary events and has an art exhibition space for hire, while the music library has a free practice piano for public use.

The conservatory (the second-largest in London) is a hidden tropical oasis, home to finches, quails, exotic fish and over 2,000 species of tropical plants and trees. Outside, the main focal point of the Centre is the lake and its neighbouring terrace and gardens, which are impressive public spaces with waterside seating and city views.

The Centre has a complex multi-level layout with numerous entrances; lines painted on the ground are designed to help visitors navigate through the labyrinthine Barbican Housing Estate. Well worth a visit, even if you get lost!

❝ *A brutal building concealing hidden treasures* **❞**

Address: **230 Bishopsgate, EC2M 4QH** (☎ **020-7392 9200,**
🖥 **www.bishopsgate.org.uk**).

Opening hours: **Box Office – Mon-Fri, 9am to 8.30pm, Sat, 10am to
5.30pm (see website for events); Library – Mon-Sat, 10am to 5.30pm
(2pm on Fri); Café – Mon-Fri, 7.30am to 10pm, Sat, 10am to 10pm, Sun,
10am to 6pm.**

Cost: **Use of the library and many events are free.**

Transport: **Liverpool Street tube station.**

BISHOPSGATE INSTITUTE

*T*he Bishopsgate Institute (Grade II* listed) is a celebrated cultural institute established in 1895 and housed in an historic 19th-century building. Described as a home for ideas and debate, learning and enquiry, and a place where independent thought is cherished, the Institute offers a cultural events programme, courses for adults, an historic library, archive collections and a community programme.

The Institute was the first of three major buildings designed by architect Charles Harrison Townsend (1851-1928), the others being the nearby Whitechapel Gallery and the Horniman Museum in south London. His work combined elements of Arts and Crafts and Art Nouveau styles, along with the typically Victorian. The Great Hall of the Bishopsgate Institute was refurbished in 2011 and a new café-bar opened.

> **The Bishopsgate Institute was created largely through the vision and dedication of Reverend William Rogers (1819-1896), who persuaded the Charity Commissioners to allocate the vast funds – assembled by St Botolph's church over 500 years – to build the Institute.**

The original aims of the Institute were to provide a public library, public hall and meeting rooms for people living and working in the City. The Great Hall in particular was 'erected for the benefit of the public to promote lectures, exhibitions and otherwise the advancement of literature, science and the fine arts'. The Institute's library is a free, independent library – open to all – which holds important historical collections about London, the labour movement, free thought and cooperative movements, as well as the history of protest and campaigning, dating from the early 19th century to the present day. The library's archives also contain a collection of over 20,000 images, including many of famous London landmarks (churches, statues, open spaces and buildings), plus social and cultural scenes from the early 20th century.

The Bishopsgate Institute hosts a range of cultural events throughout the year, including many inspired by Bishopsgate Library's historical and radical library and archive collections. These include a range of talks, walks and debates, as well as free lunch-time concerts in the Great Hall. The Institute also offers a full programme of adult courses that have been developed for complete beginners, with advanced classes in many subjects. Classes are held during lunch times, afternoons and evenings.

Whether you're visiting the Institute for the library, a course or a cultural event, or just wish to relax – you'll find the café (Bishopsgate Kitchen) a great place to unwind at any time of the day.

66 *An institution ahead of its time* **99**

Address: Newgate Street and King Edward Street, EC1A 7BA
(🖥 www.cityoflondon.gov.uk/openspaces and www.opensquares.org/
detail/christchurch.html).

Opening hours: Unrestricted access.

Cost: Free.

Transport: St Paul's tube station.

CHRISTCHURCH GREYFRIARS ROSE GARDEN

*C*hristchurch Greyfriars Rose Garden is an enchanting small garden created on the remains of Christchurch Greyfriars church on Newgate Street. The first church was constructed between 1306 and 1348 as the church of a Franciscan monastery established on the site in 1225 (the name 'Greyfriars' is from the Franciscans' grey habits). After the Dissolution of the Monasteries in 1538, Henry VIII gifted the church to the City and it reopened in 1547.

The Gothic church was destroyed in the Great Fire in 1666 and a new church was designed by Sir Christopher Wren in the neoclassical style, which was completed in 1687 with a steeple added in 1704. The church was an important centre of City society and music, and ranked among its most notable buildings and places of worship. Felix Mendelssohn played Bach's A minor fugue and other works on the organ in 1837, and Samuel Wesley also performed at the church.

The church was severely damaged in the Blitz in 1940, on a devastating night in which a total of eight Wren churches burned. The roof and vaulting collapsed into the nave, while the tower and four main walls, made of stone, remained standing but were smoke-scarred and gravely weakened. After the war it was decided not to rebuild the church, although the remains were designated a Grade I listed building in 1950 (the surviving east wall had to be demolished in 1962). In 1989, the former nave area became a public garden and memorial, while the tower and spire were converted into a private residence in 2006.

> **The wooden font cover from Wren's church – rescued from the fire in 1940 – can be seen today in the porch of St Sepulchre-without-Newgate.**

Today, Greyfriars is a lovely garden reflecting the floor plan of the original church. The nave was made into a rose garden with paths where the aisles would have been and pergolas where columns once stood. Box-hedged rose beds represent the original position of the pews, while clematis and climbing roses weave their way up ten tall wooden towers which represent the pillars that once held the roof. The garden was redesigned in 2011 in a colour scheme of mainly blue, purple and white, with shots of deep crimson, silver and lime to bring it to life. The wooden towers house a variety of discreet bird boxes to entice birdlife.

A welcome sanctuary in the City.

 One of the City's most beautiful gardens

AT A GLANCE

Address: 7 Wood St, EC2P 2NQ (☎ 020-7601 2328,
🖳 **www.citypolicemuseum.org.uk).**

Opening hours: **Tue,10am to 4pm, Wed, 11am to 4pm, Fri. 2-6pm.**
Visitors are requested to confirm opening times, which are liable to
change. Groups of more than ten are requested to make a booking.

Cost: **Free.**

Transport: **St Paul's tube station.**

CITY OF LONDON POLICE MUSEUM

*T*he City of London Police (COLP) Museum traces the history of the police force that has guarded the City of London since 1839. The COLP is responsible for law enforcement within the City of London – The Square Mile – including the Middle and Inner Temples, while the rest of Greater London is policed by the Metropolitan Police Service, a separate organisation. (For historic reasons, the City of London is administered separately from the rest of Greater London.) Nowadays the City is primarily a financial centre with a resident population of just 12,000, which is swelled by the daily influx of some 320,000 commuters who work within the City borders.

Policing in the City of London has existed since Roman times; Wood Street Police Station – the HQ of the City Police – is built on the site of a Roman fortress, which may have housed some of the first 'police' in the City. Before 1839 – when the COLP was formed – the responsibility for policing in the City was divided between the Day Police and Night Watch, primarily under two Sheriffs, which were merged into a single organisation.

The City Police HQ on Wood Street houses a small but interesting museum dedicated to the history of crime and policing in the City. The museum offers a captivating insight into the deeds of criminals and villains, from Jack the Ripper to the enigmatic Latvian revolutionary criminal Peter the Painter, and takes a look at the lives of the men and women who have guarded the City since 1839. From the first police call box in London, via the history of the police uniform and Olympic glory (gold medals won by City policemen in 1908), to the grisly stories of the City's criminal past (murders, robberies, assassinations and gun battles), you'll discover the story of crime and policing in the City of London.

The unique collection charts the development of the UK police service, from the earliest days through to modern policing methods. Guided tours led by knowledgeable volunteers provide remarkable insights into crime in Victorian London, tell how social changes affect the work of the police force, and introduce you to the curious and eclectic museum collection.

> **There's a small collection related to the Jack the Ripper murders of 1888, including photographs of the victims and information about the police investigation, plus the Houndsditch Murders of 1910, which led to the infamous Siege of Sidney Street.**

 Meet Jack the Ripper and Peter the Painter

Address: Throgmorton Avenue, EC2N 2DQ (☎ 020-7448 1304, 🖳 www.thedrapers.co.uk, ✉ banqueting@ thedrapers.co.uk).

Opening hours: Group tours (1¾ hrs) by appointment (maximum 40 people). There are no tours between the end of July and mid-September.

Cost: No formal charge, but a charity donation is requested.

Transport: Bank or Liverpool Street tube station.

DRAPERS' HALL

*T*he 18th-century Drapers' Hall is one of the grandest in the City, with lavishly decorated rooms, an extensive silver collection, and a charming garden and courtyard. The Worshipful Company of Drapers is one of the 108 Livery Companies of the City of London – its formal name is 'The Master and Wardens and Brethren and Sisters of the Guild or Fraternity of the Blessed Mary the Virgin of the Mystery of Drapers of the City of London' (phew!) – but thankfully it's usually known simply as the Drapers' Company. It ranks third in the order of precedence of the Livery Companies and is one of the historic Twelve City Livery Companies.

> Today, the company's activities include managing its endowment and acting as the corporate trustee of charities. Its members also perform important functions in the elections of the government of the City and its public servants.

An informal association of drapers has existed since at least 1180, but the company was officially founded in 1361 and received its royal charter in 1364. Originally a trade association of wool and cloth merchants, it was one of the most powerful companies in London politics. Over 100 Lord Mayors have been members of the company, which also has a long association with royalty; a number of sovereigns have been or are members, including Queen Elizabeth II and King Harald of Norway.

Like many other livery companies, the Drapers' Company is housed in a grand building named after itself. The company has owned its current site since 1543, when it purchased the mansion of Thomas Cromwell (executed in 1540) from Henry VIII. The building was destroyed in the Great Fire and rebuilt to designs by Edward Jarman. After another fire in 1772, it was rebuilt again, when the architect was John Gorham; further alterations were made in the 19th century. The Hall survived the Blitz during WWII.

The Hall includes four lavishly decorated principal rooms, which are used for the company's and client's functions. The Livery Hall can accommodate 260 guests for dinner and is often used for film locations, including *The King's Speech*, *GoldenEye* and *The Lost Prince*. The company has a unique collection of works of art, silver and artefacts, which has been accumulated and developed over the centuries.

Groups can book a guided tour of Drapers' Hall and its gardens – a rare chance to visit one of the City's great historic halls.

 A rare surviving 18th-century Livery Company hall

Address: **Great St Helen's, EC3A 6AT** (☎ **020-7283 2231,**
🖳 **www.st-helens.org.uk).**

Opening hours: **Mon-Fri, 9.30am to 12.30pm (but confirm by
telephone). See website for service times.**

Cost: **Free (but donations are welcome).**

Transport: **Liverpool Street tube station.**

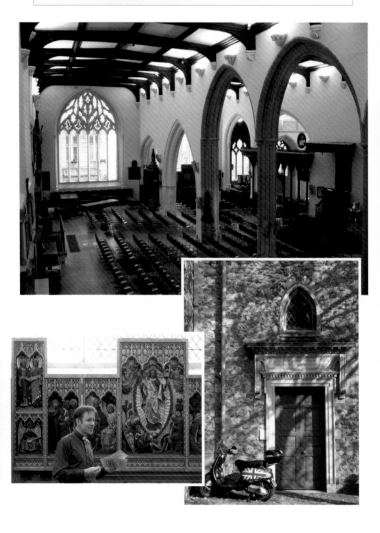

ST HELEN'S BISHOPSGATE

*S*t Helen's Bishopsgate (Grade I listed) is a 12th-century Anglican church and the largest surviving church in the City, containing more monuments than any other London church except for Westminster Abbey. The church dates from 1210 when a priory of Benedictine nuns was founded and is the only remaining building from a nunnery in the City.

St Helen's is unusual in that it was designed with two parallel naves, giving it a wide interior. Until the dissolution of the priory in 1538, the church was divided in two by a partition running from east to west, the northern half serving the nuns and the southern for the parishioners. After the Reformation, the Leathersellers' Company acquired the convent buildings and land to the north of the church. The nuns' choir became part of the parish church and the screen was removed from between the choir and the main body of the church, which is largely the building we see today.

> Among the church's many memorials are the altar tombs of Sir John Crosby (d 1476), founder of Crosby Hall, and Agnes his wife, and Sir Thomas Gresham (1519-1579), founder of the Royal Exchange.

St Helen's was the parish church of William Shakespeare when he lived in the area in the 1590s. In the 17th century, two classical doorcases were added to the otherwise Gothic church, which was heavily restored by John Loughborough Pearson (1817-1897) in 1891-1893.

St Helen's was one of only a few City churches to survive both the Great Fire of 1666 and the Blitz in WWII intact, but it wasn't so fortunate in 1992-93 when it was badly damaged by IRA bombs which exploded nearby. The roof of the building was lifted and one of the City's largest medieval stained glass windows was shattered. The church has since been fully restored, though many of the older monuments within it were entirely destroyed. Architect Quinlan Terry (b 1937), an enthusiast of Georgian architecture, designed the restoration along Reformation lines. After the bomb damage was repaired the church became a more flexible open space, lighter than previously, yet retaining its ancient grandeur.

St Helen's has a fine organ (Grade II* listed) dating from 1744, when an annuity organ made by Thomas Griffin was installed, which has undergone several restorations over the centuries.

A superb historic church and a great survivor, well worth a visit.

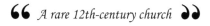

66 *A rare 12th-century church* **99**

ST BRIDE FOUNDATION & LIBRARY

*T*he St Bride Foundation – named after nearby St Bride's Church – is a stimulating cultural centre and library in the City. It was established in 1891 (as the St Bride Institute) to meet the educational, cultural and social needs of a community working within the burgeoning print industry of the Victorian era; it housed both a technical library and printing school, providing tuition for local printers and students. Today, the Foundation brings together exhibition spaces, a theatre, an educational centre and a library – one of the most significant collections of typography and historical printed reference books and documents in the world.

St Bride lies in the heart of Fleet Street, synonymous with the British press and former home to many of London's newspaper publishing houses. Though the presses have moved away (mostly to Canary Wharf), there continues to be a working community here. In the spirit of its philanthropic originators, the Foundation continues to provide a stimulating community environment that creates a focal point for encouraging and developing everyone's potential through a broad range of activities.

The processes and techniques explored at St Bride Printing School years ago are again thriving as letterpress undergoes something of a renaissance in the UK. The Foundation keeps the traditions and heritage of printing alive through a wide range of workshops, lectures, conferences and exhibitions.

The Foundation has always recognised the importance of dramatic arts in the development of the community and has produced theatrical entertainments as part of its remit for the last 115 years. Visitors can take in a free lunchtime show at the Lunchbox Theatre (1pm daily) – including everything from classics to brand new pieces by up and coming writers – or attend an evening performance in the Bridewell Theatre (one of London's few off-West End theatres). From classics to contemporary, the Bridewell plays host to a variety of companies including the Guildhall School of Music and Drama and the Artelier Dance Company. There's also the Bridewell Bar, which hosts live music and occasional special events.

Although it's often a cliché, St Bride really does offer something for everyone.

> The St Bride Library opened on the 20th November 1895 as a technical library for the printing school and printing trades. The library's collections cover printing and related subjects, including paper and binding, graphic design and typography, typefaces and calligraphy, illustration and printmaking, publishing and book-selling – and access is free to everyone.

 A unique cultural centre and font of creative inspiration

Address: Black Friars Lane, EC4V 6EJ (☎ 020-7236 1189,
🖳 www.apothecaries.org).

**Opening hours: Tours (2 hrs) can be arranged for groups with a
minimum of around 12 people.**

Cost: Tours, £10 per head.

Transport: St Paul's or Mansion House tube station.

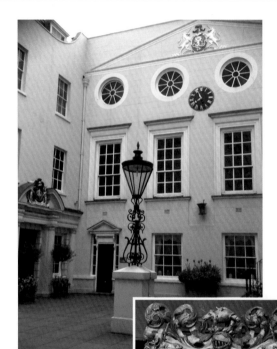

APOTHECARIES' HALL

*A*pothecaries' Hall is a splendid 17th-century building, with its original floor plan and many original features, and is one of the few halls that permits visitors. The Worshipful Society of Apothecaries is 58th in the order of precedence of the 108 Livery Companies of the City of London, and the largest. Originally, apothecaries (the word is derived from *apotheca*, meaning a place where wine, spices and herbs were stored) were members of the Grocers' Company (1345) and before that members of the Guild of Pepperers (1180). The apothecaries were granted a Royal Charter in 1617 and during the 17th century its members (including Nicholas Culpeper) constantly challenged the monopoly of the College of Physicians.

In 1704, the Society won the right to prescribe and dispense medicines, which led directly to the evolution of the apothecary into today's general practitioner of medicine. Just over a century later, as a result of the Apothecaries' Act of 1815, the Society was given the statutory right to conduct examinations and to grant licences to practise medicine throughout England and Wales.

> **The Society of Apothecaries founded the Chelsea Physic Garden in Chelsea in 1673, one of the oldest botanical gardens in Europe, and the second-oldest in Britain.**

The society's original hall was Cobham House, purchased in 1632, which was destroyed in the Great Fire in 1666. A new hall was built on the same site and completed in 1672 to the designs of Edward Jerman. An *Elaboratory* was included for the first ever large-scale manufacture of drugs (the Society manufactured and sold medicinal and pharmaceutical products at the Hall until 1922). A major restoration and building programme was carried out in the 1780s and the Hall underwent major re-development in the '80s, although its external appearance has altered little since the late 18th century.

It's the oldest extant livery company hall in the City, with the first-floor structure and arrangement of the Great Hall, Court Room and Parlour remaining as it was in 1672. The Great Hall – with its original 17th-century oak panelling – has a 24-branch candelabrum presented by Sir Benjamin Rawling (d 1775), Sheriff of London and Master, in 1736. The windows on the east and west sides of the Hall contain stained glass Coats of Arms of Past Masters and former Officers of the Society, and portraits hang on the walls.

Don't miss the rare opportunity to visit an outstanding Livery Hall.

66 *The 'bringers of help'* **99**

Address: Queen Victoria Street, EC4V 4BT (☎ 020-7248 2762, 🖳 www.college-of-arms.gov.uk).

Opening hours: Mon-Fri, 10am to 4pm, excluding Public Holidays and state occasions.

Cost: **Free.**

Transport: **Blackfriars or Mansion House tube station.**

COLLEGE OF ARMS MUSEUM

*T*he College of Arms (or Herald's College) is a royal corporation consisting of professional officers of arms, with jurisdiction over England, Wales, Northern Ireland and some Commonwealth realms (the Court of the Lord Lyon performs the same functions in Scotland). Founded by royal charter of Richard III in 1484, the College's function was the design and creation of coats of arms, which developed and diversified into genealogical research.

The College comprises 13 officers or heralds: three Kings of Arms, six Heralds of Arms and four Pursuivants of Arms. There are also seven officers extraordinary, who take part in ceremonial occasions but aren't part of the College. The entire corporation is overseen by the Earl Marshal, a hereditary office held by the Duke of Norfolk, currently Edward Fitzalan-Howard, 18th Duke of Norfolk.

The heralds are appointed by the British Sovereign and delegated authority to act on her behalf in all matters of heraldry, the granting of new coats of arms, genealogical research and the recording of pedigrees. The College maintains a registry of armorial and family records. The College of Arms also undertakes and consults on the planning of many ceremonial occasions such as coronations, state funerals, the annual Garter Service and the State Opening of Parliament. College heralds accompany the sovereign on many occasions, wearing their highly distinctive mediaeval uniform, the tabard, a coat embroidered on its front, back and sleeves with the Royal Arms.

> **In the early mediaeval period the proclamation and organisation of tournaments was the chief function of heralds, who marshalled and introduced the contestants and kept a tally of the score.**

The College, which is one of the few remaining official heraldic authorities in Europe, has had its home in the City since its foundation, and has been at its present location on Queen Victoria Street since 1555. The original building was lost in the Great Fire in 1666 and the current College dates from the 1670s, containing the Earl Marshall's Court, complete with original panelling, gallery and throne. There's an extensive library and document store. In 1941 during WWII, the College was almost consumed by fire, which had already levelled all the buildings to the east on Queen Victoria Street – the building was given up for lost, but was saved at the last minute by a change in the wind direction.

 A great institution or an anachronism?

Address: **Watling Street, EC4M 9BW (☎ 020-7248 9902,**
🖳 **http://homepage.ntlworld.com/mothersole).**

Opening hours: **Mon-Fri, 11am to 3pm. See website for service times.**

Cost: **Free (but donations are welcome).**

Transport: **Mansion House tube station.**

ST MARY ALDERMARY

*S*t Mary Aldermary (Grade I listed) is an ashlar-faced 17th-century Anglican church with a gorgeous interior, rebuilt by Wren in Gothic style after the Great Fire. There has been a church on this site for over 900 years and its name is usually taken to mean that it's the oldest of the City churches dedicated to the Virgin Mary. It's thought that the church was founded and sponsored by Benedictine monastics, although little evidence of this has survived. From the 16th century, John Stow mentioned various dignitaries buried in the early church in his 1598 Survey of London, including Richard Chaucer, vintner, a relative of the poet Geoffrey Chaucer.

> According to the art expert Nikolaus Pevsner, St Mary is 'the chief surviving monument of the 17th-century Gothic revival in the City and, along with the Collegiate Church of St Mary, Warwick, the most important late 17th-century Gothic church in England.'

In 1510, Sir Henry Keeble, a grocer and Lord Mayor, financed the building of a new church, although the tower was unfinished when he died in 1518 and wasn't actually completed until over a century later, in 1629. The church was said to have been among the largest and finest of the City's churches and a number of City notables were buried there. The parish registers date from 1558 (the year Elizabeth I ascended to the throne) and records that poet John Milton (1608-1674) married his third wife, Elizabeth Minshull, there in 1663.

St Mary Aldermary was badly damaged in the Great Fire in 1666, although parts of its walls and tower survived. It was rebuilt by Sir Christopher Wren in a Gothic style and opened in 1682. The post-fire church follows the Late Perpendicular style of the Keeble church, incorporating the walls and foundations that remained after the fire. It's the only surviving Wren church in the City built in the Gothic style; the interior is stunningly original and the mouldings and unique plaster vaulting in the nave and aisles make it a joy to visit.

St Mary Aldermary was damaged in the Blitz, when its windows were shattered and some plaster fell from the vaulting, but the building itself remained intact. It was restored in the '50s and has been sensitively repaired and restored many times over the years, most recently in 2005. It's now the home of the Moot monastic community (🖥 www.moot.uk.net).

 The most beautiful Gothic interior in the City

Address: **Abchurch Lane, EC4N 7BA** (☎ **020-7626 4481/0306,** ✉ **rector@stmagnusmartyr.org.uk**).

Opening hours: **Tue-Fri, 10am to 4pm – but confirm before travelling. See website for service times.**

Cost: **Free (but donations are welcome).**

Transport: **Monument tube station.**

ST MARY ABCHURCH

*S*t Mary Abchurch – dedicated to the Blessed Virgin Mary – is a Grade 1 listed Church of England church with an exquisite interior. One of Wren's finest and least altered churches, St Mary's has been described as a treasury of 17th-century art. The original church, dating back to the 12th century, was destroyed in the Great Fire in 1666 and rebuilt by Sir Christopher Wren in 1681-86 under the supervision of Robert Hooke (1635-1703). It has a four-storey, 51ft (15.5m) tower with a leaded spire and a pleasing red brick exterior with stone dressings. The dome, springing

> In medieval Europe, the pelican was thought to be particularly attentive to her young, to the point of providing her own blood when no other food was available, which led to the pelican becoming a symbol of the Passion of Jesus and of the Eucharist.

from four plain brick walls, has no external thrusts and measures over 40ft (12.2m) across.

As with many of Wren's churches, the plain exterior belies what awaits unsuspecting visitors, who are immediately struck by the magnificent painted dome (William Snow) depicting worship in heaven, which crowns the church. The beautiful interior was decorated by some of Wren's most talented associates; William Grey made the splendid pulpit; the fine door cases, font cover, rails and royal coat of arms are by William Emmett; and the lovely font is by William Kempster. However, the crowning glory is the grand altar-piece (reredos) by Britain's greatest woodcarver, Grinling Gibbons (1648-1721), capped by four gilded urns. This is the largest example of his work (except for St Paul's Cathedral) in any City church and the only authenticated one. Also of note are the original high pews on three sides.

The gilded 'pelican in her piety' (see box) makes its appearance both on the reredos and in the original copper weathervane made by Robert Bird (now located over the north door). The Pelican is also the badge of Corpus Christi College Cambridge, with which the church has been associated since the reign of Elizabeth I.

The church was bombed during the Blitz in 1940, which badly damaged the dome and Gibbons' reredos. The dome was repainted by Hoyle and the reredos, smashed to pieces, was painstakingly restored over a period of five years.

Don't forego an opportunity to see this magnificent Wren church and its treasures.

 A Wren masterpiece, painstakingly restored

Address: Lower Thames Street, EC3R 6DN (☎ 020-7626 4481,
🖥 www.stmagnusmartyr.org.uk).

Opening hours: Tue-Fri, 10am to 4pm, and Sun mornings. See website
for service times.

Cost: Free (but donations are welcome).

Transport: Monument tube station.

ST MAGNUS THE MARTYR

*S*t Magnus the Martyr (Grade I listed) is a beautiful church built at the north end of the old London Bridge – the main route into the City – where there has been a church for some 1,000 years. The church is dedicated to St Magnus the Martyr, the Earl of Orkney, who was executed on the island of Egilsay in 1116. Magnus had a reputation for piety and gentleness and was canonised in 1135. Early records show a Church of St Magnus existed in 1067, demolished in 1234 and replaced by a larger one.

Its position close to London Bridge played an important part in the life of the church and the City. By a decree of Pope Innocent IV in 1250, a bishop visiting his diocese was permitted to summon his clergy to one place for a general meeting, which from the 15th to the 17th centuries was St Magnus, probably due to its proximity to the river.

St Magnus narrowly escaped destruction in a fire in 1633, which consumed over 40 buildings surrounding the bridge. However, it wasn't so fortunate during the Great Fire in 1666 when it was one of the first buildings to be destroyed, being just 300m from the bakehouse in Pudding Lane where the fire started. St Magnus was one of 51 parish churches rebuilt by Sir Christopher Wren after the fire, the work spanning 1671-76, although the steeple (56m) wasn't completed until 1706.

For over two centuries, the great clock (1709) projecting from the tower was a famous London landmark (now obscured by surrounding buildings). The church survived another serious fire in 1760, and during the Blitz in 1940 a bomb fell on London Bridge, blowing out the church's windows and damaging the plasterwork and the roof of the north aisle (repaired in 1951).

Today, St Magnus welcomes visitors from around the world, who come to marvel at its magnificent interior, see the world-famous model of the old London Bridge and listen to the celebrated new ring of 12 bells (2009). The church is also noted for its 18th-century organ and liturgical music, and is the venue for a wide range of musical events.

> **The church's spiritual importance is celebrated in the poem *The Waste Land* by T. S. Eliot, who adds in a footnote that 'the interior of St Magnus the Martyr is to my mind one of the finest among Wren's interiors'.**

 A beautiful Wren church on an historic site

Address: 16-18 St-Mary-at-Hill, EC3R 8EF (☎ 020-7283 2373, 🖥 www.watermenshall.org, ✉ carol@watermenshall.org).

Opening hours: Guided tours (max. 36 people), Mon and Fri mornings, 10.30am.

Cost: Tours, £12 per head. Visitors can also enjoy lunch for an additional fee.

Transport: Monument tube station.

WATERMEN'S HALL

*T*he beautiful Watermen's Hall is the home of The Company of Watermen and Lightermen and the only original Georgian Hall in the City, a perfect example of 18th-century domestic architecture. Watermen (or wherrymen) were an essential part of early London life; using a small boat called a wherry or skiff they would ferry passengers along and across the river. With bad rural roads and narrow, congested city streets, the Thames was the most convenient highway and until the mid-18th century, London Bridge was the only bridge below Kingston.

In 1510, Henry VIII granted a licence to watermen that gave them exclusive rights to carry passengers on the river. The Company of Watermen (they combined with their colleagues in cargo to form the Company of Watermen and Lightermen in 1700) was established by Act of Parliament in 1555 to control watermen on the Thames. It remains the only ancient City Guild to he formed and controlled by an Act of Parliament. London's lack of bridges and rolling marsh-filled landscape to the south and east were perfect for access by boat and the Thames was the main thoroughfare for all kinds of traffic. In a survey of 1598 (Stow) it was estimated that some 40,000 men earned a living on or about the river.

The present Company Hall, dating from 1780, was designed by William Blackburn and remains the only original Georgian Hall in the City of London. It was extended in 1983 to include the Freemen's Room, which blends with the intimate atmosphere of the Court Room – the heart of the original building – the Silver Room (containing the company's finest silver treasures) and the Parlour Room (with its wonderful stained-glass window and collection of artefacts), to form a suite of elegant rooms.

> Young freemen of the company are eligible to participate in the Doggett's Coat and Badge Race (named after its founder, Thomas Doggett, 1640-1721) – a sculling race from London Bridge to Chelsea held annually since 1715. The winner has the honour of being awarded a scarlet coat, breeches and silver arm badge based on the original costume of 18th-century watermen.

Today, Watermen and Lightermen still work on the river, the former being concerned with passenger transport and the latter with the carriage of goods.

Don't miss a unique opportunity to visit one of the City's few surviving Georgian Livery Halls.

❝ *An intimate, original, 18th-century Livery Hall* **❞**

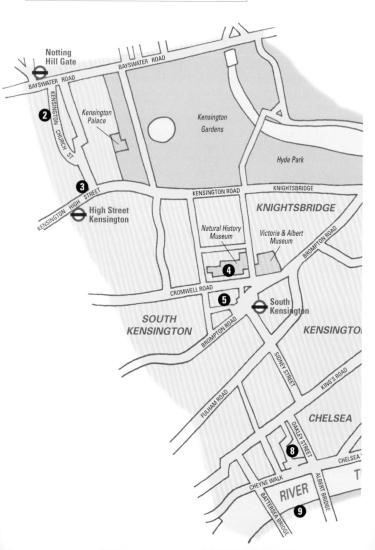

CHAPTER 3

KENSINGTON & CHELSEA

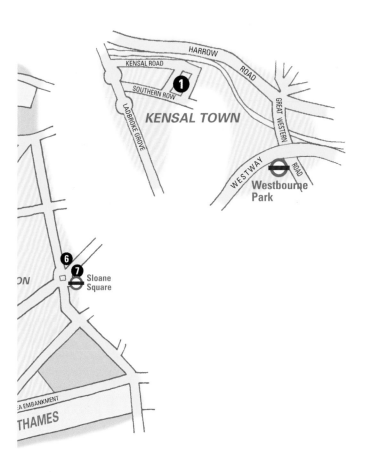

Address: **Bosworth Road, W10 5EH** (☎ **020-7361 3003**, 🖥 **www.rbkc. gov.uk and www.londongardenstrust.org/features/voysey2006.htm**).

Opening hours: **7.30am until dusk. When closed, Voysey Garden can be visited on request to the council.**

Cost: **Free.**

Transport: **Westbourne Park tube station.**

EMSLIE HORNIMAN PLEASANCE

*T*he Emslie Horniman Pleasance – the word derives from French and means 'a secluded garden' or 'enclosed plantation' – is a lovely small park (1 acre/0.4ha) containing a delightful walled Arts and Crafts style garden, the Voysey Garden (Grade II listed). Named after the London County Councillor, Emslie John Horniman MP (1863-1932) who donated the land, the park opened in 1914. It was designed by architect Charles Voysey (1857-1941) and Madeline Agar (1874-1967), with a formal Spanish-style walled garden and an area of grass, trees and shrubs. It's Voysey's only design of a park, which was partly a garden and partly a playground, with a place of relaxation for adults and a sand-pit for children.

The rectangular garden is surrounded along three sides by white lime-washed rough-cast cement walls, with shelters to the north and south with triple Tudor arches and a central entrance with a Tudor arch. Inside the shelters are wooden slatted benches. The wall along East Row is pierced with circular openings and gabled finials with iron grilles designed by William B. Reynolds – who, like Voysey, was a member of the Art Workers Guild – forming a backdrop for the planting. Working with landscape architect Madeline Agar, Voysey's rectangular flower bed is laid out around a formal pool, with flowers planted around an oak pergola flanking an oak bridge around a narrow canal of water.

After decades of neglect, the park was restored to its former glory in the '90s by Julian Harrap Architects, who not only restored the garden, but also provided new sports facilities, a children's playground, gates, signage and fencing. The remainder of the park was substantially redesigned with artist Peter Fink working as lead artist with a number of other artists involved in different aspects. The new design includes sculptural lighting, innovative gates and fences, interactive sculpture by Sophia Clist and Paul Burwell, Mediterranean inspired planting, and a strikingly-designed, colourful, children's playground. A Quiet Garden has been created in the southeast corner designed by artist Avtarjeet Dhanjal, with a sunken seating area and sculptural stone seating of different shapes.

The park also has tennis courts, five-a-side football pitches, an all-weather floodlit sports area, and changing rooms, plus a kiosk during the summer months.

> **Now famous as the starting point for the Notting Hill Carnival (August), the park is a refuge for visitors of all ages.**

❝ *A delightful haven for all ages* ❞

Address: **119 Kensington Church Street, W8 7LN** (☎ **020-7727 4242,** 🖥 **www.fullers.co.uk**).

Opening hours: **Mon-Wed, 11am to 11pm; Thu-Sat, 11am to midnight; Sun, noon to 10.30pm.**

Cost: **Free (except for a drink).**

Transport: **Notting Hill Gate tube station.**

THE CHURCHILL ARMS

*T*he Churchill Arms (originally called The Marlborough) is an attractive traditional pub offering great beers, excellent food and friendly service. In summer the pub's stuccoed Victorian exterior is a riot of colour, buried beneath an abundance of flowers in window boxes, hanging baskets and tubs, which at Christmas give way to dozens of lighted Christmas trees in a cheery festive display.

> The Churchill Arms has won numerous awards for its flower displays, including 'Boozer In Bloom' at Chelsea Flower Show 2007 and 'London in Bloom' for a number of years. It has also won Fuller's coveted Griffin Award three times and Stella's 'Love Your Local' award.

The over the top decoration continues inside this 200-year-old pub, which is bursting with character and festooned with curiosities, memorabilia and posters, There's a bewildering array of objects hanging from the ceiling, including copper vessels, hat boxes and an amazing collection of chamber pots – one for each customer – like having your own beer tankard! Every ledge, nook, cranny and inch of wall space is crammed with intriguing items, including a beautiful butterfly collection in the restaurant. Not surprisingly, numerous images of Sir Winston Churchill take pride of place, accompanied by photos of American Presidents (from Washington to Nixon), British Prime Ministers and members of the Royal Family (the late Queen mum is a favourite).

Apart from the surroundings and the excellent Fuller beers, the inexpensive authentic Thai cuisine is a major attraction, served in the pretty creeper-covered restaurant occupying the old garage 'conservatory' at the rear. From the soft and mild tasting noodles 'Pad Siew' to the hot (here hot means HOT!) jungle paste curry of 'Kaeng Par'. The heat of each dish is indicated on the menu by the number of butterflies ranging from one for spicy, two for hot and three for very (VERY) hot. Simple British bar food is also available at lunchtimes, with traditional roasts on Sundays.

The genial Irish landlord, Gerry O'Brien, is the master of ceremonies and mastermind behind the Churchill, where events are a speciality – the highlight is the celebration of Churchill Night (30th November) – plus assorted patron-saint days. The pub isn't, however, somewhere for contemplation and a quiet pint, and features large-screen TVs showing (Sky) football and other sports.

Well worth a visit, but perhaps one to avoid is you're allergic to crowds and noise.

❝ *A glorious, raucous, flamboyant British boozer* **❞**

Address: Kensington Church Street, W8 4LA (☎ 020-7937 5136,
🖥 http://smanews.weebly.com).

Opening hours: **Daily, around 7.30am to 6pm. See website for service
times.**

Cost: **Free (but donations are welcome).**

Transport: **High Street Kensington or Notting Hill Gate tube station.**

ST MARY ABBOTS

St Mary Abbots is a splendid Victorian neo-Gothic church in Early English Style, on a site where a church has stood for around 1,000 years. The manor of Kensington was given to Abrey de Vere after the Norman conquest. In around 1100, his son Godfrey was taken ill and cured by the Abbot of the great Benedictine Abbey of St Mary at Abingdon. In gratitude Godfrey bequeathed the church in Kensington to the abbey, which was dedicated to St Mary in 1262 (rebuilt 1370).

When William III established his court at Kensington Palace, the local population expanded rapidly and the medieval church became too small and was demolished in the later 17th century and replaced by a late Renaissance style church. This in turn also proved too small as the area became urbanised in the 19th century, and was replaced by the church we see today.

The current church was built in 1872 (the spire was added in 1879) by the celebrated architect Sir George Gilbert Scott (1811-1878), who also designed the Midland Grand Hotel, St Pancras Station, the Albert Memorial and the Foreign & Commonwealth Office (Durbar Court – see page 51). St Mary Abbots is characterised by a relatively plain interior in the main body of the church, which serves to focus attention on the more elaborate chancel, altar and reredos (designed by Scott but completed by his grandson, Giles). There are also some notable treasures, including a 17th-century pulpit donated by William III and a monument carved by Grinling Gibbons for Sir Hans Sloane.

Given Scott's constant involvement with church and cathedral restoration, it's inevitable that there are echoes of other older buildings, demonstrated by the west front, with its tall window and excellent carved tympanum, loosely based on Dunblane Cathedral, and the 278ft (85m) tall spire – the tallest in London – clearly influenced by that of St Mary Radcliffe, Bristol. On entering the church, the first impression is its cathedral-like size –

> **Notable parishioners have included Sir Isaac Newton, Joseph Addison, William Wilberforce, George Canning, William Thackeray, Lord Macaulay, Beatrix Potter and Diana, Princess of Wales.**

179ft (55m) in length from east to west, 109ft (34m) wide and 72ft (22m) high, seating up to 700. A cloister was added in 1889-93. The tower holds a rare ring of ten bells, half of which date from 1772, the remainder being cast in 1879.

A visit to St Mary Abbots is a rare treat.

❝ *An exceedingly magnificent Gilbert Scott church* **❞**

Address: **Cromwell Road, SW7 5BD** (☎ **020-7942 5011,**
🖥 **www.nhm.ac.uk/visit-us/whats-on/wildlife-garden-whatson**).

Opening hours: **1st April to 31st October, 10am to 5pm, including Bank Holidays. Open at other times by appointment.**

Cost: **Free.**

Transport: **South Kensington tube station.**

NATURAL HISTORY MUSEUM WILDLIFE GARDEN

*T*he Natural History Museum Wildlife Garden is a real secret garden; few people know it even exists and even fewer have visited it. The garden covers 1 acre (0.4ha) and was designed by Mark Loxton and Dennis Vickers in 1995. Located in the southwest corner next to the museum's west lawn (Orange Zone), the garden is the museum's first living exhibition, designed to show the potential for wildlife conservation in the inner city, and as an educational resource and research facility. The Garden portrays a range of British lowland habitats such as fen, reedbed, ponds, hedgerow, heathland, woodland, meadow and chalk downland. With over 2,000 plant and animal species, it has a delicacy that's rare in an urban open space.

The Wildlife Garden is an inspiration to anyone wishing to create a space for wild plants and animals. Dragonflies, moorhens, moths, butterflies, foxes, robins, marsh marigolds, primroses, lime, hornbeam, and even grazing sheep are just some of the abundant wildlife that lives in or visits the garden. Many birds visit the bird feeders including blue tits, great tits, greenfinches, coal tits and robins, while on the ground are feeding dunnocks, and squirrels and mice invade the garden shed. Whatever the time of the year, the garden is buzzing with life.

The meadow attracts many insects including the common blue butterfly (*Polyommatus icarus*), whose caterpillar feeds off bird's-foot-trefoil. During May and June azure damselflies (*Coenagrion puella*) may also be seen foraging amongst a variety of plants, while tiny froglets and toadlets migrate to the meadow in June and July. There's also a Butterfly House with exotic butterflies, allowing you to get close to some of the world's most beautiful butterflies and moths; visitors can lean about the insects living in the wildlife haven from the museum's resident scientists.

> **The Wildlife Garden is a slice of rural magic in the heart of the city – guaranteed to delight children and grown ups alike.**

Spring wildlife displays, workshops, activities and talks are regularly held, while during the summer term the garden organises a range of activities for school groups. The garden has earned a number of Green Flag awards, which recognise the best green spaces in the country. The museum has published a book about the garden – *Wildlife Garden* – by Roy Vickery.

❝ *A secret garden in the heart of Kensington* **❞**

Address: 17 Queensberry Place, SW7 2DT (☎ 020-7871 3515, 🖥 www.institut-francais.org.uk).

Opening hours: Mon-Fri, 9am to 11pm, Sat, 10am to 11pm, Sun – opens one hour before the first event. For other times, see website.

Cost: Free to visit and use the restaurant/bar.

Transport: South Kensington tube station.

INSTITUT FRANÇAIS DU ROYAUME-UNI

*T*he Institut français du Royaume-Uni (French Cultural Institute in the UK) is the official French government centre of language and culture in the UK, occupying a handsome Art Deco building in Kensington containing a cinema/theatre, library, bistro and reception rooms. The Institut was founded in 1910 by Marie d'Orliac – now a worldwide organisation with over 150 centres – who was eager to introduce Londoners to French writers, thinkers and artists.

The Institut occupied a number of buildings before its current home was commissioned from French architect Patrice Bonnet (1879-1964) and inaugurated by President Albert Lebrun and HRH Princess Mary on 21st March 1939. Inside, a sweeping staircase leads from the foyer area to the first floor, decorated by the famous Rodin statue L'Age d'Airain and a tapestry by Sonia Delaunay. The building's distinctive red-brick exterior is decorated with columns incised with delicate lattice work, and with brickwork and beige ceramic plaques depicting the Graces of Minerva, the goddess of intelligence.

During its 100-year history many great names have passed through the doors, including Jean Renoir, Eugène Ionesco, Catherine Deneuve and Michel Tournier. The Institut français exists to promote French language and culture and encourage cross-cultural exchange. This is reflected in the programme of talks and films, with speakers from both sides of the Channel meeting regularly in discussion, and screenings of films from all corners of the world. The Institut's twice-monthly wine-tasting sessions provide a valuable insight into this vital part of French culture.

Some 7,000 students enrol annually on courses at the Institut's Language Centre, which in addition to traditional language courses, offers courses in business French and on different aspects of French culture and current affairs. The centre also has a media lending library (*La Médiathèque*) containing some 50,000 books, DVDs and CDs. A window onto contemporary France, the library contains the largest free-access collection of French material in the UK, including feature films, documentaries, music, poetry, novels, comic books and children's books.

The public cinema, *Ciné lumière*, has 240 seats, and is one of the UK's best repertory cinemas, screening a mix of French, European and world feature films and documentaries. It shows both classics and new releases, and regularly hosts special events such as premières, retrospectives and themed seasons.

A ray of French sunshine in west London.

> **The Institut has an inexpensive French restaurant – Le Bistrot – and bar open for breakfast, lunch and dinner.**

 A taste of La Bonne Vie in Kensington

Address: **Sloane Square, Sloane Street, SW1X 9BZ** (☎ **020-7730 7270,** 🖥 **www.holytrinitysloanesquare.co.uk**).

Opening hours: **Daily, from around 7.30am to 6pm (it's advisable to check at weekends). See website for service times.**

Cost: **Free (but donations are welcome).**

Transport: **Sloane Square tube station.**

HOLY TRINITY SLOANE SQUARE

*H*oly Trinity Sloane Square (Grade 1 listed) is a ravishing Victorian Anglican parish church built in a striking Arts and Crafts style. Designed by John Dando Sedding (1836-1891), it was built in 1888-90 and financed by the 5th Earl Cadogan in whose London estate it lay. It replaced an earlier building only half its size which, at the time of its demolition, was less than 60 years old.

Holy Trinity was built on a grand scale, suddenly becoming, if not the longest church in the capital then, strangely, the widest, eclipsing even St Paul's Cathedral by nine inches. However, it's the internal fittings that make Holy Trinity stand out as one of the finest Victorian churches in England, the work of leading sculptors and designers of the day, including F. W. Pomeroy, H. H. Armstead, Onslow Ford and Hamo Thornycroft. In 1891 Sedding died (his memorial can be seen in the Lady Chapel) and Henry Wilson completed the interior decoration to the original design.

The church has an important collection of stained glass, including an enormous east window by Edward Burne-Jones and William Morris; and other windows by William Blake Richmond (including some highly decadent imagery), Powells (architects, the Memorial Chapel) and Christopher Whall (the incomplete clerestory sequence and two striking windows on the south side of the nave).

Holy Trinity was badly damaged by incendiary bombs in WWII (thankfully most of the glorious stained glass windows survived intact) and there was an attempt to demolish it and replace it with something smaller, thwarted by a campaign led by former Poet Laureate John Betjeman – who dubbed Holy Trinity the 'Cathedral of the Arts and Crafts Movement' – and the Victorian Society.

Holy Trinity has one of the finest and largest organs of any parish church in England, made by J. W. Walker & Sons – recently completely rebuilt – and a reputation for the excellence of its music and outstanding choirs.

Treat yourself to a visit to Holy Trinity – preferably when the choir is in full voice – and it will uplift your spirits.

> **Many notable figures have worshipped and assisted at Holy Trinity, including Prime Minister William Gladstone and Liberal and reformist politician Sir Charles Wentworth Dilke MP. The church also attracted Bohemian artists and poets, some of whom clustered loosely around Oscar Wilde.**

 The cathedral of the Arts and Crafts movement

AT A GLANCE

Address: Sloane Square, SW1W 8AS (☎ **020-7565 5000, restaurant 020-7565 5058,** 🖥 **http://royalcourttheatre.com).**

Opening hours: **See website for programme. The café/bar is open Mon-Sat, lunch and dinner, noon to 8pm. Behind-the-scenes tours (1½ hrs) are held periodically (see website).**

Cost: **Free. Building tours £7, £5 concessions. All seats in both theatres are priced at just £10 for Monday performances.**

Transport: **Sloane Square tube station.**

ROYAL COURT THEATRE

*T*he Royal Court Theatre (Grade II listed) is a splendid Victorian-era theatre that's the de facto home of modern English theatre. The current theatre replaced an earlier building and opened on 24th September 1888 as the New Court Theatre. Designed by Walter Emden and Bertie Crewe, it was built of fine red brick with a stone façade in free Italianate style. It had a chequered life for the first 70 years of its existence, serving variously as a receiving house, a producing venue (home to some of George Bernard Shaw's greatest works, including *Major Barbara* and *Man and Superman)* and a cinema, before falling into disuse after bomb damage during WWII.

In the '90s the theatre was completely rebuilt, reopening in February 2000, with the 370-seat proscenium-arch Jerwood Theatre Downstairs and the 85-seat Jerwood Theatre Upstairs.

After the war the interior was re-constructed by Robert Cromie and the theatre re-opened in 1952. George Devine became artistic director and in 1956 his English Stage Company – Britain's first national subsidised theatre company – set up home at the Royal Court and began producing radical new work. Devine aimed to create a writers' theatre, seeking to discover new writers and produce serious contemporary works – he produced John Osborne's *Look Back in Anger* in 1956, which was later seen as the starting point of modern British drama.

In addition to premiering works by numerous local writers, the Court's early seasons included new international plays by Bertolt Brecht, Eugene Ionesco, Samuel Beckett, Jean-Paul Sartre and Marguerite Duras. The Rocky Horror Show premiered at the theatre in 1973, while *Owners* by Caryl Churchill was another early production (she went on to write 17 plays for the Royal Court).

The Royal Court remains dedicated to promoting new work by innovative writers from the UK and around the world, and its Young Writers Programme works to develop new voices with a biennial festival and year-round development work for writers aged under 26. The theatre's role in promoting new voices is undisputed, so much so that *The New York Times* described it as 'the most important theatre in Europe'.

The Royal Court has a first-rate café/bar/restaurant (in the 19th-century auditorium pit) open for lunch and dinner, plus an excellent bookshop.

A theatre that's an inspiration to writers, actors and audiences alike – worthy of any theatre lover's support.

66 *London's coolest theatre with a great tradition* **99**

Address: 1 Lawrence Street, Chelsea, SW3 5NB (☎ 020-7349 9111, 🖥 www.thexkeys.co.uk).

Opening hours: Bar – daily, noon to midnight; Restaurant – Mon-Tue, 6-10.30pm, Wed-Sat, noon to 3pm and 6-10.30pm, Sun, noon to 3.30pm.

Cost: Free (except for a drink or meal).

Transport: South Kensington or Sloane Square tube station.

THE CROSS KEYS

*T*he Cross Keys is a delightful 18th-century pub and restaurant – its history can be traced back to 1708 – close to the River Thames in Chelsea. Famous locals who've (allegedly) enjoyed a pint here include Dante Gabriel Rossetti, Dylan Thomas, JMW Turner, James Whistler, William Holman Hunt, John Singer Sargent, George Meredith, Thomas Carlyle, Agatha Christie and members of the Rolling Stones, many of whom lived nearby in Cheyne Walk.

The exuberant exterior decor and relief sculptures – there also used to be swans and cygnets and a fox, but these were removed when the current owners renovated the pub a few years ago – are inspired by the pub's name. Crossed keys are a Christian sign (depicted on the Vatican City's coat of arms) symbolising the keys which Jesus gave to St Peter so that he could control who entered the Kingdom of Heaven.

The cosy bar at the front has comfy sofas as well as tables for lounging, where the crowning glory is a table (the 'Tabletap') with its own beer taps! The first of its kind in London, you help yourself from a choice of beers and it's recorded on a digital display.

Inside, the pub has flagstone floors, green Chesterfields, tarnished mirrors and whitewashed walls, which blend well with the artistic theme created by co-owner and celebrated sculptor Rudy Weller, who created *The Four Bronze Horses of Helios* in Haymarket (Piccadilly Circus) and *The Three Graces* (or *Daughters of Helios*) leaping from the roof of the nearby Criterion Building (Jermyn Street). For The Cross Keys he's created a 'magical kingdom' throughout the four rooms: the bar, the conservatory restaurant, gallery and a room at the top, the latter two being 'events' rooms for hire. The large conservatory restaurant has a retractable roof for those blessed days when the sun shines.

The modern European menu is based on what's seasonal and includes such English classics as Cornish pan-fried scallops with chorizo, pea purée and champ; ham wrapped pork loin, lemon grass dauphinoise, purple sprouting broccoli and apple red wine sauce; glazed duck breast with braised red cabbage; and Wagyu burger served with truffle fries. There's also a bar menu offering more traditional pub fare such as fish and chips and traditional roasts on Sundays.

Not the cheapest place around, but a great venue to enjoy a good meal or a family celebration.

66 *A beautiful historic Chelsea pub* **99**

AT A GLANCE

Address: The Couper Collection Barges, Battersea Beach, Thames Riverside Walk, Hester Road, SW11 4AN (🖥 www.coupercollection.org.uk, ✉ info@coupercollection.org.uk).

Opening hours: Tue-Fri, 10am to 4pm and by appointment.

Cost: Free.

Transport: Bus routes: 19, 49, 239, 319, 345 to the south side of Battersea Bridge.

COUPER COLLECTION

*T*he Couper Collection exhibits artwork and installations by London artist Max Couper, as well as hosting exhibitions and events by other artists. However, what makes the gallery unique is that the artworks are made and displayed on board a fleet of permanently-moored Thames' barges – a secret world of fictional charts, sculptures and artefacts that take inspiration from the Thames.

The Collection's barges are London's last remaining fleet of historic Thames barges on their ancient moorings, which were continuously in use from the 18th century until the '80s. The barges encompass a variety of types dating from 1908 to 1974, including the last two barges built on the Thames – a pair of 1,000 ton wheat barges. London's barges, also known as lighters, were originally responsible for the prosperity of the city. They were finally made redundant by the advent of containerisation in the '80s, when thousands of barges disappeared for ever from the Thames in central London.

The Collection includes work shown in 1996 and 1997 at Couper's one-man exhibitions at The Museum of Contemporary Art (Antwerp), The Lehmbruck Museum of Sculpture (Duisberg), and The Sprengal Museum of Modern Art (Hanover), plus work shown in New York and London installations since 1978. The Collection was opened on the site in 1998 as a permanent public trust in association with Wandsworth Council.

The Collection includes 'The Museum of First Art', which exhibits work by young London artists under the age of

> In 2000, the barges were the venue for the 'Fleeting Opera 2000', a contemporary Floating Opera for the River Thames performed by The Royal Opera, The Royal Ballet and Dame Judi Dench.

18. It began as an educational Focus event of The London String of Pearls Jubilee Festival in two parts, entitled 'Archetypes and Local Heroes' by the Couper Collection and the National Portrait Gallery, funded by the Heritage Lottery Fund, London Arts and the Corporation of London. The project initially involved five schools in the London boroughs of Kensington & Chelsea, Wandsworth and Southwark, and is central London's only facility where the public and schools can enjoy art and culture on the Thames.

The Collection has a changing programme of live events, new artists' exhibitions, discussions, educational collaborations and ecology.

This unique gallery also offers superb views of Cheyne Walk, Chelsea Riverside and the Albert Bridge.

66 *A floating gallery on the Thames* **99**

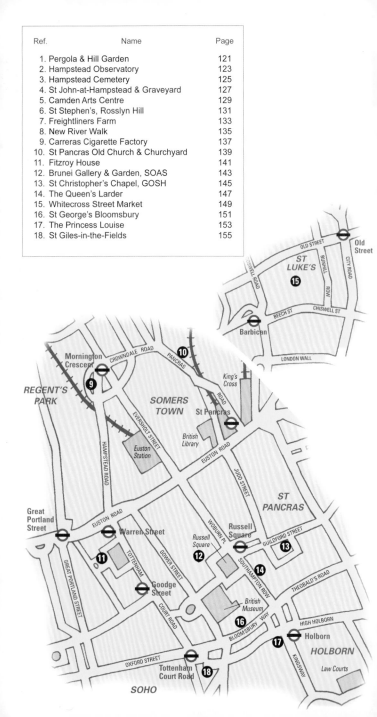

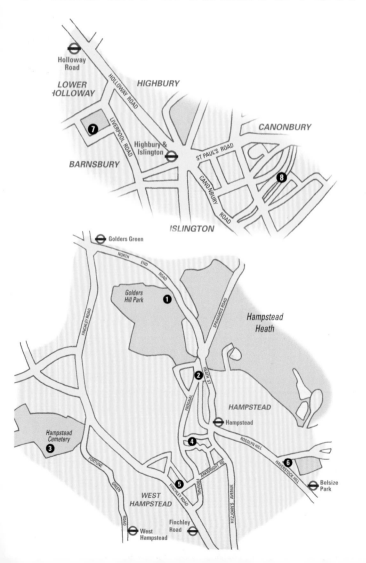

AT A GLANCE

Address: Inverforth Close, off North End Way, NW3 7EX
(🖥 www.cityoflondon.gov.uk and www.londongardenstrust.org/index.
htm?joining.htm).

Opening hours: **Daily, dawn to dusk.**

Cost: **Free.**

Transport: **Golders Green or Hampstead tube station.**

HILL GARDEN & PERGOLA

*T*he beautiful Pergola (Grade II listed) – 800ft (244m) in length – and charming Hill Garden are among the hidden delights of Hampstead Heath. This formal Arts and Crafts garden was created between 1906 and 1925 by celebrated landscape architect Thomas Mawson (1861-1933) for the soap magnate Lord Leverhulme (1851-1925). It's situated at the rear of Inverforth House, formerly The Hill, which Leverhulme purchased in 1904 for his London residence. He subsequently acquired some adjoining land, which led to the creation of the Pergola. The first part of the project was completed in 1906 and then extended in 1911, but it wasn't finally completed until 1925, shortly before Lord Leverhulme died. The Hill was then purchased by Baron Inverforth (and renamed Inverforth House), who lived here until his death in 1955.

Mawson brought architectural treatment and formality to garden design, and the Pergola and gardens were destined to become the best surviving examples of his work. He overcame the difficulty of the public right of way between the two parts of the structure by building a fine stone bridge. The Pergola was a magnificent Edwardian extravagance and became the setting for garden parties and summer evening strolls. The Pergola walk, linking the formal gardens of the main house and the more gentle lawns of the lower garden, was a master stroke, enhanced by the dramatic contrast between the towering trees of West Heath and the exotic plants climbing the graceful Pergola.

WWII and subsequent years weren't kind to the Pergola and gardens, which were purchased by the London County Council in 1960, when they were in an appalling state. The area was restored and opened to the public in 1963 as the Hill Garden. Since 1989 it has been owned and managed by the City of London Corporation, which restored the Pergola in 1995.

In late spring and early summer the raised, covered Pergola is festooned with fragrant flowers, including jasmine, buddleia, sage, honeysuckle, vines, clematis, kiwi, potato vine, lavender and wisteria. Visit during the early evening and you may even see roosting long-eared bats. In contrast to the wild decadence of the Pergola, Hill Garden is beautifully manicured and designed and a slice of paradise, offering panoramic views of London.

> **A favourite haunt of local artists, the Pergola and Hill Garden are a delightful sanctuary and a perfect antidote to the stresses of modern life.**

 A secret, magical gem of a garden

Address: Corner of Heath Street and Hampstead Grove, Lower Terrace, Whitestone Pond, Hampstead, NW3 (💻 www.hampsteadscience.ac.uk, ✉ info@hampsteadscience.ac.uk).

Opening hours: Usually Fri-Sat evenings from October to April/May on clear nights. Check website for opening times, as they vary according to the season and planetary movements. Maximum around 12 people.

Cost: Free (donations are invited).

Transport: Hampstead tube station.

HAMPSTEAD OBSERVATORY

*T*he Hampstead Observatory is one of the only observatories in the world situated in the centre of a huge city, and the only observatory in London offering regular free viewings of the night sky. Located (since 1910) at Whitestone Pond in Hampstead at the highest point in the city, it's owned and operated by the Hampstead Scientific Society founded in 1899. Alongside the Observatory is a weather station, which has been checked daily since 1910, providing the longest continuous record of meteorological readings in the country.

The telescope is a fine six-inch Cooke refracting telescope – built in 1898 by Thomas Cooke of York and presented to the society in 1923. It's viewed on a modern equatorial mounting, made by the society in the '70s, featuring a remote-controlled guidance system. It's equatorial because, as the earth rotates beneath your feet, the stars move east-west and quickly drift out of view. The telescope is placed on an axis and is driven by a motor so that it tracks the stars as they move across the sky. The Cooke telescope is a first class instrument and suitable for an urban location where light pollution is an ever increasing problem, and visitors can only view the brighter, deep sky objects. Nevertheless, under average conditions it provides wonderful views of the moon, planets and brighter stars.

During open sessions, the Observatory is manned by a demonstrator and an assistant who are members of the society and are on hand to show visitors interesting objects through the telescope and to answer questions. In addition to its regular viewing dates – which are restricted to the winter months as the sky isn't dark enough in summer for stargazing – the Observatory is also open during eclipses, appearances of comets and at other times of special interest. It isn't necessary to pre-book, so occasionally it gets crowded, but usually everyone gets a look in.

> The society (membership £10 per annum) aims to promote an interest in all branches of science and caters for laymen as well as those with specialist knowledge. It has both astronomical and meteorological sections, and runs a programme of lectures (see website) and talks on various scientific topics, which are open to the general public.

If you're interested in our solar system and the universe, a visit to the Hampstead Observatory is a must.

 Heavenly bodies in Hampstead

Address: Fortune Green Road, West Hampstead, NW6
(☎ 020-7527 8300, 🖳 www.camden.gov.uk/cemeteries and www.thefriendsofhampsteadcemetery.com).

Opening hours: Weekdays from 7.30am, Sat from 9am and Sun and Public Holidays from 10am. Closing time is around dusk, i.e. 4pm from November to January and 8.30pm from May to July (see website for other months).

Cost: Free.

Transport: West Hampstead tube or rail station.

HAMPSTEAD CEMETERY

*H*ampstead Cemetery is a beautiful historic cemetery (situated in Finchley), jointly managed by Islington and Camden Cemetery Service. It was opened in November 1876 on a 20-acre/8ha site (extended to 26 acres/10.5ha in 1901) with eastern and western sections divided by a public footpath. An estimated 60,000 people are buried here and grave spaces are no longer available, though there's an area for cremated remains.

The cemetery has an entry lodge and a pair of Gothic-style mortuary chapels (Grade II listed), made of Kentish ragstone and Bath stone. The chapels share a porch or portico (*porte-cochère*), a feature of many late 18th- and early 19th-century mansions and public buildings. The southern chapel was used for burials in consecrated ground south of the main avenue, while the other was for burials in unconsecrated ground to the north.

A large number of Celtic crosses are found in the area to the southwest of the chapel, marking the presence of several Scottish families. The north-eastern corner has some notable examples of modern and Art Deco stonemasonry – including 18 listed by English Heritage – and several graves noted for their humorous or bizarre inscriptions.

The eastern part of the cemetery is home to the so-called Bianchi Monument, a large triangular grave for the Gall family, executed in the finest Art Deco style. The most prominent feature of the grave – a stylised sculpture of a female angel raising her hands to heaven – has

> The cemetery has a large number of trees, including ash, cedar, yew, oak, Scots pine, lime, sycamore, Norwegian maple, silver birch, Lombardy poplar, purple cherry-plum, weeping willow and Swedish whitebeam.

become famous in its own right, and often adorns the covers of local guidebooks. Similarly, the tomb of James Wilson ('Wilson Pasha'), Chief Engineer to the Egyptian Government (1875-1901), executed in red marble and also found in the eastern section, has a striking Egyptian appearance.

A wildlife area in the northern part of the eastern half of the cemetery has been planted with shrubs and wild flowers that are particularly attractive to wildlife; a variety of butterflies are found here, including small white, speckled wood, holly blue, meadow brown and small copper. The cemetery is also home to (or visited by) many bird species.

Hampstead Cemetery is a lovely tranquil spot to while away an hour or two at any time of the year.

66 *A lovely Victorian cemetery* **99**

ST JOHN-AT-HAMPSTEAD & GRAVEYARD

St John-at-Hampstead (dedicated to St John the Evangelist) is a sumptuous Georgian Church of England church with a stunning interior. There's likely to have been a church on this site for over 1,000 years, when a charter was granted to the Benedictine Monks of Westminster in 986, although the first record of one is from 1312, when it was recorded that John de Neuport was its priest. On the Dissolution of the Monasteries, the Abbot was replaced by the Bishop of Westminster, Thomas Thirlby, who also served as St John's rector. The see (and title) was abolished in 1551 by Edward VI, with the manor and benefice of Hampstead being granted to Sir Thomas Wrothe.

As Hampstead grew in popularity and size as a health resort, the small medieval church became inadequate and run down and was declared unusable in 1744. Pictures from this time show the church to be part stone and part timber, with a small wooden tower. The present building was built to designs by Henry Flitcroft (1697-1769) and John Sanderson (1730-1774), and dedicated on 8th October 1747, but again proved too small and was extended 30ft (9.1m) westwards in 1844 by means of transepts, providing 524 extra seats.

Gas lighting was installed and in 1853 the first Willis organ was built, with Henry Willis himself employed as the organist. The famous organ has been much altered over the years and in 1997 was restored (more or less) to its original Willis sound. The church was enlarged again in 1878 to include a new chancel and sanctuary, and a side chapel was added and consecrated in 1912. In 1958 the dark Victorian interior scheme was removed and the original lighter, whitewashed scheme reinstated – today, the interior is that of an opulent Georgian town church with a Baroque twist.

Perhaps more famous today than St John's church is its tranquil, magnificent graveyard, whose monuments and gravestones include many of great historic significance, notably that of romantic painter John Constable. Other notables buried here include novelist and historian Walter Besant, writer and comedian Peter Cook, actress Kay Kendall, Labour Party leader Hugh Gaitskell, inventor of the marine chronometer (and longitude) John Harrison, and various members of the distinguished du Maurier family.

> **The churchyard is designated a Site of Nature Conservation Importance and noted for its wildlife, providing a refuge for a wealth of rare and protected plants and animals.**

 A handsome church and equally famous graveyard

AT A GLANCE

Address: Arkwright Road, NW3 6DG (☎ 020-7472 5500,
🖳 **www.camdenartscentre.org).**

Opening hours: **Tue-Sun, 10am to 6pm (Wed until 9pm). Closed Mondays.**

Cost: **Free.**

Transport: **Finchley Road tube station.**

CAMDEN ARTS CENTRE

*C*amden Arts Centre – housed in a splendid Victorian Gothic building (Grade II listed) – is one of London's best contemporary art spaces and the largest arts venue in north London. Built in 1897 as the Hampstead Public Library, the building became the Hampstead Arts Centre in 1965 and was taken over by the local council in 1967 and renamed the Camden Arts Centre. Exhibitions in the larger galleries were the responsibility of the Arkwright Arts Trust, which were often ambitious and portrayed well-known artists. These aspects of the Centre relocated – along with most of the local artists who had frequented the Centre – to the Hampstead School of Art in 1992.

Director Jenni Lomax joined Camden Arts Centre in 1990 and led the organisation through a major building refurbishment scheme, completed in 2004 by Tony Fretton Architects. The beautiful and sensitively designed building now combines the original Victorian Gothic features with a contemporary urban design to enhance the space and light. The centre piece of the scheme is a new public concourse on the ground floor which visibly connects the neighbourhood to the café and garden. The new galleries attract artists of the highest calibre and are able to display a broad range of work, including installations, film and video, light sensitive drawings and sculpture.

The Centre has developed an internationally acclaimed programme of exhibitions, artist residencies, off-site projects and artist-led activities, thus ensuring it remains a leading hub for seeing, making and discussing contemporary art. The exhibition and education programmes have equal importance and are continually intertwined.

> **Exhibitions feature a mix of emerging artists, international artists showing for the first time in London, significant historic figures who inspire contemporary practice, and artist selected group shows relevant to current debate.**

Off-site artists' projects include new commissions and performance in strategic areas such as King's Cross and local schools and community centres, while educational activities include a regular series of talks and discussions, film screenings and live art performances, alongside activities for families and schools, and participation projects led by artists. The Centre also runs a variety of public events including talks and debates, live-art performances, film screenings and family open days.

The Camden Arts Centre has a good bookshop and an excellent café – why not pop along for some stimulating art followed by some refreshment in the lovely garden.

❝ *One of London's best contemporary art spaces* **❞**

ST STEPHEN'S, ROSSLYN HILL

*S*t Stephen's (Grade I listed) is a beautiful former church designed in English Gothic Revival (or Neo Gothic) style by Samuel Sanders Teulon (1812-73), who considered it the best of the his 114 churches, calling it his 'mighty church'. Work began in 1869, with consecration at the end of the year, though the church wasn't fully completed until 1870. Unlike so many Victorian churches which remained uncompleted, St Stephen's was completed within three years of its consecration, with the clock and carillon installed in 1873. Soon after completion a school was established in the crypt and the church has continued to be used for educational purposes ever since.

St Stephen's is markedly French in outline, with steep roofs and a massive square tower. When Teulon was first offered the commission, he particularly requested that the church should be built of brick. For the exterior, he chose brick from Dunstable, which when new was described as varying in colour from pale grey to Indian red, giving the church a mottled appearance. The decorative stone bands on the exterior are of Kentish ragstone from Maidstone and, as if to contrast with the exterior, the inside walls are faced with grey, tallow and white bricks from Huntingdonshire, laid in stripes and panels. The most spectacular ornamental brickwork is found under the tower and in the transepts, and is slightly Moorish in style. In addition the sculptural and mosaic decoration is unusually rich and varied, much of which was created by Thomas Earp and Antonio Salviati.

The church was built on a steep slope and prone to subsidence, and by the late '60s there were concerns about its structural integrity, and with maintenance costs rising and its congregation dwindling, it was closed in 1977. St Stephen's was saved from demolition (to provide a car park for the nearby hospital) or being made into flats in the late '70s, although it fell into slow decay (with squatters) before being deconsecrated and finding a new use. It was finally leased to the St Stephen's Restoration and Preservation Trust in 1999, which raised over £4m to restore the building to its former glory.

> Some stained glass windows have survived, as has the impressive wooden beamed roof, but stripped of its decoration it's the building itself that's the star.

Now used as a local community centre and venue, St Stephen's is a remarkable building.

 *A strikingly beautiful former Gothic Revival church*

Address: **Sheringham Road, N7 8PF** (☎ **020-7609 0467,**
🖥 **www.freightlinersfarm.org.uk).**

Opening hours: **Daily, autumn/winter, 10am to 4pm; spring/summer, 10am to 4.45pm. Closed Mondays, except on Bank Holidays, and during the Christmas/New Year period.**

Cost: **Free (but donations are encouraged).**

Transport: **Holloway Road or Highbury & Islington tube station.**

FREIGHTLINERS FARM

*F*reightliners Farm is an outstanding urban farm in the heart of Islington, one of only half a dozen in inner London. The farm was founded on former wasteland behind King's Cross Station in 1973 – its name came from the railway goods vans that originally housed the animals. The farm moved to its present site in 1978 and purpose-built farm buildings were erected in 1988. The site is currently 1.2 acres (0.5ha), but there are plans to expand it further.

Freightliners allows individuals and groups to learn from and interact with their environment and each other through animal care, horticulture and sustainable practices. The farm offers a wide-ranging educational programme in its fully-equipped classroom, where school groups can take part in workshops, including bread-making, cooking, gardening, composting, arts and crafts, spinning and weaving. Freightliners also offers educational courses in carpentry, cooking, animal care, horticulture, beekeeping, and health and safety on the farm, while regular volunteers get the chance to join in the farm's accredited horticulture training scheme.

The farm has a wide variety of animals ranging from cows to rare breed pigs and goats, to new born lambs and chicks, many of which can be adopted through the farm's 'Adopt an Animal Scheme' (you can even adopt an apple tree!). The farm also keeps and sell chickens, ducks, geese, goats, sheep, turkeys, guinea fowl, quail, pigeons, doves, rabbits and guinea pigs.

> None of the animals are slaughtered, so you don't need to worry about that fluffy lamb or cute piglet ending up in your lunch!

In the animal village, children have the opportunity to get up close and personal with many animals in the petting area. The farm also keeps bees, and visitors can learn about the secret world of the honey bee, in addition to buying delicious honey and products made from beeswax such as candles and furniture polish.

Visitors can enjoy the ornamental garden, with its array of colourful flowers and plants, and gain tips and ideas from the kitchen garden with its wide selection of herbs, fruit trees and bushes (there's a gardening club on Wednesday afternoons). The Farm produces a range of fruit and vegetables for sale in the farm shop, from potatoes and onions to rhubarb. There's also a café.

A great place to get a taste of country life in the city – not just for kids but for all the family.

66 *A taste of rural life in the city* **99**

AT A GLANCE

Address: Canonbury Grove, N1 (☏ 020-7527 2000, 🖳 www.islington. gov.uk – see parks).

Opening hours: Daily, 8am to dusk.

Cost: Free.

Transport: Highbury & Islington tube station or Essex Road rail station.

NEW RIVER WALK

*N*ew River Walk – neither new or a river! – is a delightful public park of 3.48 acres (1.4ha) in Islington that's part of the New River Path and a tranquil oasis for wildlife. The New River was an aqueduct commissioned in 1613 by Sir Hugh Myddleton (1560-1631) – whose statue stands at the southern tip of Islington Green – to bring water from the River Lee in Hertfordshire to central London. The aqueduct still supplies water today, accounting for some 8 per cent of London's consumption, though it now terminates at Stoke Newington.

The New River Path is 28mi (45km) long, following the course of the New River from Hertford to Islington, linking the inner city to the open countryside. It was developed between 1991 and 2003 at a cost of over £2m, in a partnership including Thames Water, Groundwork, the New River Action Group and others.

> The narrow pathway winds intriguingly over pretty bridges, while benches are strategically placed for rest stops and to enjoy the views.

Wherever possible, the route follows the historic water channel, as well as some straightened and piped sections between the New River's starting point near Hertford to its original end in Islington. The route is waymarked throughout its length by signs displaying the NR Path logo.

The section of the New River Path that comprises the New River Walk runs between Islington and Canonbury. The park follows the New River as it runs above ground between St Pauls Road and Canonbury Road in Islington. The charming linear park is landscaped along the river and is around 4mi (7km) in length, exploring some of Islington's many and varied squares and garden spaces. Much of the route is along service paths on private land running beside the watercourse, while other sections follow public rights of way – the 'heritage' section south of Stoke Newington uses paths through parks and along streets.

The park is a haven for wildlife and is landscaped with native English plants and specimen trees, including swamp cypress, dawn redwood and weeping willows; signboards provide information about the local flora and fauna. The river teems with life and you're likely to encounter ducks, coots and moorhens, plus – if you're lucky – rarer species such as sparrowhawks, grey wagtails, firecrests and grey herons.

A popular walk is from Canonbury Square to Newington Green, where you can enjoy lunch in one of the area's many excellent eateries.

❝ *A magical, secret watery 'park' in Islington* **❞**

Address: **180 Hampstead Road, Mornington Crescent, NW1 7AW**
(🖳 **http://en.wikipedia.org/wiki/carreras_cigarette_factory**).

Opening hours: **Unrestricted exterior access from public road.**

Cost: **Free.**

Transport: **Mornington Crescent tube station.**

CARRERAS CIGARETTE FACTORY

*T*he Carreras Cigarette Factory – or Camden Arcadia Works – is a large (550ft/168m long) Art Deco building in Camden; a striking example of early 20th-century Egyptian Revival architecture. It was built in 1926-28 by the Carreras Tobacco Company on the communal garden area of Mornington Crescent. The architects were M. E. and O. H. Collins and Arthur George Porri, who adapted the Collins' design, which was inspired by the contemporary fashion for Egyptian-style buildings and decorative arts.

As the demand for cigarettes increased in the early 20th century, particularly after WWI, the Carreras Tobacco Company outgrew its Arcadia cigarette factory in City Road, and in 1928 moved production to its new Arcadia Works in Mornington Crescent. The building was faced in Atlas White cement, coloured to look like sand, while the front of the building was lined with a colonnade of 12 large papyriform columns, painted in bright colours with Venetian glass decoration. Dominating the entrance to the building were two large (8.5ft/2.6m tall) bronze statues of cats, stylised versions of the Egyptian god Bastet (or *Bubastis*/*Bast*), which were cast at the Haskins Foundry in London.

The main entrance was approached by a staircase, the handrails designed in the shape of serpents mounted on the wall with bronze human hands. The entrance itself was designed in the style of a tent, similar to the cavetto-moulded lintels seen in architecture dating from the Old Kingdom (Sneferu, 26th century BC). Above the door was a carved Horus of Behdet, a symbol of the winged disk of the sun.

In 1960-62 the Camden Arcadia Works were converted into offices. The famous building was refurbished and stripped of its Egyptian decoration in an attempt to give it a simpler, more Modernist appearance.

> The image of a black cat was a branding device which Carreras used on the packets of their Craven A range of cigarettes.

However, in 1996 the building was purchased by Resolution GLH, who commissioned architects Finch Forman to restore the building to its former glory. The restorers recreated some 85 per cent of the original Art Deco features, including installing replicas of the famous black cat statues. The building is now offices and isn't open to the public, but can be admired from the road.

If you're a fan of Art Deco, then the Carreras Cigarette Factory is a rare treat.

66 *An Art Deco tour de force* **99**

Address: **191 Pancras Way, NW1 1UL** (☎ **020-7424 0724,**
🖥 **http://oldstpancrasteam.wordpress.com/old-st-pancras**).

Opening hours: **Open daily from around 9am to dusk. See website for service times.**

Cost: **Free (but donations are welcome).**

Transport: **St Pancras tube station.**

The Hardy Tree

ST PANCRAS OLD CHURCH & CHURCHYARD

S t Pancras Old Church (Grade II* listed) is a beautiful and historic Church of England parish church. The church – not to be confused with St Pancras New Church – is dedicated to the Roman martyr St Pancras, after which the surrounding area is named. It's believed to be one of the oldest sites of Christian worship in England; documentary evidence for the early history of the church is scant, but it's believed to have existed since AD314. Remnants of medieval features and references in the *Domesday Book* (1086) suggest it pre-dates the Norman Conquest (1066).

> **The churchyard contains the self-designed mausoleum of architect Sir John Soane (Grade I listed) and his wife, which allegedly provided the inspiration for the design by Sir Giles Gilbert Scott of the iconic red telephone box.**

By the early 19th century, the church – then known simply as St Pancras Church – was too small for the parish and its parochial rights were transferred to the larger St Pancras New Church in nearby Euston Road, consecrated in 1822. St Pancras church was renamed St Pancras Old Church and became a chapel of ease, eventually falling into disuse. As it stood in the early 19th century, the church consisted of an un-aisled nave, a chancel without a chancel arch and a western tower. The south porch had served as a vestry since the 18th century.

By 1847 the Old Church was derelict, but as the local population grew it was decided to restore it. The architect of the alterations was Alexander Dick Gough (1804-1871) who removed the old tower – allowing the nave to be extended westwards – and built a new tower on the south side; the south porch was also removed and a new vestry added on the north side. There were further restorations in 1888 and 1925 – when the plaster ceiling and the side galleries were removed – and in 1948 following WWII bomb damage.

The recently restored St Pancras churchyard – almost as famous as the church – is the largest green space in the locality, with some fine mature trees. Among the notables buried here are Sir John Soane (see box), the composer Johann Christian Bach, the sculptor John Flaxman and William Franklin, the last colonial Governor of New Jersey, and illegitimate son of Benjamin Franklin. There's also a memorial tomb for philosophers and writers Mary Wollstonecraft and William Godwin.

A rare and lovely old church with a delightful historic churchyard.

 One of the oldest Christian sites in Britain

L. Ron Hubbard

FITZROY HOUSE

*S*et in the heart of Fitzrovia, Fitzroy House is a fine example of an 18th-century Georgian townhouse. Built in 1791, it imitates the designs of Robert Adam, the famous Georgian period architect, who, along with his brother, designed Fitzroy Square. The house is one of the last remaining structures on the block that retains its original exterior.

At first glance the building is indistinguishable from its neighbours, but Fitzroy House is famous for its former inhabitants, which include Irish playwright George Bernard Shaw, who lived on the first floor with his mother in 1881-2. (Fitzrovia has been home to many famous artists and writers, including H. G. Wells, George Orwell, Charles Dickens and Virginia Woolf.)

> With 19 *New York Times'* bestsellers and three literary Guinness World Record Titles including 'Most Published Author' (an astonishing 1,084 publications), he's one of the most prolific writers of all time.

Today, Fitzroy House is better known as the former home of controversial American writer and philosopher L. (Lafeyette) Ron Hubbard (1911-1986), who wrote many of his best-known works here. Nowadays most famous as the founder of Dianetics and Scientology, L. Ron Hubbard cannot be easily pigeon-holed. While first and foremost a writer, he worked in many fields including photography and horticulture, and as a sailor, aviator, musician and explorer, not to mention his work in the humanitarian fields of drug rehabilitation, criminal reform and education.

In the '50s, L. Ron Hubbard, lived and worked at Fitzroy House for almost three years, and today it's a museum dedicated to his life and work. One floor is devoted to an exhibition of his early life, from Boy Scout to explorer, and top pulp fiction writer of the '30s and '40s to his later achievements as a humanitarian. Visitors are invited to step into this '50s time capsule where they can view its faithfully restored communications office equipment (including Adler typewriters, Grundig tape recorder and a Western Union Telefax), original manuscripts, rare first edition books and artefacts relating to the life of one of the most prominent authors of the 20th century. The second floor is dedicated to his literary works.

A fascinating peek behind the scenes of a splendid Georgian house and the works of one of the 20th-century's most prolific writers.

66 *Former home to literary giants* **99**

AT A GLANCE

Address: **School of Oriental and African Studies (SOAS), University of London, Thornhaugh Street, Russell Square, WC1H 0XG (☎ 020-7637 2388, 🖥 www.soas.ac.uk).**

Opening hours: **Tue-Sat, 10.30am to 5pm (late night Thu until 8pm). Groups of ten or more are requested to book in advance. Closed Sundays, Mondays and Bank Holidays.**

Cost: **Free.**

Transport: **Russell Square or Goodge Street tube station.**

BRUNEI GALLERY & GARDEN, SOAS

*T*he Brunei Gallery at the School of Oriental and African Studies (commonly abbreviated to SOAS) hosts a programme of changing contemporary and historical exhibitions from Asia, Africa and the Middle East.

Founded in 1916, the SOAS is a public research university and a constituent college of the University of London, specialising in law, politics, economics (specifically development economics), humanities and languages relating to Asia, Africa and the Middle East. It has produced several heads of state, government ministers, ambassadors, Supreme Court judges, a Nobel Peace Prize Laureate, and many other notable leaders.

The Gallery was built as a result of an endowment from the Sultan of Brunei Darussalam and inaugurated by the Princess Royal in 1995. The Gallery's aim is to present and promote the cultures of Asia, Africa and the Middle East, as both a student resource and a public facility. It incorporates exhibition spaces on three floors, a bookshop, a lecture theatre, and conference and teaching facilities.

There's a permanent display of 'Objects of Instruction: Treasures of the School of Oriental and African Studies' in the new Foyle Special Collections Gallery, aimed at publicising the school's remarkably rich but little known collections. It contains a wide range of interesting and beautiful objects from across Asia and Africa, including illustrated Islamic manuscripts; Chinese and Japanese paintings and prints; Middle East and East Asian ceramics; decorative Buddhist manuscripts and sculptures from Southeast Asia; contemporary African paintings and textiles; and important archaeological collections. Content is rotated periodically, thus ensuring the vitality and continued appeal of the permanent display.

The Gallery's Japanese-style roof garden was built during the Japan 2001 celebrations and was officially opened by its sponsor, Haruhisa Handa, an honorary fellow of the school. The garden is dedicated to forgiveness, which is the meaning of the kanji character engraved on the garden's granite water basin. The designer, Peter Swift, conceived the garden as a place of quiet contemplation and meditation, as well as a functional space complementary to the Gallery and its artistic activities. The garden offers a tranquil area away from the noise and bustle of London's streets, where visitors can relax.

> **The Gallery stages a comprehensive programme of temporary exhibitions, both historical and contemporary, which reflect subjects and regions studied at SOAS.**

The school also stages a wide range of public events from conferences to lectures and workshops.

 A stimulating and tranquil retreat

AT A GLANCE

Address: **Great Ormond Street Hospital, Great Ormond Street, WC1N 3JH** (☎ **020-7405 9200,** ⌨ **www.gosh.nhs.uk/about-us/our-history/gallery**).

Opening hours: **24 hours a day.**

Cost: **Free.**

Transport: **Russell Square tube station.**

ST CHRISTOPHER'S CHAPEL, GOSH

*S*t Christopher's Chapel (Grade II listed) – dedicated to St Christopher as the Patron Saint of children – at the Great Ormond Street Hospital (GOSH) is a stunningly decorative building, and the most sumptuous hospital chapel in the country.

Great Ormond Street Hospital for children was created in response to the shocking mortality rate in the mid-19th century, which meant that only half of all babies born into poverty would celebrate their first birthday. Desperate to save children's lives in the capital, Dr George West campaigned for a specialist hospital to be built. In 1852, he got his wish and with ten beds, two physicians and five nurses, GOSH was born.

Built in the High Victorian style, the stunning Chapel interior – in elaborate 'Franco-Italianate style' – may remind you of Pugin's work, which isn't surprising as it was designed by Edward Middleton Barry (1830-1880), third son of Sir Charles Barry, who along with Pugin, designed the Houses of Parliament. Completed in 1875, the Chapel is dedicated to the memory of Caroline, wife of William Henry Barry (eldest son of Sir Charles Barry) who donated £40,000 to build the Chapel and provided a stipend for the chaplain.

The Chapel is small, with just four rows of seats on either side of the main aisle, with a dramatic altar at the end. The beautiful terrazzo floor is by the Italian mosaicist Antonio Salviati, said to be modelled on St Mark's, Venice. The stained glass depicts the nativity, the childhood of Christ and biblical scenes connected with children, above which is a series of angels holding tablets inscribed with the Christian virtues.

> **The Chapel's small size adds to the intimate atmosphere and makes the stunning decoration less intimidating than it might otherwise be.**

When the old GOSH was replaced by a new hospital in the '90s, there was no question of demolishing the Chapel, which was 'simply' moved! A concrete cast was laid under the Chapel, supported by jacks, and the whole building was placed in a giant waterproof 'box' and moved by sliding it along a purpose-built runway, pushed by hydraulic ram-jacks; a world first and an amazing feat of engineering. Restored to its former splendour, the Chapel was officially reopened by Diana, Princess of Wales, on Valentine's Day 1994.

A moving Chapel (in more ways than one) and a magical place that's well worth a visit.

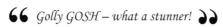

❝ *Golly GOSH – what a stunner!* **❞**

AT A GLANCE

Address: 1 Queen Square, Bloomsbury, WC1N 3AR (☎ **020-7837 5627,** 🖳 **www.queenslarder.co.uk**).

Opening hours: Mon-Sat 11.30am to 11pm, Sun noon to 10.30pm.

Cost: Free (apart from a drink).

Transport: Russell Square tube station.

THE QUEEN'S LARDER

*T*he Queen's Larder is an historic, attractive corner pub in Bloomsbury, which is known to have existed since 1720, when it was a humble alehouse without a sign. The pub takes its name from Queen Charlotte, wife of 'Mad King' George III, who received treatment for his apparent insanity at a doctor's house in the square towards the end of his reign. The Queen assisted in the nursing of her husband, by cooking for him and she rented a small cellar beneath the pub, where she kept special foods for him – hence the 'Queen's Larder'. The square was previously named Queen Anne's Square because a statue contained within it was misidentified as depicting Queen Anne, though it's now believed to be a portrayal of Queen Charlotte,

Originally an ancient village called Lomesbury, Bloomsbury was mostly fields until the 17th century when a number of manor houses were built in the area. During the 18th and 19th centuries, hospitals and universities dominated the scene, which helped Bloomsbury develop its cultural reputation. The area was home to the Foundling Hospital (est. 1739), London's first home for abandoned children – at the time of its construction, around 75 per cent of London's children died before they were aged five. The hospital is now a poignant museum, while its former grounds include Coram's Fields, a children's park with a paddling pool, animal enclosure and playground (adults only admitted with a child). Bloomsbury is also noted for its artistic and literary connections, not least for the Bloomsbury Group, a group of artists and writers (which included Virginia Woolf and E. M. Forster) who were politically vocal, sexually uninhibited and Bohemian long before it became fashionable.

The Queen's Larder is a tiny, intimate pub, characterised by its club-like atmosphere, with a small ground floor bar clad in wood with olde worlde décor, including theatre and ballet posters on the walls; upstairs there's a charming dining room, while outside is a large seating area overlooking the square. It's a cosy spot in winter and a delightful place to watch the world go by in the summer, while enjoying excellent real ales – including Greene King IPA and Old Speckled Hen – and traditional pub grub such as spam fritters, roast beef sandwiches, ploughman's and sausage and mash.

> A classic, traditional pub, frequented by staff from nearby Great Ormond Street Hospital – handy when you fall off your stool!

 A great historic pub in a lovely location

AT A GLANCE

Address: Whitecross Street, Islington, EC1 (☎ 020-7527 1761, 🖥 www.whitecrossstreet.co.uk).

Opening hours: **General market – Mon-Fri, 10am to 4pm; Food market – Thu-Fri, 11am to 4pm.**

Cost: **Free.**

Transport: **Old Street or Barbican tube station.**

WHITECROSS STREET MARKET

*W*hitecross Street Market is one of London's coolest markets with the best street food in town. It's also home to a general market on weekdays, but it's the superb food market on Thursdays and Fridays that really draws the crowds – and which has been instrumental in revitalising the area. Like most market streets, it has an eclectic, independent feel that's missing from many of the capital's high streets.

Whitecross Street Market begun trading in the 17th century, making it one of London's oldest markets. But by the end of the 19th century the area had become a by-word for poverty and alcohol abuse, and it became known locally as Squalors' Market. However, after decades of decline the street is now enjoying an upturn in its fortunes, having benefited from a programme of investment and regeneration in recent years.

Whitecross Street has become a favourite destination for street food on Thursdays and Fridays, with stalls selling every sort of street food under the sun – it's London on a (paper) plate. There are also stalls offering great coffee (some of the best in London), freshly squeezed juices, home-made cakes, proper cheeses, authentic Italian charcuterie, plump olives and real bread and more. However, it's the authentic street food that packs them in with a United Nations of stalls including Thai, Caribbean, Italian, Chinese, Turkish, Portuguese, various Indian, Brazilian, French, German – even British – great salads, salt beef and burgers, wild game, home-made pork pies, pie and mash, hog-roast sandwiches, plus cakes and cookies (e.g. from Comptoir Gourmand and Galeto) and much more.

You don't even have to eat it in the rain as the local pub, The Two Brewers, will let you bring in your market food provided that you buy a drink. The nearby Barbican Centre also has plenty of seating and if it's a sunny day, Fortune Street Park is just a stone's throw away – with grassy areas and park benches – as is scenic Bunhill Fields cemetery.

> There's more to Whitecross Street than simply its market, and it boasts a wide range of shops, art galleries, and some great traditional places to eat and drink; if it's raining or you fancy being waited on instead of waiting in line, there's a wealth of cafés, restaurants and pubs within a few minutes.

Whitecross Street also hosts street entertainment, food festivals, an open-air art gallery and the famous Whitecross Street Party in July. Come. Eat. Enjoy.

" *Street food heaven!* **"**

Address: **6-7 Little Russell Street, WC1A 2HR** (☎ **020-7242 1979,**
🖥 **www.stgeorgesbloomsbury.org.uk**).

Opening hours: **Usually daily from 1-4pm (but it's advisable to check
before travelling). If it isn't open, you can visit the church office at the
back (via Little Russell Street gate) and ask someone to open it. See
website for service times.**

Cost: **Free (but donations are welcome).**

Transport: **Holborn or Tottenham Court Road tube station.**

ST GEORGE'S BLOOMSBURY

*S*t George's Bloomsbury (Grade I listed) is a grand English Baroque church built 1716-1731 and the parish church of Bloomsbury, consecrated in 1730. It was designed by Nicholas Hawksmoor (1661-1736), pupil and former assistant of Sir Christopher Wren, the leading architect of English Baroque. It's the architect's most idiosyncratic work, combining Baroque splendour with classical references, topped by the most eccentric spire in London. This was the sixth and last of Hawksmoor's London churches, though his work as a surveyor for the church Commissioners continued until his death in 1736.

The stepped tower – topped with a statue of George I in Roman dress – is believed to have been influenced by Pliny the Elder's 's description of the mausoleum at Halicarnassus. Its statues of fighting lions and unicorns symbolise the end of the First Jacobite Rising, while the portico is thought to be based on that of the Temple of Bacchus in Baalbek, Lebanon. The tower is depicted in William Hogarth's well-known

> **The Victorian novelist Anthony Trollope (1815) was baptised at St George's and the funeral of Emily Davison, the suffragette who died when she was trampled by the King's horse during the 1913 Derby, also took place here.**

engraving 'Gin Lane' (1751), while Charles Dickens used St George's as the setting for 'The Bloomsbury Christening' in Sketches by Boz.

Despite the grandeur of Hawksmoor's design, the parish vestrymen were incensed that it provided so little accommodation (just 447 seats compared, for example, with 2,000 in Wren's St James's Piccadilly); as a result, the church was enlarged and reorientated in 1781 along a north-south axis. Other changes were made to Hawksmoor's original design during the late 18th and the 19th centuries.

St George's recently underwent major restoration, re-opening in 2006, during which Hawksmoor's original design and configuration was reinstated, including reorientation. The interior was restored to its original decorative plaster ceiling, windows, railings, floors and furnishings, and a 17th-century Dutch chandelier – on loan from the Victoria and Albert Museum , where it formerly graced the Grand Entrance.

Today, St George's is a thriving parish church, concert venue, and centre for community arts and education. There's an exhibition about the church, 'Hawksmoor and Bloomsbury', housed in the undercroft.

A visit to this unique church – one of the capital's most striking buildings and a monument to Hawksmoor's genius – is highly recommended.

66 *A work of startling originality* **99**

Address: **208-209 High Holborn, WC1V 7BW** (☎ **020-7405 8816**).
Opening hours: **Mon-Sat, 11am to 11pm; closed Sundays.**
Cost: **Free (except for a drink).**
Transport: **Holborn tube station.**

THE PRINCESS LOUISE

*T*he Princess Louise (Grade II listed) is a Victorian public house that's famous for its remarkable original 'gin-palace' interior, considered by many to be the best preserved and most attractive in London. Named in honour of Queen Victoria's fourth daughter, it was built in 1872 and refitted in 1891 by architect Arthur Chitty (during the golden age of Victorian pub design). He employed the finest craftsmen of the age; tiles by Simpson & Sons; glasswork by Morris & Son and joinery thought to be by Lascelles. This beautiful pub is a testament to the skills of those Victorian craftsmen.

Every inch of the walls is covered in the finest cut glass and gilt mirrors, sumptuously decorated tiles, ornate plasterwork and the highest quality oak-panelling. Even the toilets are a work of art with their original Victorian fittings (and smells!). With half-a-dozen ornately carved, sumptuously-tiled bar areas under one high, stucco ceiling, the Princess Louise is a classic example of a Victorian public house where drinkers were segregated according to their social status. From its unprepossessing exterior with 'Princess Louise' etched in gold on a black masthead, it's difficult to imagine the treasures that lie within. The Princess is dimly lit, which adds to its historic feel, and initially it's like a maze, with an island bar in the middle of the room and the rest divided into traditional partitions.

> The Princess Louise is also notable for having been the venue for a number of influential folk clubs run by Ewan MacColl (1915-1989) and others, which played an important part in the British folk revival of the late '50s and early '60s.

The Princess was restored in 2007 to her original Victorian layout by its owner (since 1997), Yorkshire brewer, Samuel Smith (established 1758). They opted for restoration rather than simply refurbishment and lavished a fortune on their flagship London pub. The most notable change was the reinstatement of the discreet cubicles that were removed several decades earlier. In June 2009, the pub was joint winner of the best refurbishment class in the 2008 Pub Design Awards, presented annually by CAMRA.

Food is served but receives mixed reviews – the best thing that can be said about it is that it's typical British pub grub. However, people don't come here to eat but for the reasonably-priced beers and to soak up the friendly, magical atmosphere.

66 *A beautiful gem of a pub, fit for a princess* **99**

Address: 60 St Giles High Street, WC2H 8LG (☎ 020-7240 2532, 🖥 www.stgilesonline.org).

Opening hours: Mon-Fri, 9am to 6pm. See website for service times.

Cost: Free (but donations are welcome).

Transport: Tottenham Court Road tube station.

ST GILES-IN-THE-FIELDS

St Giles-in-the-Fields is a beautiful, historic (Grade I listed) 18th-century church built in 1734 in the Palladian style. There has been a house of prayer on this site since 1101, when Queen Matilda, wife of Henry I, founded a leper hospital here. The chapel probably became the church of a small village, which serviced the hospital, with the lepers screened off. In common with other monasteries, the hospital was dissolved by Henry VIII in 1539 and its lands sold. The hospital chapel became a parish church with the first Rector of St Giles being appointed in 1547, when the words 'in-the-fields' were added to its name.

In the early 17th century, the church fell into disrepair and a Gothic brick structure was built between 1623 and 1630. Some of the first victims of the Great Plague in 1665 were buried in St Giles's churchyard and by the end of the year there were 3,216 recorded plague deaths in the church's parish alone (which had fewer than 2,000 households).

By 1711, the church suffered badly from damp and a new church was built in 1730-34, designed by Henry Flitcroft (1697-1769) – the first English church built in the Palladian style. The parish's population grew considerably in the 18th and 19th centuries, exceeding 30,000 by 1831.

St Giles escaped severe damage in WWII but lost most of its Victorian glass. It underwent a major restoration in 1952-53, described by Poet Laureate John Betjeman as 'one of the most successful post-war church restorations'. Since the '50s the area has changed enormously and now has a resident population of less than 5,000.

> **St Giles was the last church on the route between Newgate Prison and the gallows at Tyburn, and the churchwardens paid for the condemned to have a drink – popularly named 'St Giles' bowl' – at the Angel pub next door, before they were hanged.**

The church has a fine 17th-century organ built in 1678, which has been rebuilt and restored many times over the centuries, but still retains much of its original pipework. The church also has a wealth of memorials from the 18th-20th centuries.

St Giles is known as 'The Poets' Church' (it has associations with John Milton and Andrew Marvell) and the Poetry Society holds its annual general meeting in the vestry house. The church also stages concerts and events, and hosts a theatre club and professional choir.

 The poets' church with a turbulent history

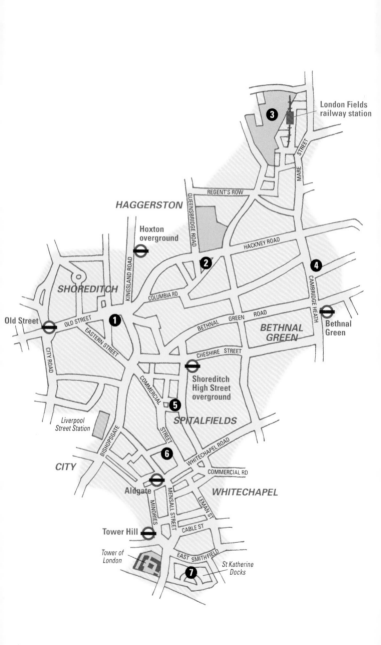

London Fields railway station

3

HAGGERSTON

Hoxton overground

REGENT'S ROW

QUEENSBRIDGE ROAD

MARE STREET

HACKNEY ROAD

2

4

SHOREDITCH

KINGSLAND ROAD

COLUMBIA RD

CAMBRIDGE HEATH

Old Street

OLD STREET

EASTERN STREET

1

BETHNAL GREEN ROAD

BETHNAL GREEN

Bethnal Green

CITY ROAD

CHESHIRE STREET

COMMERCIAL STREET

Shoreditch High Street overground

Liverpool Street Station

5

SPITALFIELDS

BISHOPSGATE

6

WHITECHAPEL ROAD

COMMERCIAL RD

Aldgate

MENSALL STREET

WHITECHAPEL

MINORIES

LEMAN ST

Tower Hill

CABLE ST

Tower of London

EAST SMITHFIELD

7

St Katherine Docks

CHAPTER 5

EAST LONDON

N.B. See next page and individual pages for maps

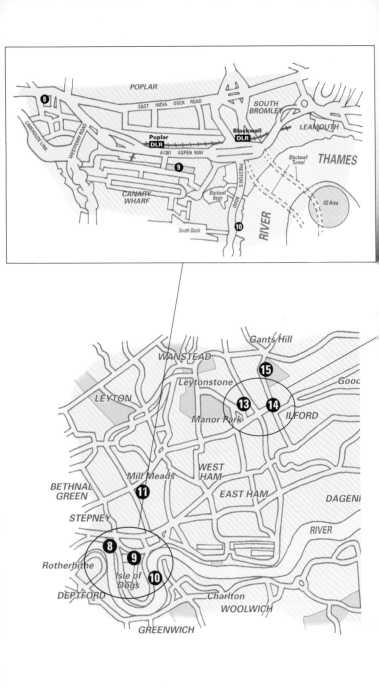

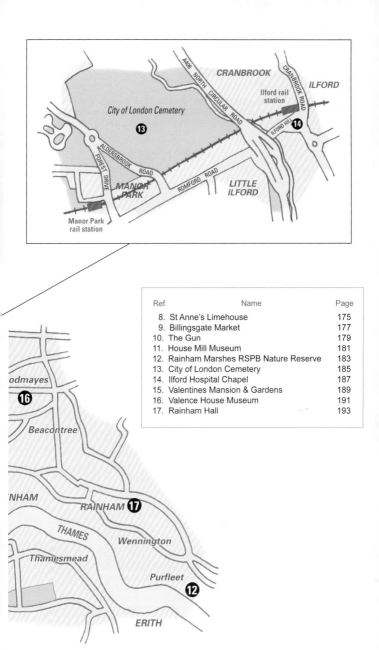

N.B. See individual pages for detailed maps for nos 11, 12, 15, 16 & 17

Address: Rivington Place, EC2A 3BA (☎ 020-7749 1240, 🖥 www.rivingtonplace.org).

Opening hours: Exhibitions – Tue, Wed and Fri, 11am to 6pm, Thu 11am to 9pm, Sat noon to 6pm. Closed Sundays, Mondays and Bank Holidays. **Library** – Tue to Fri, 10am to 1pm and 2-5pm.

Cost: Free.

Transport: Old Street or Shoreditch High Street tube station.

RIVINGTON PLACE GALLERY

*R*ivington Place Gallery is an international art gallery in the heart of Shoreditch, East London, home to Iniva (Institute of International Visual Arts) and Autograph ABP's (💻 www.autograph-abp.co.uk) dynamic artistic programmes, and the UK's first permanent public space dedicated to cultural diversity in the visual arts. The RIBA award-winning building was designed by leading architect David Adjays, influenced by African and contemporary art as well as by the history of the local area. It cost £8m and opened on 5th October 2007 – the first publicly-funded building of its kind since The Hayward Gallery over 40 years ago.

Rivington Place is a new kind of visual arts space, with a programme of exhibitions and events which engage with new ideas and emerging debates in contemporary visual arts, reflecting the cultural diversity of contemporary society. The vision is to create a centre of excellence for the presentation and dissemination of ideas and practices in contemporary visual arts, which have been marginalised by mainstream cultural institutions.

Rivington Place also contains the Stuart Hall Library, named after the eminent cultural theorist, Professor Stuart Hall, which focuses on contemporary African, Asian, Latin American and European Art, and the work of British artists from different cultural backgrounds. Run by Iniva, the library contains exhibition catalogues, monographs on critical and cultural theory, and periodicals. It also has audio-visual material on DVD and CD, and a substantial collection of slides and ephemera. The library also hosts talks and events, stimulating debate and engaging leading thinkers.

Exhibitions at Rivington Place include artists who raise issues from different parts of the world such as Zineb Sedira, Hew Locke, NS Harsha, Donald Rodney and James Barnor. Exhibitions in 2011/2012 included the first UK solo show by Rabih Mroué, an overview of the work of photographer Romtimi Fani-Kayode, the group show Social Fabric and the annual commission for the Gallery's large street-facing window.

> Rivington's award-winning learning and research programme involves people of all ages, locally and internationally, which is reflected in activities in Iniva's Education Space and off-site locations.

The building houses exhibition and installation spaces, seminar and screening space, multimedia facilities, photography archive, learning space, meeting room, workspaces, a bookshop and a café/bar (open from 8am) with a seasonal menu using local suppliers.

Rivington Place, through both its architecture and curatorial programming, provides a hub for the ever-rotating world of visual arts.

 Cutting edge art in an award-winning building

Address: **Columbia Road, E2** (🖥 **http://columbiaroad.info**).

Opening hours: **Sundays, 8am to 3pm.**

Cost: **Free.**

Transport: **Hoxton rail station and 26, 48 and 55 buses.**

COLUMBIA ROAD FLOWER MARKET & SHOPS

*C*olumbia Road Flower Market is a colourful street market in East London and the city's only dedicated flower market. On Sundays the street is transformed into an oasis of foliage and flowers – everything from bedding plants to 10-foot banana trees. The market was established as a covered food market in 1869 by the heiress and philanthropist Angela Burdett-Coutts (1814-1906); Columbia Road was named in her honour after she instituted a Bishopric in British Columbia (Canada). The food market closed in 1886 after which the buildings were used as warehouses and small workshops, and was finally demolished in 1958.

The Flower Market began as a Saturday trading market, but as the local Jewish population grew a Sunday market was established, and the Saturday market lapsed, which also (conveniently) provided the opportunity for Covent Garden and Spitalfields' traders to sell their stock left over from Saturday. The demand for cut flowers and plants among East Enders was created by Huguenot immigrants, together with a fascination for caged song birds, a reminder of which is the pub at the end of the market – The Birdcage.

The market went into a long decline during WWII, when a civilian shelter beneath the market suffered a direct hit during the Blitz. From the '60s, new rules forced traders to attend regularly, although the whole area deteriorated in the '70s and faced demolition. The market enjoyed a resurgence in the '80s with the increasing popularity of television gardening programmes and today a wide

> A great place to chill out on a Sunday morning, followed by lunch in one of the local eateries or a curry in nearby Brick Lane.

range of plants, bedding plants, shrubs, bulbs and freshly cut flowers is available at competitive prices (even lower near closing time); many traders are also growers and are second or third generation.

The area offers much more than a flower market and encompasses over 50 independent, mostly Victorian, shops, making it one of London's most interesting shopping streets. Outlets include tiny art galleries, cup cake vendors, perfumers, vintage clothing boutiques, homeware retailers, English and Italian delis, garden accessory sellers, jewellery makers and antique dealers, plus more unusual wares such as hand-made soap, candlesticks and Buddhist artefacts. There's also a wealth of great pubs, cafés and restaurants. Not surprisingly, the market is popular with photographers and television companies, who regularly film here.

 London's most colourful and fragrant market

Address: **London Fields Westside, E8 3EU** (☎ **020-7254 9038,**
🖥 **www.hackney.gov.uk/london-fields.htm, www.gll.org/centre/london-fields-lido.asp and www.londonfieldsusergroup.org.uk**).

Opening hours: **Park – unrestricted access; Lido – Summer, Mon-Fri, 6.30am to 8pm, Sat-Sun 8am to 5pm; other times vary depending on the season – see website for details.**

Cost: **Lido: non-members, adults £4.30, juniors (15 and under) £2.60.**

Transport: **London Fields rail station.**

LONDON FIELDS & LIDO

*L*ondon Fields (31 acres/12.5ha) is one of East London's most popular green spaces and also the name of an area of Hackney with many interesting shops. Due to its proximity to the City of London, Hackney was a favourite of wealthy Londoners from the Middle Ages until the 19th century, and became increasingly attractive following the Great Plague in 1665 and the Great Fire in 1666. Wealthy residents who wished to be close to the court, entertainment and London's financial centre, but also enjoy country living, built large houses here. Though it seems hardly credible today, in 1756 Hackney was declared to excel all other villages in the kingdom in the opulence of its inhabitants.

London Field (as it was then called) was first recorded in 1540, at which time it was common ground extending to around 100 acres (40ha), used by drovers to pasture their livestock before taking them to market in London. It's uncertain how the name London Field came into being, but it was probably due to the field's position on what had for centuries been the main footpath from the village of Hackney (and beyond the River Lea, from Essex) to the City of London. When travellers crossed this field they were only two miles from the City gate.

London Fields has a lido (see below), a much-used cricket pitch, soccer pitches, a BMX track, two tennis courts, a table tennis table and two children's play areas with a paddling pool (open May to September).

> **A much-used cycle path runs from the Pub on the Park – a popular local watering hole – to Broadway Market (🖥 www.broadwaymarket.co.uk), a mouth-watering food market on Saturdays from 9am to 5pm.**

London Fields lido first opened in 1932 but closed in 1988, only reopening in 2006 following a determined local campaign after being neglected for 18 years. It has been rebuilt to modern standards and is the only heated, outdoor, 50-metre, Olympic-size swimming pool in London. One of only ten survivors from the original 68 lidos in the Greater London area, it's open year round and supervised by lifeguards. There's a café which also caters for park visitors.

London Fields is a beautiful green space with extensive grassy areas and many beautiful trees (notably plane trees), and has won a number of Green Flag awards. It's a great place to play sports, swim, enjoy a picnic or just chill out.

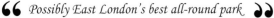

66 *Possibly East London's best all-round park* **99**

Address: **Patriot Square, Bethnal Green, E2 9NF (☎ 020-7871 0460, 🖳 http://townhallhotel.com and www.viajante.co.uk)**.

Opening hours: **Exterior – unrestricted access, interior – bar-restaurant hours unless you're a resident (see website).**

Cost: **Free (apart from a drink or meal).**

Transport: **Bethnal Green tube station.**

TOWN HALL HOTEL

*T*he Town Hall Hotel (Grade II listed) in Bethnal Green is a beautiful landmark Edwardian building, which has been converted into a luxurious five-star hotel, combining architectural splendour with cutting-edge design. The Town Hall offers a range of spacious serviced apartments, stylish hotel bedrooms and spectacular suites.

The original Town Hall opened in 1910, during the heyday of Edwardian architecture and British power. The building reflected a new confidence and wealth and the council spent lavishly on fine architects, craftsmen and artists to decorate it. In 1937 the Town Hall was extended onto Patriot Square – where the neoclassical entrance to the new hotel can now be found – during which splendid Art Deco interiors were added. The building fell into disuse in 1993 and for 14 years was used only as a location for television and films – including *Atonement* and *Lock, Stock and Two Smoking Barrels* – until being purchased by Singaporean hotel magnate Peng Loh.

The architectural expert Nikolaus Pevsner called the internal decoration 'subtle but expensive Art Deco style'. Australian walnut wood was used to panel the council chamber and mahogany in the mayoral office, green and white marble lined the staircase, while even the air vents were covered with exquisitely patterned brass grilles. Highlights include the sculpture on the frontage to Cambridge Heath Road by Henry Poole (1873-1928), the De Bathonia (a local nobleman in the time of Henry III) coat of arms in the windows facing Patriot Square, and stained glass windows and carvings showing scenes from the ballad of the Blind Beggar of Bethnal Green.

Upon entering the hotel you're immediately drawn to the beautiful domed roof of the elegant Art Deco entrance hall, the massive marble staircase and period ornamentation. The hotel's Viajante restaurant – a rare East End gem – and its talented Portuguese chef Nuno Mendes, won a Michelin star within nine months of opening. The hotel also has a bistro (The Corner Room) and an innovative cocktail bar offering over 200 spirits, beers and cocktails.

> **The Town Hall building in Bethnal Green has been beautifully restored and won the RICS London Award for Building Conservation, creating a unique designer hotel which fuses old and new.**

A bit off the beaten track, the Town Hall Hotel is well worth a trip to the East End for a drink or a superb meal – or even an overnight stay – not to forget a peek at this architectural delight.

 A gem of an Edwardian/Art Deco building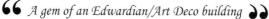

Address: **19 Princelet Street, E1 6QH** (☎ **020-7247 5352,**
🖥 **www.19princeletstreet.org.uk**).

Opening hours: **Group visits (1-2 hrs) by appointment. Also open
during London Open House weekend (🖥 www.londonopenhouse.org).**

Cost: **No set fee, but most groups (maximum of 30-40 people) are
expected to make a 'donation' of at least £5 per person or a minimum
of £100 per group.**

Transport: **Shoreditch High Street tube station.**

MUSEUM OF IMMIGRATION AND DIVERSITY

*T*he Museum of Immigration and Diversity is a unique museum – Europe's only cultural institution devoted to the movement of people in search of a better life – in one of East London's prettiest streets. It's situated in Spitalfields, which has been home to waves of dispossessed immigrants from Ireland, Europe and beyond, from the 17th century to the present day; nowadays it's home to Bangladeshi, Bengali and Somali communities.

> **In keeping with the house's multicultural past, it's now owned by a charity established to preserve the building, and to remember and celebrate the lives of those who lived, worked and worshipped here over the centuries.**

The Museum is housed is an unrestored (Grade II* listed) house built in 1719, which was home to a Huguenot silk merchant, Peter Abraham Ogier, fleeing religious persecution in France. With the decline of the British silk weaving industry as the Industrial Revolution gathered pace, the Huguenots moved on and were replaced by Irish immigrants escaping the potato famine that swept Ireland in the mid-19th century. The Irish provided local industrialists with a vast supply of cheap labour for East London's docks and factories.

Between 1870 and 1914, thousands of Jewish settlers arrived from Eastern Europe, fleeing appalling conditions, growing anti-Semitism and Tsarist pogroms in Russia. By the 1930s, the Jewish community was well established in East London, many working in cabinet making, the fur trade and tailoring. Houses like this one, where Huguenots once wove silk, now became workplaces and homes for Jewish families. Life was hard for new arrivals and a Jewish self-help group called the Loyal United Friends leased rooms at number 19, which they converted into a synagogue with a meeting place in the basement. The synagogue remained in use until the '70s, when the congregation dwindled.

The moment you step through the door of 19 Princelet Street you realise that you're entering a rare and remarkable building, made all the more poignant by it's fragile state and air of decay. There's a touching exhibition entitled 'Suitcases and Sanctuary', exploring the history of the waves of immigrants who shaped Spitalfields, seen through the eyes of today's children. The building is in desperate need of restoration – which is why it's only open infrequently – and the charity hopes to restore it and create a permanent exhibition. One hopes that its unique atmosphere won't be lost in the process.

 A unique and moving museum and house

AT A GLANCE

Address: London Metropolitan University, 25 Old Castle Street, E1 7NT (☎ **020-7320 2222**, ⌨ **www.londonmet.ac.uk/thewomenslibrary**).

Opening hours: Tue to Fri, 9.30am to 5.30pm (Thu 8pm), Sat, 10am to 4pm. Closed Mon and Sun.

Cost: **Free.**

Transport: **Aldgate tube station.**

WOMEN'S LIBRARY

*T*he Women's Library is the UK's main library and museum resource about women and the women's movement, especially concentrating on Britain in the 19th and 20th centuries. The Library contains over 60,000 books and pamphlets, which include scholarly works on women's history, biographies, popular works, government publications and works of literature.

The Library's origin derives from the London National Society for Women's Suffrage, established in 1867, though the Library wasn't formally created until the 1920s, and the first Librarian, Vera Douie, wasn't appointed until 1st January 1926. At this time it was called the Women's Service Library. Vera Douie remained in her post for 41 years, during which time she took a small but interesting society library and created a major resource with an international reputation.

The Library was originally housed in a converted tavern in Marsham Street, Westminster, which in the 1930s developed into the Women's Service House, a major women's centre within walking distance of Parliament. Members of the society and Library included writers such as Vera Brittain and Virginia Woolf, as well as politicians, most notably Eleanor Rathbone. During WWII it suffered bomb damage and the Library had no permanent home until 1957, when it moved to Wilfred Street, near Victoria railway station. By this time, the society and Library had changed their names to the Fawcett Society and the Fawcett Library, in commemoration of the non-militant suffrage leader Millicent Garrett Fawcett, and of her daughter, Philippa Fawcett.

> **The collections span a variety of topics, such as women's rights, suffrage, sexuality, health, education, employment, reproductive rights, the family and the home – and is of 'outstanding national and international importance'.**

In 1977, the Library was rescued by the then City of London Polytechnic (now the London Metropolitan University) and languished for over 20 years in a cramped basement until receiving a grant of £4.2m in 1998 from the Heritage Lottery Fund towards a new home on the site of the old East End public wash houses in Old Castle Street. The new Library opened in February 2002 and changed its name to 'The Women's Library'.

The Library hosts a changing programme of exhibitions in its museum space, where topics have included women's suffrage, beauty queens, office work, '80s politics and prostitution. It also hosts public talks, films, reading groups and short courses, and offers free guided tours. Use of the Reading Room is free and open to everyone.

 A rare institution celebrating British women's history

ST KATHARINE DOCKS

*S*t Katharine Docks were one of the commercial docks that formed the Port of London, situated just east of the Tower of London and Tower Bridge. The foundations of today's buildings can be traced back to the 10th century, when King Edgar gave 13 acres (5.3ha) of land to 13 knights to use for trade. There's evidence of there having been a dock at St Katharine's since 1125, and it has also housed a hospital and monastery; in fact the Docks took their name from the former hospital of St Katharine by the Tower, built in the 12th century.

The first use of the name St Katharine Docks can be traced to Elizabethan times, when the area around the hospital was thriving with busy wharves. By the end of the 18th century, St Katharine's was a prosperous settlement with its own court, school and almshouses, and along with the hospital was home to some 3,000 people. However, when the government wanted to expand the Docks the area was earmarked for redevelopment; construction commenced in 1827 with the demolition of 1,250 slum houses and the medieval hospital of St Katharine.

The scheme was designed by celebrated engineer Thomas Telford (1757-1834) – his only major project in London – with the Docks' warehouses (designed by Philip Hardwick) built on the quayside so that goods could be unloaded directly into them. The

> **The Docks have their own pier serving boats to Westminster and Greenwich, while boats to other destinations call at nearby Tower Millennium Pier (see 🖥 www.tfl.gov.uk/river).**

Docks opened in 1828 and although well used, they weren't a huge commercial success, being unable to accommodate large ships. However, they gained a reputation for handling valuable cargoes and as late as the 1930s were described as a focal point for the world's greatest concentration of portable wealth. They were badly damaged in WWII and never fully recovered, and were among the first London docks to be closed in 1968. Most of the original warehouses were demolished when the docks were redeveloped in the '70s,

Today, St Katharine Docks features offices, luxury warehouse apartments, a large hotel, shops, a Friday food market (10am to 4pm), bars, restaurants, cafés and a pub (The Dickens Inn, a former brewery dating to the 18th century), a yacht marina and other recreational facilities.

A great place for a family day out in the city.

 From bustling docks to tranquil yachting haven

Address: 5 Newell Street, E14 7HP (☎ 020-7515 0977, 🖥 http://stanneslimehouse.org).

Opening hours: Sunday mornings from 10.30am. Access can be arranged at other times by contacting the church office. See website for service times.

Cost: Free (but donations are welcome).

Transport: Westferry DLR station.

ST ANNE'S LIMEHOUSE

St Anne's Limehouse (Grade I listed) is a splendid Baroque Anglican church designed by the celebrated architect Nicholas Hawksmoor (1661-1736), a pupil of Sir Christopher Wren. The huge church was one of Queen Anne's 'Fifty New Churches' designed to serve the needs of the rapidly expanding population of London in the 18th century, of which only 12 were built. Consecrated in 1730, it was Hawksmoor's earliest church (1725) and must have appeared overwhelming to local residents in its day.

The church's crowning glory is its entrance front and magnificent tower; it also has a beautiful vestibule but the spacious interior is rather plain, although there are plans to restore it to Hawksmoor's original design. The churchyard contains a distinctive pyramid, originally planned to be installed atop the tower, and a cruciform 1918 war memorial of white stone and bronze (both Grade II listed). St Anne's boasts the second-highest church clock in London after Big Ben – the 197ft (60m) tower is a 'Trinity House mark' for identifying shipping lanes on the Thames and thus flies the Royal Navy's white ensign.

St Anne's has a long-standing association with the Royal Navy and its current rector is the RN's honorary Chaplain. The church has two specially-designed exhibition cabinets: one contains the pre-1801 battle-sized White Ensign of the Royal Navy and the other HMS Ark Royal's 18 x 9ft (5.5 x 2.75m) battle Ensign, plus the cap of a rating with the Ark Royal cap tally (name), pictures, the ship's crest and brief histories of all five ships that have born the name Ark Royal.

The church was gutted by fire in 1850 and restored between 1851 and 1854 by Philip Hardwick and John Morris. St Anne's underwent a major restoration in recent decades when Julian Harrap architects (1983-1993) added tubular steel trusses to support the roof; between 1999 and 2009 further restoration included the front end of the church, the organ, extensive exterior cleaning and the churchyard.

The Gray and Davison pipe organ in St Anne's won first prize in the Great Exhibition of 1851 at Crystal Palace, and is much prized by musicians. Fully restored in 2009, the church became the main rehearsal venue for the recently formed Docklands Sinfonia Orchestra, and hosts occasional classical concerts.

> There's a link to Greenwich time at the top of the tower: a weight falls when a signal comes from Greenwich (line of sight).

 Hawksmoor's towering achievement!

AT A GLANCE

Address: **Trafalgar Way, E14 5ST** (☎ **020-7987 1118,** 🖥 **www. billingsgate-market.org.uk).**

Opening hours: **Tue-Sat, 5-8.30am. Closed Sun-Mon and the Tuesday after a Bank Holiday Monday.**

Cost: **Free.**

Transport: **Poplar DLR station.**

BILLINGSGATE MARKET

*S*ituated in East London, Billingsgate Fish Market is the UK's largest inland fish market and takes its name from Billingsgate – originally known as Blynesgate and Byllynsgate – in the City of London, where the riverside market was originally established. The (general) market rights of the City of London were based on a charter granted by Edward III in 1327, which prohibited the establishment of rival markets within 6.6mi (10.6km) of the City, this being the distance a person could be expected to walk to market, sell his produce and return in a day.

Billingsgate Wharf, close to Lower Thames Street, became the centre of a fish market in the 16th and 17th centuries, but didn't become formally established until an Act of Parliament in 1699. In 1849 the fish market – the largest in the world at the time – was moved off the streets into its own riverside building, which was demolished in 1873 and replaced by an arcaded market hall designed by City architect Sir Horace Jones in 1875. This building, now known as Old Billingsgate Market (⌨ www.oldbillingsgate.co.uk), is now used as a corporate events venue.

In 1982, the Market was relocated to a new 13-acre (5.3ha) complex close to Canary Wharf in Docklands. Most of the fish sold through the Market now arrives by road, from ports as far afield as Aberdeen and Cornwall, while live imports include lobsters from Canada and eels from New Zealand. The ground floor of the building consists of a large trading hall with around 100 stands and 30 shops, including two cafés. Some 25,000 tonnes of fish and fish products are sold annually at Billingsgate, about 40 per cent imported from abroad, with an annual turnover of around £200m.

> In 2012, the City of London withdrew the trading licences from Market porters, thus ending a centuries-old tradition whereby porters had the sole licence to transport fish within the Market. Under the portering system, merchants paid porters a fixed retainer and the fishmonger or customer paid a bobbin (18 pence today) per stone of fish delivered.

The Billingsgate Seafood Training School provides tailor-made courses and demonstrations in fish recognition, knife skills, presentation, cooking and nutrition.

Billingsgate Market is open to the general public and is an interesting place to visit – but if you're shopping for fish you need to arrive early for the best selection.

 Providing London with fresh fish for over 300 years

AT A GLANCE

Address: **27 Coldharbour, Docklands, E14 9NS** (☎ **020-7515 5222,** 💻 **www.thegundocklands.com**).

Opening hours: **Mon-Sat, 11am to midnight, Sun, 11am to 11pm. Bookings advisable if you're planning to eat anything other than bar food.**

Cost: **Free (apart from a drink).**

Transport: **Blackwall DLR station or Canary Wharf pier and taxi (free for diners).**

THE GUN

*T*he Gun (Grade II listed) is an 18th-century, Thameside gastropub – serving award-winning modern British cuisine – with a intriguing 250-year history. It takes its name from a cannon fired to celebrate the opening of the West India Import Docks in 1802 (though the pub is earlier); a fitting name in an area which was once home to the iron foundries that made the guns for the Royal Navy fleets in the 18th and 19th centuries. In the late 18th century, Lord Horatio Nelson acquired a property just up the road (still known as Nelson's House) and regularly visited the docks to inspect the guns up until his death at the Battle of Trafalgar in 1805. He was a regular patron of The Gun, where he allegedly had assignations with Lady Emma Hamilton in the upstairs room, now called The River Room.

In 2001, a fire destroyed much of the interior of the old building and the pub remained closed for three years. The current owners, brothers Tom and Ed Martin, acquired the premises and spent around nine months painstakingly restoring it, opening the doors in 2004. The Gun now has a dining room in the main bar (with a roaring log fire in winter), a back bar with two snugs and two private dining rooms. There's also a large riverside terrace seating 50, which is used from May-September for al fresco drinks and BBQs, while enjoying panoramic views of the river and O2 Arena.

The pub has three handpumps offering fine ales (from, for example, Dark Star and Adnams) and imaginative cooking, which, although not cheap, is light years away from standard pub fare. As an added incentive, when you book a table in the dining room from Mon-Fri (not available weekends/Bank Holidays), lunchtime diners travelling from Canary Wharf or the Isle of Dogs can claim a taxi to the pub and back – free of charge! What are you waiting for?

> **The Gun also has a long association with smugglers landing contraband on the site and distributing it via a hidden tunnel. There's a spy-hole in the secret circular staircase used to keep a lookout for 'The Revenue Men'. As the docks on the Isle of Docks flourished so did the pub, becoming the local for dockers, stevedores and boatmen.**

 Love nest of Admiral Nelson and Lady Hamilton

AT A GLANCE

Address: Three Mill Lane, Bromley-by-Bow, E3 3DU (☎ 020-8980 4626, 🖳 www.housemill.org.uk).

Opening hours: Sun, May to October, 11am to 4pm and the first Sundays in March, April and December. Guided tours last around 45 mins (last tour 3.30pm).

Cost: Adults £3, concessions £1.50, children free.

Transport: Bromley-by-Bow tube station.

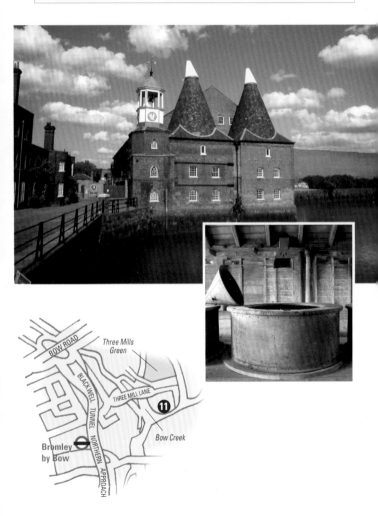

HOUSE MILL MUSEUM

*T*he House Mill is a Grade 1 listed 18th-century tidal mill set in a beautiful riverside location in the heart of London's East End – believed to be the largest tidal mill still in existence in the world. The mill was built in 1776 by Daniel Bisson, on the site of an earlier mill, between two houses occupied by the miller and his family, hence its name. It's a timber framed building clad in brick on three sides.

In addition to flour-making, the mill also prepared grain for a (gin) distillery next door on Three Mills Island. Built across the River Lea, the mill trapped the sea and river water at high tide to turn the water wheels on the ebb. The outflowing water turned four large wheels driving twelve pairs of millstones, all of which survive together with other historic machinery (though it isn't currently operational). The mill ceased operation in 1941 after the area was bombed during WWII.

In medieval times the site was known as Three Mills and provided flour for the bakers of Stratford-atte-Bow, who in turn supplied bread to the City of London. In 1728, Three Mills was purchased by Peter Lefevre, a Huguenot, who entered

> The *Domesday Book* (1086) recorded eight mills in this area – among the earliest known tide mills in England – and as windmills came later these must have been tidal water mills on the River Lea.

into partnership with Daniel Bisson and several others. The mills cooperated with a distillery and the company had its own carpenters and coopers, and also operated a large piggery fed on the mills' waste products.

In the mid-'70s, House Mill was threatened with demolition and was saved by the intervention of the governors of the Passmore Edwards Museum (Newham). In 1989 work began on the House Mill, the fabric of which has been fully restored. The Miller's House was rebuilt in 1995 with a modern interior but retaining the original façade, and now has a visitor, information and education centre and a small café.

Nowadays, the mill is owned by The River Lea Tidal Mill Trust, which plans to reinstate the water wheels and other machinery in order to demonstrate grinding, and together with modern turbines (installed at the rear of the building), the wheels will also be used for hydro power generation.

A fascinating historic mill well worth visiting.

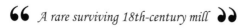

66 *A rare surviving 18th-century mill* **99**

Address: New Tank Hill Road, Purfleet, RM19 1SZ (☎ 01708-899840,
💻 www.rspb.org.uk/reserves/guide/r/rainhammarshes).

Opening hours: 1st November to 31st March, 9.30am to 4.30pm; 1st
April to 31st October, 9.30am to 5pm. Closed Christmas Day and
Boxing Day.

Cost: Non-RSPB members, adult £3, child £1.50, family £9 (two adults
and up to four children). Free to RSPB members and local residents.

Transport: Purfleet rail station, but best reached by car. Car park,
voluntary £1 donation.

RAINHAM MARSHES RSPB NATURE RESERVE

Rainham Marshes RSPB (Royal Society for the Protection of Birds) Nature Reserve is a wetland on the upper Thames Estuary and a magnet for bird lovers and nature enthusiasts. Previously used as a firing range by the Ministry of Defence, the marshes were closed to the public for over 100 years until being acquired by the RSPB in 2000 and opening in 2006. The reserve is one of the few ancient medieval landscapes remaining in the London area, and the largest area of wetland on the upper region of the Thames Estuary, taking in Wennington, Aveley and Rainham Marshes.

The RSPB has transformed the reserve into a unique marshland with a wide variety of wetland plants, teeming with wildlife, from birds and mammals (it's home to one of the country's most dense water vole populations) to insects – dragonflies and butterflies abound – and reptiles.

Needless to say, the stars are the reserve's wealth of bird life, which includes breeding waders, such as redshank and snipe, as well as large numbers of wintering wildfowl, finches and birds of prey. Among the leading attractions are avocet, lapwing, little egret, peregrine and ringed plover. Each season brings a different experience. In spring, the air is filled with birdsong as birds compete to establish territories and attract a mate, while in summer you can see fledglings making their first venture into the outside world. Autumn brings large movements of migrating birds – some heading south to a warmer climate, while others seek refuge in the UK from the cold Arctic winter – and in winter there are large flocks gathering to feed or flying at dusk to form large roosts to keep warm.

The reserve organises a number of regular events for birdwatchers, from novice to expert, throughout the year, including weekly Wednesday guided birding walks, dawn chorus walks, winter spectacle birding events and a bird watching club for children. There's also an innovative visitor centre, with huge picture-windows looking out onto the marshes and hides affording great views of the reserve. The visitor centre is packed with environmentally-friendly features and boasts a number of prestigious architectural awards.

> **With around 2.5mi (4km) of trails, a children's adventure play area, wildlife garden, marshland discovery zone, shop and café, the reserve offers something for everyone and is a haven for families, walkers, cyclists, wildlife enthusiasts and school groups.**

❝ *A nature lover's delight* **❞**

Address: Aldersbrook Road, Manor Park, E12 5DQ (☎ 020-8530 2151, 🖳 www.cityoflondon.gov.uk > Cemetery and Crematorium).

Opening hours: Winter – daily, 9am to 5pm (Christmas and Boxing Day, 3pm); summer – Mon-Fri, 9am to 7pm, weekends, 9am to 5pm. Walking tours on the third or fourth Sunday of the month from 10am to noon (see website or telephone to book). No dogs allowed.

Cost: Free.

Transport: Manor Park rail station or East Ham or Wanstead tube station and 101 bus.

CITY OF LONDON CEMETERY

*T*he City of London Cemetery and Crematorium (Grade I listed) is one of London's most appealing cemeteries, owned and operated by the City of London Corporation. Designed by William Haywood and opened in 1856, the 200-acre (81ha) site is a picturesque parkland with beautiful formal gardens, tree-lined avenues and an interesting local heritage. A crematorium (now a chapel) opened on 25th October 1904 and was replaced by a new one in 1971. The cemetery is one of the largest municipal cemeteries in Europe – over 500,000 people have been interred here – and is non-denominational, although there was originally an Anglican chapel with a 61ft (19m) spire and an unusual round Dissenter's chapel.

The cemetery is rich in architecture, ecology, geology, horticulture and history, and was the first to be awarded the prestigious Green Flag. It contains over 3,500 trees, memorial gardens (see below), a woodland area, water features, ponds and a nature area, which is home to a wide variety of birds, insects and mammals (including squirrels, terrapins, frogs, bats, hedgehogs and moles). There's also a Chapel of Remembrance and a columbarium (storage for cremated remains). The cemetery is one of only a few in London containing catacombs, although they proved unpopular and were partly converted into columbarium space. In 1937, a Garden of Rest was created, followed by a series of glorious memorial gardens, which now extend to 32 acres (13ha) containing some 20,000 rose bushes.

Among the estimated 150,000 gravesites are those of Elizabeth Ann Everest, nanny to Winston Churchill; World Cup hero Bobby Moore; philosopher and inventor Sir Robert Hooke; actress Dame Anna Neagle; and Jack the Ripper victims, Mary Ann Nichols and Catherine Eddowes. One of the best ways to explore the cemetery is to join a walking tour. Highlights include a glimpse of 150 years of the Burial and Cremation registers; insights into striking mausoleums and memorials marking historical moments; famous tombs and graves; exploring some of the Grade II listed chapels and catacombs; and hearing fascinating stories of the siege of Sidney Street and of Edith Thompson, who was one of the last women hanged in the UK in the 20th century for the murder of her husband, Percy, who's buried here.

> **One of London's most interesting and beautiful burial grounds, the City of London Cemetery is a peaceful place for quiet enjoyment and contemplation – and a lovely spot to visit at any time of the year.**

❝ *A fine resting place for both the living and the dead* **❞**

Address: 48 Ilford Hill, Ilford, IG1 2AT (☎ 020-8590 2098, 🖥 www.ilfordhospitalchapel.co.uk).

Opening hours: Open day on the second Saturday of each month from March to November, 10am to 4pm. Private tours (15-20 people) can also be arranged. Visitors are also welcome to take part in services (see website for times).

Cost: Free (but donations are welcome).

Transport: Ilford rail station.

ILFORD HOSPITAL CHAPEL

*I*lford Hospital Chapel – or to give it its full name, the 'Ilford Hospital Chapel of St Mary the Virgin and St Thomas of Canterbury' – is a gem of a building (Grade II* listed). Known locally as 'The Hospital Chapel', it was founded around 1145AD by Adelicia (Adeliza), Abbess of Barking, as a hospice for 13 aged and infirm men. The nave and chancel of the present Chapel were built during the 14th century or earlier, and the north wall was formed by the original Norman wall when the Chapel was built. In those days Barking Abbey was a wealthy and influential nunnery, established in 666AD and endowed with the Manor of Barking (including Ilford and Dagenham).

> The Chapel was dedicated first to St Mary the Virgin, though later Mary Becket became Abbess in succession to Adelicia and arranged for the name of her brother, Thomas à Becket, to be added to the dedication in his memory.

By 1219 the Chapel was admitting lepers, although little medical treatment could be offered – only shelter and spiritual comfort. An archaeological investigation of the courtyard during 1959-1960 revealed between 22 and 25 burials to the left of the porch and more recent examination has shown that several suffered from leprosy. These remains lay at a lower level than the surviving foundation of the Chapel or at least earlier than the 14th century.

The ancient Abbey of Barking was dissolved by Henry VIII in 1539 during the Reformation and demolished between 1540 and 1541. However, the Ilford Hospital Chapel with its own endowments and constitution, survived this fate and also the abolition of Chantries in 1547, probably due to its function as a chapel-of-ease as well as a hospice. Since the 15th century the Chapel has had a number of owners and patrons, and is now owned and administered by the Abbess Adelicia Charity.

The complex consists of the Chapel itself plus almshouses on either side, which were quarters for the poor brethren and the chaplains, recently converted into modern flats. The hospital was governed by a master, originally appointed by the abbess, who in later times at least, was provided with a large house (demolished in 1905) to the east adjoining Ilford Lane.

Ilford Hospital Chapel is a charming building containing some splendid stained glass windows – the finest in Ilford – and well worth the trip.

❝ *A magical, charming 14th-century chapel* **❞**

VALENTINES MANSION & GARDENS

*V*alentines Mansion (Grade II* listed), set in formal gardens (Grade II listed), is a splendid William III country house, recently restored to its former glory. The Mansion was built in 1696-7, probably by James Chadwick, son-in-law of John Tillotson, the Archbishop of Canterbury, whose widow Lady Elizabeth owned the estate.

City merchant and banker Robert Surman bought the estate in 1724 and enlarged and improved the house and gardens, creating the walled gardens, dovecote and grottoes. In 1754, Sir Charles Raymond purchased Valentines and continued reconstructing the house, giving it its Georgian appearance; the date 1769 with his family crest is on the rainwater heads above the drainpipes. Externally the house is an 18th-century structure, but some features inside the house are earlier, including much of the panelling and joinery.

> By 1912 the council had acquired the Mansion and its grounds, since when it has been used as a home for wartime refugees, a hospital, a public health centre and a council housing department (until 1994).

By the time Sir Charles Raymond died in 1788 the estate had been greatly enlarged, and the new owner, Donald Cameron, presided over 400 acres (162ha). Valentines changed hands many times over the next century until being left by Charles Holcombe to his niece in 1870, when it became the permanent home of the Ingleby family. It remained a family house until 1906, when Sarah Ingleby, its last inhabitant, died. In 1899 47 (19ha) acres of the grounds were sold by Mrs Ingleby to Ilford Urban District Council and opened as a public park.

After being neglected and standing empty for 15 years, both the park and Mansion were restored thanks to a grant of several million pounds from the Heritage Lottery Fund and additional funding from the borough of Redbridge. Today, Valentines features a recreated Victorian kitchen and Georgian rooms, with glorious views over the surrounding parkland. The gardens include an exceptional formal 18th-century garden, an historic herb/kitchen garden, an old English walled garden and a Victorian rose garden. There's also a dovecote, canal and a café.

Additional attractions include contemporary art exhibitions, family Sunday activities on the first Sunday of each month and a farmer's market on the fourth Sunday of the month, while the grounds host county cricket matches and the Redbridge Town Show (see website for information).

A lovely historic home that makes a great day out for all the family.

 A beautiful country house with fine gardens

Address: Becontree Avenue, Dagenham, RM8 3HT (☎ 020-8227 5222, 🖥 www.lbbd.gov.uk/museumsandheritage/valencehousemuseum/pages/home.aspx).

Opening hours: Mon-Sat, 10am to 4pm. Closed on Sundays and Public Holidays.

Cost: Free.

Transport: Chadwell Heath rail station.

VALENCE HOUSE MUSEUM

*V*alence House Museum is the attractive local history museum of Barking and Dagenham housed in a 15th-century (Grade II* listed) manor house, the only survivor of five manor houses that once stood in Dagenham. The timber-framed museum building, still partially surrounded by a moat, is situated in Valence Park (28.7 acres/11.25ha). The existing structure dates from the 15th century, with additions or remodelling made in every century since it was built. A survey of 1649 reveals a house much larger than today with parlours, a dining-room, bedchambers and a variety of domestic offices.

A house was first established here in the 13th century, first mentioned in a property transaction of 1269, when Robert de Dyne (or Dyve) conveyed it to Gillian, widow of Hugh de Dyne. The area and surrounding roads take their names from later tenants of the estate, Agnes de Valence and her brother Aylmer, Earl of Pembroke, who occupied the land in the early 1300s. Agnes and Aylmer came from a wealthy family, with royal connections, originally from the Valence province of France. It passed through several owners until 1475 when the estate became the property of the Dean and Chapter of Windsor and remained in their ownership until 1867, when it passed to the Church Commissioners. The last person to use Valence House as a home was Thomas May, who lived there with his wife, their 12 children and his mother-in-law from 1878 until 1921.

In 1921, the London County Council purchased the building and estate and Valence House was later used as local council offices and library headquarters, before becoming Barking and Dagenham's Local History Museum in 1974. The Museum underwent extensive restoration in 2007-2010, which included new galleries, a purpose-built archive and a local studies centre. It contains permanent exhibitions on history and life in Barking and Dagenham, including the rise and fall of Barking Abbey, industrial innovation and sporting heritage. The Valence House gallery traces the history of the house and surrounding land, and looks at many of the people who have called Valence House home. You can also explore its beautiful oak-panelled rooms and view a newly-discovered 400-year-old wall painting.

> **Valence House is a great day out for the family and has a delightful al fresco café, peaceful walled herb garden, medieval moat and a beautiful public park, with many ancient trees.**

 One of the best local history museums in London

Address: **The Broadway, Rainham, RM13 9YN** (☎ **020-7799 4552,** 💻 **www.nationaltrust.org.uk/main/w-rainhamhall**).

Opening hours: **Saturdays and Bank Holiday Mondays, from 7th April to 3rd November (2012), 2-5pm, plus May Day and Rainham Christmas Fair. See website for further information.**

Cost: **Adult £2.80, child £1.60, family £7.20. Free for National Trust members and on a few days a year.**

Transport: **Rainham rail station.**

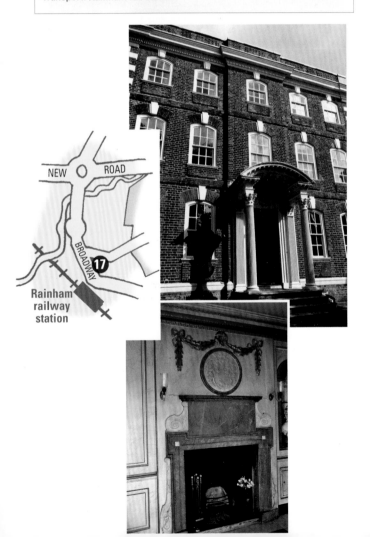

RAINHAM HALL

*S*ituated in the centre of Rainham Village, Rainham Hall (Grade II* listed) is a charming and remarkably original Georgian merchant's house dating from the early 18th century, owned by the National Trust since 1949. Built in 1729 for Captain John Harle, a master mariner and wealthy merchant, it held a pivotal place in Rainham Village for two centuries, connecting village life with river commerce until the 1920s.

The Hall and its coach house were a focal point for Captain Harle's trading activities, which were an important factor in the development of Rainham village in the 18th century. Such close grouping of an owner's domestic and commercial premises was normal at this time, but what makes Rainham Hall significant is that it's a rare intact survivor of a practice that was once widespread. It's also a scarce witness of the river trade (on the River Ingrebourne) which forms such an important aspect of local and regional history.

Set in a large garden, the elegant Queen Anne Hall was built in the (then fashionable) Dutch Domestic style, characterised by red brick and decorative stonework; the house contains many surprising features and excellent craftsmanship using the finest materials. The Hall comprises three storeys and is entered through a classical doorway of Corinthian pilasters. Other features include ornamental stonework, a fine carved wooden porch, authentic Georgian interior decor, splendid 18th-century plasterwork, a beautiful carved wooden staircase and wonderful painted walls.

> **Many people believe that Colonel Mulliner, who lived in the house in the early 20th century, haunts the home. He's said to look dapper in his fine collar and grey tweeds. Oddly enough, it appears that the ghost may be afraid of the dark, as he has never been seen after sunset.**

The spectacular 18th-century, wrought-iron railings (the gateway contains the intertwined initials of John Harle and his wife Mary) at the front of the house represent some of the finest work of London smiths. Also of note are the Victorian dog kennels, which have recently been restored. Comprising 2 acres (0.8ha), the lovely garden is an additional feature and contains a 30-tree orchard (recently replanted) and a huge mulberry tree.

A great day out for all the family – you can combine a visit with the nearby 12th-century Norman church of St Helen and St Giles (where Captain Harle is buried) and round off your day with lunch in a local hostelry.

66 *A rare, original 18th-century merchant's house* **99**

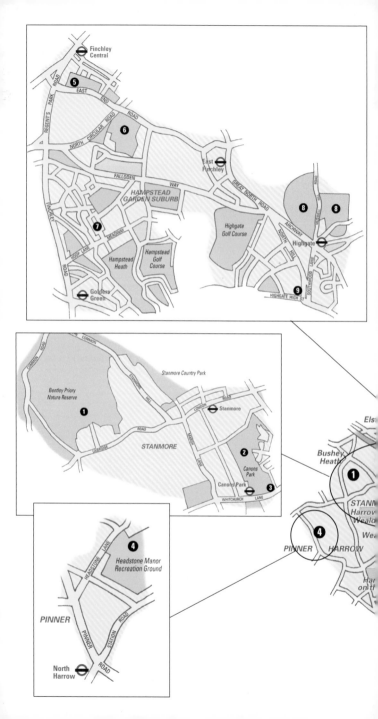

CHAPTER 6

NORTH LONDON

N.B. See next page for more maps

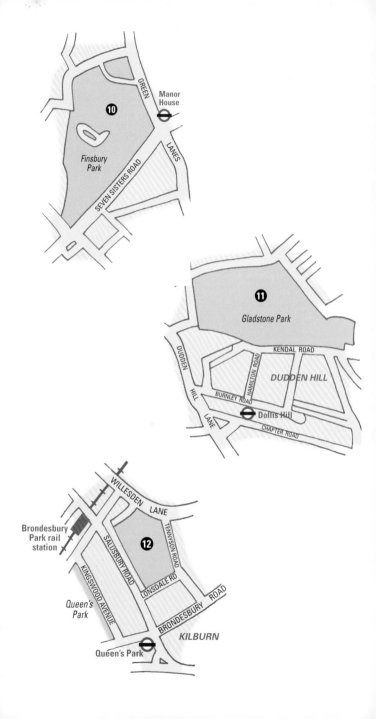

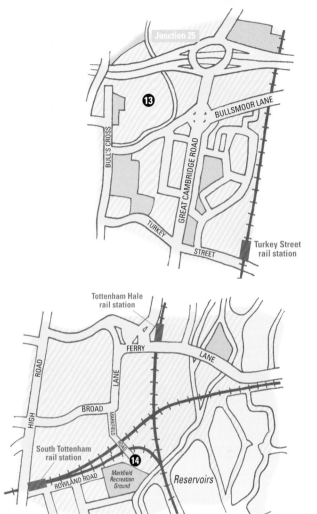

N.B. See previous page for overview map

Address: **Stanmore, HA7 (☏ 020-8954 2918 for nature reserve, ⌨ www.bentleypriory.org and www.harrowncf.org/bp_home.html).**

Opening hours: **Reserve – unrestricted access.**

Cost: **Free.**

Transport: **Stanmore tube station, but best reached by car.**

BENTLEY PRIORY & NATURE RESERVE

*B*entley Priory (Grade II* listed) is an 18th-century building which gets its name from an Augustinian priory of Canons dating from the Middle Ages, which was believed to have been founded in 1170 by Ranulf de Glanville. In 1546, after the Dissolution, Henry VIII gave the priory to private owners. In 1766, the estate was sold to James Duberly, who demolished the original Priory and built the current Bentley Priory in 1776 to a design by Sir John Soane (1753-1837). It was significantly extended in 1788 by Soane for John Hamilton, 1st Marquess of Abercorn. The Priory was the final home of the Dowager Queen Adelaide, queen consort of William IV, who died here in 1849.

Between 1882 and 1922 the Priory was used as a hotel and girl's school until 1926, when the estate was divided, with one parcel (comprising the Priory buildings and around 40 acres/16.2ha of land) being sold to the Air Ministry and becoming RAF Bentley Priory, which it remained until 2008. RAF Bentley Priory is famous as the headquarters of Fighter Command from July 1936 until April 1968. It was here during WWII that the Battle of Britain was masterminded by Lord Dowding – the Officers' Mess (Dowding's office) still remains and contains Dowding's office, along with its original furniture and furnishings.

The land south of the house is now the Bentley Priory Nature Reserve, a Site of Special Scientific Interest maintained by Harrow Heritage Trust. It's a 163-acre (66ha) mosaic of ancient woodland, unimproved natural grassland, scrub, wetland, streams and an artificial lake – an unusual combination of habitats in Greater London. The Bentley Priory area contains a number of woods, including Heriot Wood, where the dominant tree is hornbeam, a species characteristic of ancient woodlands, while to the west of Summerhouse Lake stands the 'Master', a mighty oak at least 500 years old.

> **The Bentley Priory site is being redeveloped for private housing, but the Officers' Mess will become the Battle of Britain museum in 2013, along with the Victorian Italianate gardens.**

The reserve is noted for its abundance of coarse grasses, which includes traditional grassland that has never been treated with fertilisers, and hence is rich in wild flowers. There's a wealth of wildlife, particularly birds, which include buzzards, spotted flycatcher and bullfinch, while in summer whitethroat, garden warblers, blackcaps, chiffchaffs and willow warblers can be heard.

A lovely day out for all the family.

❝ *A magical spot with an illustrious place in history* **❞**

Address: Donnefield Avenue, Harrow, HA8 6QT (☎ 020-8424 1754, 🖥 www.friendsofcanonspark.org.uk and www.harrow.gov.uk/info/200073/parks_and_open_spaces).

Opening hours: Daily, 8am to dusk.

Cost: Free.

Transport: Canons Park tube station.

CANONS PARK

*C*anons Park (Grade II listed) is a delightful 44.5-acre (18ha) slice of 18th-century parkland between Stanmore and Edgware, containing several listed buildings. The land which became Canons Park belonged, until the Dissolution of the Monasteries, to the Priory of St Bartholomew the Great ('Canons' refers to the canons or monks). In 1709, the Cannons estate (later changed to Canons) was acquired through marriage by James Brydges (1673-1744), first Duke of Chandos, who built a palace in 1713-25 designed by James Gibbs. Brydges hired some of the best builders, landscape gardeners and craftsmen of the day to create the splendid grounds, which contained fountains, canals, pools, lakes, avenues, formal gardens and a kitchen garden. Today you can still see the avenue that led from the palace to the church (St Lawrence's – see below) in the form of a raised causeway along which the duke and his family would proceed to church on Sunday. The basin, on what is now Canons Drive, was one of the duke's pools.

James Brydges lost part of his vast fortune in the South Sea Bubble and the second Duke was unable to maintain the house and abandoned it. It fell into ruin and was rebuilt on a smaller scale in around 1754 by William Hallett, a prominent cabinet maker, much of which still exists as part of the North London Collegiate School which now occupies the site.

The undeveloped part of the estate was acquired by Harrow Council in 1936 and became the current public park, combining 18th-, 19th- and 20th-century landscape designs. The crowning glory is the walled King George V Memorial Garden – part of the duke's original kitchen gardens – which was re-designed in the 1930s after the park became public. It reflects the 1930s period, with a structure of evergreens highlighted by seasonal displays, featuring a central square pool surrounded by a raised terrace with steps, formal flower beds and a pavilion.

Following a Heritage Lottery Fund grant of almost £1m, the gardens and buildings were comprehensively restored in recent years (completed in 2008), including new entrance gates, re-laid paving, replanted flower-beds and stylish topiary.

Today Canons Park – awarded a Green Flag in 2010 and 2011 – is a delightful haven for both people and wildlife (the 'Friends of Canons Park' organise regular bird watching walks), with a children's playground and café in summer.

Why not combine a visit with nearby St Lawrence Whitchurch (see below)?

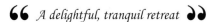

66 *A delightful, tranquil retreat* **99**

Address: Whitchurch Lane, Edgware, HA8 6QS (☎ 020-8952 0019, 🖥 www.little-stanmore.org – Internet Explorer only).

Opening hours: Guided tours, Sundays, 2-5pm in summer and 2-4pm in winter. Also tours by special arrangement. See website for service times.

Cost: Free (but donations are welcome).

Transport: Canons Park tube station.

ST LAWRENCE WHITCHURCH

*S*t Lawrence Whitchurch – also know as St Lawrence, Little Stanmore – is a splendid Grade 1 listed church. St Lawrence was a deacon in Rome who was martyred in 258AD. Before being executed he was purportedly commanded to bring the riches of the church with him; Lawrence had already given away the church's wealth, so arrived with a crowd of the poor, blind, sick and crippled, who to him were the church's true riches.

With the exception of the 14th-century tower, the church was completely rebuilt in a unique Continental Baroque style in 1714-16 for James Brydges, 1st Duke of Chandos. The walls and ceiling of the dramatic interior are covered with paintings; the panels on the ceiling are attributed to Louis Laguerre and show miracles from St John's Gospel, while the ceiling above the altar depicts the *Adoration of Jehovah*. Behind the altar is an imitation sky, lit by a concealed window which is characteristic of the Baroque *trompe l'oeil* (trick of the eye) style of continental Europe. The paintings of the *Nativity* and the *Descent from the Cross*, on either side of the altar, and the *Transfiguration* above the Duke's Pew, are attributed to Antonio Bellucci. Most of the interior woodwork is original and attributed to master woodcarver Grinling Gibbons, including the organ case, carved with cherubs, pea pods and other typical Gibbons' decorations.

The famous composer George Frideric Handel (1685-1759) was employed by Brydges in 1717-18 as his composer-in-residence. At the time, Brydges had yet to be elevated to the dukedom, but he commissioned 11 anthems from Handel, known as the 'Chandos Anthems'; they were almost certainly performed at the church with Handel directing the singers and a small orchestra employed by his patron. A new organ was made for St Lawrence in 1994, based on the surviving parts of the 1716 Gerard Smith organ used by Handel.

> **St Lawrence was martyred on a griddle and is reputed to have told his executioners to turn him over, as he was 'done on that side'. It perhaps isn't surprising that he's known as the patron saint of cooks and restaurateurs!**

On the north side of the church is the Chandos Mausoleum, built to the order of the first Duke of Chandos. The centrepiece by Grinling Gibbons (1648-1721) is a Baroque monument to the duke and his first two wives.

Why not combine a visit with nearby Canons Park (see above)?

66 *Where Handel played the organ* **99**

AT A GLANCE

Address: **Headstone Manor, Pinner View, HA2 6PX (☎ 020-8861 2626, 🖥 www.harrow.gov.uk > harrow_museum_buildings).**

Opening hours: **April to October, Mon and Wed-Fri, noon to 5pm; weekends and Bank Holidays, 10.30am to 5pm. November to March, Mon and Wed-Fri, noon to 4pm; weekends and Bank Holidays, 10.30am to 4pm. Closed on Tuesdays. Tours of the manor house at 3pm (1 hr) during summer weekends only. Private tours (min. 6 people) can also be arranged.**

Cost: **Free. Tours of Headstone Manor £3 (children free).**

Transport: **North Harrow tube station.**

HARROW MUSEUM BUILDINGS

*H*arrow Museum Buildings – comprising four remarkable buildings: Headstone Manor, the Tithe Barn, the Small Barn and the Granary – make up the absorbing local authority museum of the borough of Harrow. Situated in the beautiful manor grounds, the museum has been described as 'one of the most interesting domestic complexes in the whole country', containing examples of master craftsmen's workmanship dating from the 14th, 17th and 18th centuries.

The land on which Headstone Manor stands is recorded as having been owned in 825AD by Wulfred, Archbishop of Canterbury. The moated Headstone Manor (Grade I listed) was built around 1310 and is the earliest-surviving timber-framed building in the area. The moat is the only surviving filled moat in north London and was constructed as a status symbol to reflect the wealth of the owner, the Archbishop of Canterbury, John Stratford. The manor remained in the ownership of the Archbishops of Canterbury until 1546, following the Dissolution, when it was surrendered to Henry VIII. Soon after, Henry sold it to one of his court favourites and it remained in private ownership for almost four centuries.

The numerous owners of Headstone Manor made dramatic extensions and changes to the building, such as adding extra wings and changing the appearance of the interior and exterior of the building. Examples include the panelling of the great hall in 1631, and the addition of a fashionable brick façade in the 1770s, which gives Headstone Manor the appearance it has today.

Headstone Manor was a working farm, and consequently was surrounded by farm buildings, although by the early 20th century most had fallen into a state of disrepair and were demolished. Today, only two survive, including the impressive Tithe Barn (Grade II* listed). Built in 1506, the barn has a framework made entirely from English Oak, measuring an impressive 141ft (43m) long and 29.5ft (9m) high. The foundations of the Small Barn (Grade II listed) date from the 14th century, but it appears to have been built in the same period as the 16th-century Tithe Barn. The Small Barn stands opposite the giant Tithe Barn and was originally two buildings standing end to end.

> The collection at Harrow Museum is comprised of objects and artefacts with strong links to the Harrow area. The museum also hosts a number of temporary exhibitions and has a café and shop.

A fun day out for all the family.

 Majestic buildings housing an interesting collection

Address: 17 East End Road, Finchley, N3 3QE (☎ 020-8346 7812, 🖥 www.avenuehouse.org.uk and http://friendsofavenuehouse.org).

Opening hours: House – see public events on the website; Gardens – around 7.30am to dusk; Stephens Collection – Tue-Thu, 2-4.30pm; Café – daily, 10am to 5pm.

Cost: Free.

Transport: Finchley Central tube station.

AVENUE HOUSE & ARBORETUM

*A*venue House (Grade II listed) is an imposing Victorian (allegedly haunted) mansion in Finchley set in 10 acres (4ha) of beautiful grounds. Originally owned by the Bishop of London, the land on which Avenue House stands used to be known as Temple Croft Fields, after the Knights Templars who were granted it in 1243. From 1312 it belonged to the Knights Hospitallers until their estates were seized by Henry VIII in 1540. It then passed through various hands until being purchased by Thomas Allen in 1732. The first house on the site was built by the Rev. Edward Cooper in 1859, a relative of the Allen family, which later became known as Avenue House.

The estate was purchased in 1874 by Henry Charles (Inky) Stephens, son of the inventor of the famous blue-black ink. He engaged Robert Marnock (1800-1889), reportedly the best landscape gardener of his time, to design the gardens. Stephens died in 1918 and bequeathed Avenue House to the people of Finchley. A small display and archive of material relating to the Stephens Ink company and the Stephens' family, called the Stephens Collection (see 🖥 www.london-northwest.com/sites/stephens), is on display at the House.

The grounds became a public park on 3rd May 1928, almost ten years after Stephens' death. The estate contains an arboretum, with rare and unusual trees from as far afield as China and California, including a Pocket Handkerchief Tree, Redwood, Gingko and the memorably-named Wing-Nut Tree, as well as many varieties of native trees. One of the main features of the grounds is The Bothy, built as a large walled garden in the shape of a castle sometime in the late 1870s. It's one of the earliest non-Roman concrete structures in England, though in a state of disrepair; the Avenue House Estate Trust hopes to conclude an agreement with a tenant who will restore it. There's also a children's playground and a café. The Bothy garden, once the vegetable garden for Avenue House, is now a hidden oasis with a lawned area and a wild garden.

> In 1989 the house was ravaged by fire and refurbished By Barnet Council. It's now held in trust for the people of Finchley and run by the Avenue House Estate Trust as a venue for private, community and business functions, meetings and classes.

A beautiful park and mansion with an interesting history – and a wonderful local resource.

 An imposing mansion and spectacular arboretum

AT A GLANCE

Address: **East End Road, N2 0RZ** (☎ **020-8567 0913**, 🖥 **www. westminster.gov.uk/services/communityandliving/burials/eastfinchley**).

Opening hours: **Winter (Nov-Feb) – Mon-Fri, 8.30am to 4.30pm, weekends and Public Holidays, 11am to 4pm. Spring to autumn – Mon-Fri, 8.30am to 6pm, weekends and Public Holidays, 11am to 6pm.**

Cost: **Free.**

Transport: **East Finchley tube station.**

EAST FINCHLEY CEMETERY

*E*ast Finchley Cemetery is a relatively unknown Victorian (1855) cemetery and crematorium (opened in 1937), and one of London's most beautiful – named Cemetery of the Year in 2007. It ought to be on the list of 'must-visit cemeteries' in London but is often over-looked in favour of the magnificent seven (Abney Park, Brompton, Highgate, Kensal Green, Nunhead, Tower Hamlets and West Norwood). Created to serve the affluent suburbs of Marylebone, Highgate and Hampstead, it contains many spectacular memorials.

Originally called St Marylebone Cemetery, East Finchley was previously managed by St Marylebone Borough Council but became the responsibility of the City of Westminster following a local government reorganisation in 1965. The name formally changed to East Finchley when Westminster City Council re-acquired it in the early '90s. The cemetery contains over 22,000 private grave spaces and is still used for burials today.

East Finchley Cemetery contains a number of splendid bronzes, including that of Australian engineer Sir Peter Nicol Russell's (1816-1905) tomb near the entrance, which depicts a young engineer being lifted to heaven by an angel, with a bust of Sir Peter on a pillar above them. It was designed by Sir Edgar MacKennal, who also designed the effigies of Edward VII and Queen Alexandra in St George's Chapel (Windsor Castle). Two more notable bronzes – facing each other towards the northwest of the main chapel – adorn the graves of Thomas Tate (a reclining youth pointing to heaven), and Harry Ripley (a mourning woman). The 'chapel' (Grade II listed) at the centre of the cemetery, is in fact a mausoleum for Lord Borthwick, owner of *The Morning Post*.

Although a number of grave markers and monuments are broken and decayed, and some have been vandalised (or precious metals stolen), East Finchley Cemetery has generally been superbly maintained, attested to by the annual award of a Green Flag annually from 2007-2011. It's also a local nature reserve and contains a number of specimen trees, including two splendid Cedar of Lebanon trees planted on the front lawn in 1856.

> **Notable burials include conductor Leopold Stokowski, Sir Robert Harmsworth (newspaper publisher with a memorial by Edwin Lutyens), Lord Northcliffe (founder of the *Daily Mail*), Melanie Appleby (of pop duo Mel and Kim), scientist Thomas Henry Huxley, and artist and cartoonist Heath Robinson. There are also many soldiers' war graves from both WWI and WWII.**

❝ *A fitting place to be laid to rest* **❞**

Address: Hampstead Garden Suburb, NW11 7AH (☏ 020-8455 1025, 🖳 www.stjudeonthehill.com).

Opening hours: Sundays, noon to 5.30pm from 25th March to 21st October. Group visits can be arranged at other times. See website for service times.

Cost: Free (but donations are welcome).

Transport: Golders Green tube station (15 minutes walk or take the H2 bus).

ST JUDE-ON-THE-HILL

*S*t Jude-on-the-Hill (St Jude's) is the gorgeous parish church of Hampstead Garden Suburb. The community was founded in 1907 by Henrietta Barnett (1851-1936) as a model 'village' where all classes of people (provided they were wealthy!) could live together in attractive surroundings and social harmony.

The church was designed by Edwin Landseer Lutyens (1869-1944), the leading architect of the early 20th century, in what Simon Jenkins described as 'the confident application of Queen Anne Revival to traditional church form'. Building began in 1909 and the church was consecrated in May 1911, though the west end wasn't completed until 1935. Externally it's 200ft (61m) long, while the spire rises to 178ft (54.3m). The ceiling is barrel-vaulted and domed and there are three vaults between the west end and the crossing, a saucer dome over the crossing plus a further vault, and a saucer dome over the sanctuary.

The splendid murals and paintings are by Walter Starmer (1877-1961), who began with the Lady Chapel in 1920, finishing with the apse in 1929, The west window (dedicated 1937) is also to the design of Starmer and depicts St Jude holding the cross in his right hand and St Jude's church

> The church hosts the annual Proms at St Jude's music festival in June-July, a nine-day midsummer music and culture festival (see 🖳 www.promsatstjudes.org.uk).

in his left. Below is his symbol, the ship, while above is Christ in glory surrounded by the traditional symbols of the four evangelists. The ceiling panels over the centre aisle depict the wise men and the shepherds, Christ feeding the multitude and stilling the storm, Christ healing the blind and lepers, the crucifixion (dome) and the entry into Jerusalem with Christ carrying the cross (chancel). The fine iron screens that flank the sanctuary are much older than the church and bear the name Matthias Heit and the date 1710.

St Jude's contains a wealth of fine memorials, including (on the north side of the west door) one to the millions of horses killed in WWI made in 1970 by Rosemary Proctor (died 1995); it replaced the original bronze model of a horse by Lutyens' father, and its replacement, both of which were stolen.

The superb Father Willis organ came from St Jude's church in Whitechapel, where Canon Samuel Barnett, husband of Henrietta Barnett (founder of Hampstead Garden Suburb) was vicar.

A glorious church and Lutyens' pièce de résistance.

❝ *Lutyens' ecclesiastical masterpiece* **❞**

Address: **Muswell Hill Road, N10 3JN (☎ 020-8444 6129,** 💻 **www.cityoflondon.gov.uk, www.haringey.gov.uk > Parks and Open Spaces and www.fqw.org.uk).**

Opening hours: **Highgate Wood – daily, 7.30am to sunset, which can be as early as 4.30pm in winter and as late as 9.45pm in summer. Queen's Wood – unrestricted access.**

Cost: **Free.**

Transport: **Highgate tube station.**

HIGHGATE & QUEEN'S WOODS

*H*ighgate Wood and Queen's Wood (separated by Muswell Hill Road) are two stunning preserved segments of the ancient Forest of Middlesex, which covered much of London and was mentioned in the *Domesday Book*. Both woods are a wildlife oasis and Local Nature Reserve, designated a Site of Metropolitan Importance for Nature Conservation.

Highgate Wood – owned and managed by the City of London Corporation – covers an area of 70 acres (28ha) rich in oak, holly and hornbeam trees, plus the rare wild service tree, the presence of which commonly indicates an ancient woodland. The wood is home to over 50 other tree and shrub species and is rich in wildlife, including five species of bat, foxes, grey squirrels, over 70 bird species and more than 250 species of moths.

Excavations show that Romano-Britons were producing pottery from local materials here between AD 50-100, and there are ancient earthworks that may have formed part of an enclosure for deer during the medieval period, when the Bishop of London owned the wood. Between the 16th and 18th centuries the wood, then known as 'Brewer's Fell', was leased to various tenants who managed (coppiced) the wood and produced timber (particularly oak) for the Crown to construct ships and for church buildings. In 1886, the City of London Corporation acquired the wood, then known as Gravelpit Wood, for public use and renamed it Highgate Wood.

> In addition to football and cricket pitches, Highgate Wood also has a children's playground, a café and an information centre, while Queen's Wood has a café and an organic community garden.

Queen's Wood is owned and managed by the borough of Haringey. It covers an area of 51 acres (21ha) and was known as Churchyard Bottom Wood (possibly due to the discovery of human bones, thought to be a burial pit for victims of the bubonic plague in 1665) until being purchased by Hornsey Council in 1898, when it was renamed Queen's Wood in honour of Queen Victoria. Like Highgate Wood, it's ancient woodland, featuring English oak and the occasional beech, which provide a canopy above cherry, field maple, hazel, holly, hornbeam, midland hawthorn, mountain ash, lowland birch and the rare wild service tree. Queen's Wood reportedly has a greater diversity of flora and fauna than Highgate Wood, as it's wilder and has greater structural diversity and a denser shrub layer.

Visit Highgate and Queen's Woods and prepare to be enchanted.

 A captivating glimpse of London's ancient forests

Address: Highgate Village, N6 4BD (☎ **020-8340 8054, 020-8340 3488 (box office),** 🖥 **www.upstairsatthegatehouse.com**)

Opening hours: **Mon-Thu and Sun, 9am to 11pm, Fri-Sat, 9am to midnight.**

Cost: **Free (except for a drink).**

Transport: **Highgate tube station.**

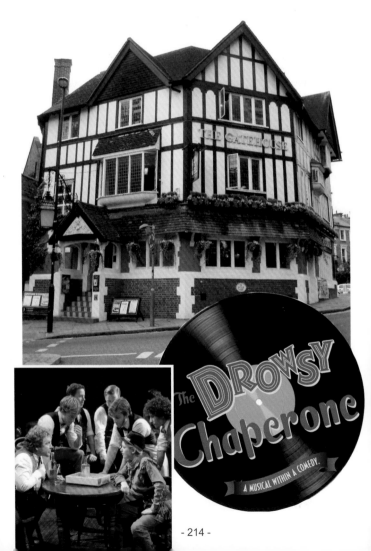

THE GATEHOUSE

*T*he Gatehouse is a rare combination of a (historic) pub and an award-winning fringe theatre, producing a varied programme of drama, musicals and fringe theatre productions. The (Wetherspoon's) Gatehouse is reportedly the oldest pub in Highgate – it's thought to have been the site of an inn as far back as the 14th century – although the mock Tudor façade only dates back to 1905. The earliest mention of The Gatehouse in licensing records is in 1670, when an Edward Culter was the landlord.

A curious fact about The Gatehouse is that the borough boundary between Middlesex and London ran directly through the building; when the hall was used as a courtroom, a rope divided the sessions to make sure prisoners didn't escape to the neighbouring authority's area! This problem continued as the authorities changed, most recently with Camden and Haringey sharing the building, until, in 1993, the border was moved a few feet to allow one licensing authority overall control.

From its days next to the toll gate, through its use as a meeting house and courtroom, The Gatehouse has had a chequered history. Lord Byron, George Cruikshank, Dick Turpin and Charles Dickens were reportedly regulars, and the Highgate Literary and Scientific Institution's inaugural meeting took place in the pub on 16th January 1839. At the turn of the century, The Gatehouse was famous throughout London for its 'shilling ordinaries' – gigantic lunches which filled many a Victorian stomach.

The auditorium that now houses the theatre opened in 1895 as 'a place suitable for balls, Cinderellas and concerts', and its various uses have included a Victorian Music Hall, a cinema, a Masonic Lodge and a venue for amateur dramatics. In the '60s, a jazz and folk club famously featured Paul Simon (of Simon and Garfunkel fame).

The Upstairs at the Gatehouse Theatre was established in 1985 and is managed by Ovation Theatres. It has a knack of finding future smashes, such as recent musicals based upon Take That (*Never Forget*) and *Big Brother the Musical* – perfect fringe theatre but with mainstream appeal. The Gatehouse stages the Camden Fringe in July-August.

The pub serves a great selection of ales and typical (i.e. mediocre) pub grub, but it's the pub's charm, beer garden and the theatre that makes this pub so special.

> The pub is allegedly haunted by the ghost of Mother Marnes, a murdered widow.

 A charming pub and fringe theatre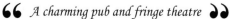

AT A GLANCE

Address: **Endymion Road, Seven Sisters Road and Green Lanes, N4** (☎ **020-8489 0000,** 🖥 **www.haringey.gov.uk > greenspaces and www. finsburyparkpeople.co.uk**).

Opening hours: **Daily, dawn to dusk.**

Cost: **Free.**

Transport: **Manor House tube station.**

FINSBURY PARK

*F*insbury Park (Grade II listed) is a beautiful 115-acre (46ha) public park in the borough of Haringey – one of the first great Victorian parks. Officially opened in 1869, Finsbury Park was one of many 'People's Parks' created to provide Londoners with open spaces as an antidote to the city's ever-increasing urbanisation. Today it's one of London's most diverse parks with a rich tapestry of landscapes, serving a wide range of communities.

Throughout the late 19th and early 20th centuries, the park was a respectable and beautifully manicured space for people to relax and exercise; in the early 20th century it also became a venue for political meetings, including pacifist campaigning during WWI. The park deteriorated after WWII, though still much loved and used by the local community; it was restored to its former glory after a £5m Heritage Lottery Fund award in 2003. Restoration included re-landscaping the American Gardens and Alexander McKenzie's historical flower gardens, cleaning the lake, a new café and children's playground, creating a new skate park and repairing the tennis courts. The park has a mix of open ground, formal gardens, avenues of mature trees and an arboretum area containing rare trees. It was awarded the prestigious Green Flag in 2007 and has retained it ever since.

> **The Parkland Walk (** ⌨ **www.parkland-walk.org.uk) starts in Finsbury Park – a lovely 4.5mi (7.2km) linear green pathway following the route of the old rail line from Finsbury Park to Alexandra Palace.**

Finsbury Park has long been an established music venue, attracting many famous artists and bands, including Jimi Hendrix (1967), Ian Dury and The Blockheads, Morrissey and Madness (1992) and Bob Dylan (1993, 2011). The park hosted the annual Fleadh Festival from 1990 to 2004; originally the acts were meant to be Irish or Irish-related but the festival featured artists as diverse as Sting and the Sex Pistols. Other concerts and large public events have included the Big Gay Out, Party in the Park and Rise: London United.

The park offers a wealth of sports facilities including soccer pitches, a bowling green, an athletics track, an outdoor gym, and tennis and basketball courts. Unusually for London, the park also provides venues for American sports: an American football field, Much more than just a concert venuebaseball 'diamonds' (it's home to the London Mets, also UK national champions).

A welcome retreat from north London's urban landscape.

 Much more than just a concert venue

Address: **Dollis Hill Lane, NW2** (☏ **020-8937 5619**, 🖳 **www.brent.gov.uk/
pks.nsf/parks/lbb-39 and www.gladstonepark.org.uk**).

Opening hours: **Unrestricted access; walled garden dawn to dusk.**

Cost: **Free.**

Transport: **Dollis Hill tube station.**

GLADSTONE PARK

*G*ladstone Park, a beautiful 97-acre (39ha) oasis in Dollis Hill, administered by the borough of Brent. The park provides a diverse environment comprising a formal garden, duck pond, varied terrain, woodland, hedgerows and open ground, which constantly change with the seasons. On clear days it offers a panoramic vista of London from the top of the hill, 213ft (65m) above sea level, including a fine view of Wembley Stadium.

The core of Gladstone Park was formed from the parkland of Dollis Hill House, once an extensive estate. Unfortunately the historic house was allowed to deteriorate (not helped by two arson attacks) until it could no longer be economically preserved, and was demolished in 2011. Owned by the Earl of Aberdeen in the late 19th century, the Liberal leader and Prime Minister William Gladstone was often a guest here, as was the great American writer Mark Twain. Initially the park was to be called Dollis Hill Park, but its associations with Gladstone were so strong that it was decided to name the park after him.

In 1898, the house and land south of Dollis Hill Lane were acquired by Willesden Rural District Council for £50,000 and opened by the Earl of Aberdeen in 1901. Many of its features date from that time, such as the fine tree-lined avenues, and retained landscaping where the house stood, including the lake and walled garden. Additional attributes included a swimming pool, opened in 1903 (now a bowling green), flower beds and a formal terraced garden. There's a Holocaust Memorial (Paula Kotis, 1968) in the northwest of the park.

Gladstone Park offers a range of sports facilities, including ten tennis courts, football pitches, a rugby pitch, a cricket pitch, netball courts and a bowling green. Other facilities and attractions within the park include two children's playgrounds, an obstacle course, a zip slide, tree carvings, a duck pond, a terraced garden, a wildlife area and allotments. There's also a café (Karmarama, open Fri-Sun, 11am to 5pm) and, in the northeast corner, Stables Gallery and Arts Centre (🖳 www.brentarts.org.uk), Brent's contemporary art gallery.

A lovely park offering something for everyone.

> **The tranquil walled garden is a former winner of the 2005 'London in Bloom' competition, plus a number of Green Flag awards, where you can relax and enjoy the fine lawns, flowerbeds, shrubs and trees that give the gardens a unique atmosphere.**

 One of north London's most attractive parks

Address: **Willesden Lane, Kilburn, NW6 7SD** (☎ **020-8902 2385,** 🖥 **www.brent.gov.uk/cemetery.nsf/cemeteries/lbb-7**).

Opening hours: **Daily, 9am to between 4 and 8pm (closes at 4pm from November-February, 5pm October, 6pm March, 7pm April-September and 8pm May-August), including Bank Holidays.**

Cost: **Free.**

Transport: **Brondesbury Park or Queen's Park tube station.**

PADDINGTON OLD CEMETERY

*P*addington Old Cemetery is a lovely small Victorian cemetery – covering an area of 25 acres (10ha) – with a pair of stunning chapels (one still in use). Opened in 1855, primarily (as the name suggests) to bury the dead of Paddington, despite being situated in Kilburn; it was named for the Paddington Burial Board who opened it and Brent Council retained the name.

The Old Cemetery was one of the first to be opened by the Burial Board, established following the 1852 Metropolitan Interment Act to address the acute problem of over-flowing urban churchyards. Designed by Thomas Little (1802-1859) – who was also responsible for Nunhead Cemetery – the original path layout in the shape of a horse-shoe still remains. Specimen trees were planted along the paths, many of which remain, including oak, lime, horse chestnut, yew, field maple, London plane and Scots pine, plus at least one oak tree that dates from before the cemetery was laid out. Today there are over 500 mature trees, which are an oasis for wildlife in this heavily built-up area. An apiary is situated within the cemetery – the bees are essential for the cross-pollination of the cemetery's abundant wild flowers – and 'tombstone honey' is a favourite with local people.

Little designed two lodges, now in private use, and a fine pair of chapels (Grade II listed) with port cochère and central belfry in 13th-century Gothic style, constructed from Kentish ragstone and linked by arches. The one to the west was a Church of England chapel, while the other was for non-conformists. The original cemetery is almost full but a new section has been opened in the north, where mounding of public graves and reclamation of space enables its continued use. In the eastern corner is an area known as 'God's Acre', with a stone cross commemorating those buried here. This is now overgrown and part of the nature area comprising woodland with mature trees.

> **The cemetery was featured in the Doctor Who story, *The Remembrance of the Daleks*.**

A war memorial lies close to the western entrance, within a small rectangular area next to formal rose beds, and there are also formal rose gardens near the eastern lodge. The cemetery is enclosed within brick perimeter walls and has imposing iron gates with piers topped by draped urns.

Paddington Old Cemetery is a welcome refuge from the stresses of modern life.

66 *A poignant reminder of our mortality*

Address: Bullsmoor Lane, Enfield, EN1 4RQ (☎ 08456-122 122,
🖥 www.capelmanorgardens.co.uk).

Opening hours: November to February, Mon-Fri, 10am to 5pm; March to October, daily, 10am to 5.30pm. Closed 25th December to 1st January.

Cost: Adults £5.50, concessions £4.50, children £2.50 (5 and under free), family £13.50 (2 adults and up to 3 children). For special musical and theatrical events, see website.

Transport: Turkey Street rail station (20 minutes walk) or by car.

CAPEL MANOR GARDENS

*C*apel Manor Gardens is a stunning 30-acre (12.1ha) estate surrounding a Georgian manor house and Victorian stables. The Gardens feature a variety of richly-planted themed gardens, including historical gardens, an Italianate maze, a Japanese garden, Kim Wilde's Jungle Gym Garden and many others. They also contains the Gardening Which? Magazine demonstration and trial gardens and the National Gardening Centre, which includes specially designed gardens such as Sunflower Street – seven front and back gardens designed by former students. The latest addition is the gold-medal-winning Australian Garden from the 2011 RHS Chelsea Flower Show.

The history of Capel Manor dates back to 1275 when the land, then known as 'Honeylands and Pentriches', was held by Ellis of Honeyland. There's evidence of a manor house at this time but the one you see today was built in the 1750s. In 1486, Sir William Capel became the owner of the house here, which remained in his family (later Lords of Essex) until the 16th century, when Sir Giles, Sir Henry and Edward Capel surrendered it to the crown.

The estate then passed through a succession of owners until, in 1932, Lt Col Sydney Medcalf occupied it and remained here until his death in 1958. The last private owner of Capel, Colonel Medcalf had a passion for horticulture but is best remembered for his association with the breeding of Clydesdale horses, having established a stud farm at Capel House. Capel Manor became a National Centre for Clydesdale horse breeding and the Medcalf cup is still awarded today. Colonel Medcalf left the house to the Incorporated Society of Accountants and in 1965 the contents were sold at auction.

Today, Capel Manor is a college of horticulture and London's only specialist centre for land-based studies. Capel Manor College is a working estate where students and staff gain 'hands-on' experience in all aspects of land-based studies, including horticulture, arboriculture (tree surgery), garden design, floristry, animal care, saddlery and environmental conservation.

The Animal Corner has Kune Kune pigs, goats, poultry, rabbits, pygmy goats and guinea pigs, while Clydesdale horses can be seen working and exercising in the grounds. There's also a varied programme of shows and events throughout the year, while the Hessayon (visitors) Centre contains a garden gift shop with plant sales in summer.

> **Enjoy the stunning scenery, picnic by the lake or have lunch in the Terrace restaurant – a perfect day out for budding horticulturalists.**

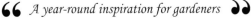 *A year-round inspiration for gardeners*

Address: **Markfield Road, Tottenham, N15 4RB** (☎ **01707-873628,** 🖥 **www.haringey.gov.uk > Parks and Open Spaces and www. markfieldpark.org.uk).**

Opening hours: **Park – unrestricted access; Beam Engine Museum – October to March, second Sunday of the month, 11am to 4pm; April to September, second and fourth Sunday of each month, 11am to 5pm. See website for steaming dates** (🖥 **www.mbeam.org).**

Cost: **Free.**

Transport: **Tottenham Hale tube and rail station and South Tottenham rail.**

MARKFIELD PARK & BEAM ENGINE MUSEUM

*M*arkfield Park is a lovely 18.8-acre (7.6ha) park located within the Lee Valley Regional Park in the borough of Haringey, which was officially opened as Markfield Recreation Ground King George's Field in 1938. It's situated on a flood plain with two major watercourses flowing through it; the culverted Stonebridge Brook and the open channel of the Old Moselle Brook, which discharge into the River Lee forming the park's eastern boundary.

There are various different areas and facilities within the park, including soccer pitches, open grass and picnic areas, a children's playground, rose and community gardens, a lawn bowls club, BMX area and even graffiti walls. There's also a café with free wi-fi in the museum.

The park is most famous for the Markfield Beam Engine and Museum, a 'Site of Industrial Heritage Interest'. The Tottenham and Wood Green sewage treatment works and pumping station was opened here in 1864, while the Markfield Beam Engine was built between 1886 and 1888 and commissioned on 12th July 1888. It's a 100 horsepower beam pumping engine housed in a Victorian engine house (both Grade II listed), which saw continuous service from 1889 until late 1905, when it was relegated to standby duty for storm water pumping. The engine ceased operation in 1964 but was recently restored to full working order and can be seen operating under steam power on 'steaming' days.

The beam engine is a free-standing engine of the compound rotative type with two cylinders, arranged to be double-acting and compounded. It's believed to be the last engine produced by Wood Bros. of Sowerby Bridge, Yorkshire, and is the only surviving eight-column engine in its original location. The engine's beam drives two pumps of the single-acting plunger type, each of 26" diameter with a 51" stroke. At a working speed of 16rpm, the pumps could handle 4m gallons in 24 hours over a relatively low head. The engine's flywheel is 27ft in diameter and weighs around 17 tons.

In recent years, £3.8m has been spent on restoration, including renovating and restoring the beam engine and heritage building works to the Markfield Museum, a new café and toilets, an improved sports pavilion, a new playground and general landscape improvements throughout the park. The park improvements were recognised In 2010 and 2011 with the award of a Green Flag.

 A park for nature lovers and engineering fans

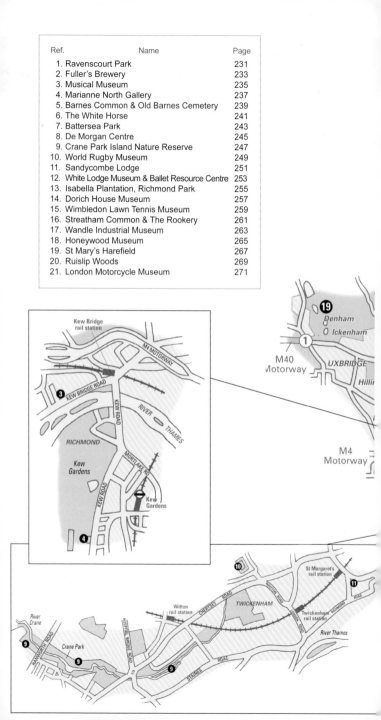

CHAPTER 7

WEST & SOUTHWEST LONDON

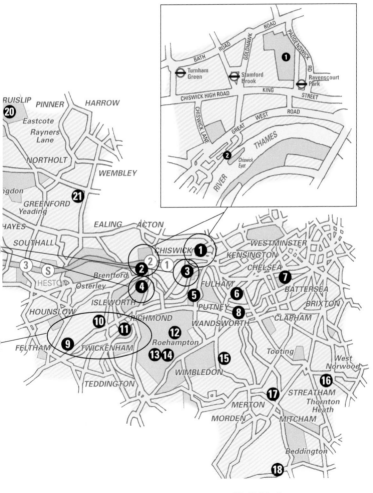

N.B. See next page for more maps and individual pages for detailed maps for nos 5 to 8.

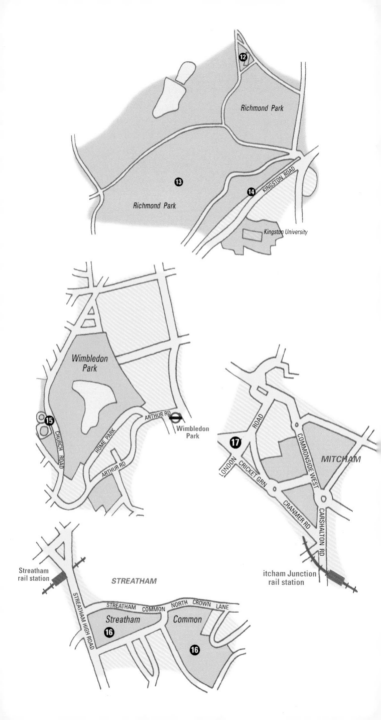

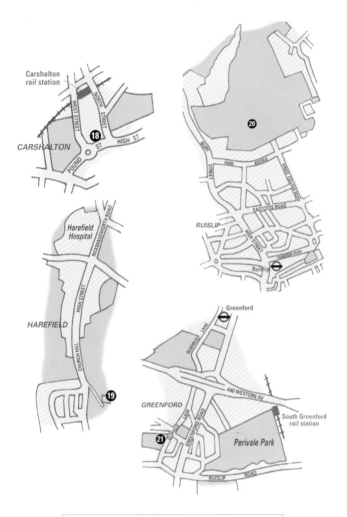

N.B. See previous page for overview map

Address: **Ravenscourt Park, W6** (🖥 **www.lbhf.gov.uk** and **http://s295963082.websitehome.co.uk/forp**).

Opening hours: **Daily, 7.30am to sunset, e.g. 10pm (summer) and 4.30pm (winter).**

Cost: **Free.**

Transport: **Ravenscourt Park tube station.**

RAVENSCOURT PARK

*R*avenscourt Park is a beautiful 32-acre (13ha) public park and garden established in 1888 and designed by J. J. Sexby on land surrounding Ravenscourt House. The origins of Ravenscourt Park lie in the medieval manor and estate of Palingswick (or Paddenswick) Manor, first recorded in the 12th century. By the 13th century the manor house was a mansion surrounded by a moat fed by Stamford Brook. Edward III's mistress Alice Perrers lived in the manor during the 14th century. The manor house was rebuilt in 1650 and in 1747 was sold to Thomas Corbett who named it Ravenscourt, probably derived from the raven in his coat of arms, which was itself a pun on his name, as *corbeau* is French for *raven*.

In 1812, the house and estate were purchased by their final private owner, George Scott, a builder and philanthropist who developed nearby St Peter's Square. Scott employed leading landscape architect Humphry Repton to design the gardens, and encouraged the building of houses along their edges. In 1887, the Scott family sold the estate to a developer, but it was then purchased by the Metropolitan Board of Works (later the London County Council), which established a public park in 1888, now owned and managed by the borough of Hammersmith and Fulham. Ravenscourt House was demolished after being severely damaged during WWII; only the stable block remain, which is now the park's café.

The park combines attractive landscaping and a range of wildlife habitats, and was awarded a Green Flag in 2011. Its crowning glory is the magical, scented walled garden, secreted in the northeast corner of the park. Originally the kitchen garden of the house, it's laid out in a traditional Victorian symmetrical design with rose beds and rose arches, and exotic herbaceous beds featuring yuccas, giant poppies, irises and gunnera. It's bordered below the wall with shrubs, while scented plants such as lavender and honeysuckle make it a real treat for the nose as well as the eyes. The garden is a wonderful, Zen-like retreat, with benches and bowers.

A park for all seasons and for everyone to enjoy.

> **The park offers a wide range of leisure facilities, including tennis and basketball courts, bowling and putting greens, multiple play areas and a tea-house. Annual events include a spectacular bonfire night, Carter's Steam Fair and an alfresco opera season.**

66 *A lovely park with a secret garden* **99**

Address: The Griffin Brewery, Chiswick Lane South, W4 2QB (tours, ☎ 020-8996 2175, 🖥 www.fullers.co.uk).

Opening hours: Tours (approx. 1½ hrs), Mon-Fri, 11am, noon, 1pm, 2pm and 3pm, except Public Holidays (must be pre-booked). Shop, Mon-Fri, 10am to 8pm, Sat, 10am to 6pm.

Cost: Tours, adults £10, children (16-17) £7. Under 16s not permitted. Vintage ale tour £15 (see website).

Transport: Turnham Green tube station.

FULLER'S BREWERY

*F*uller's historic brewery in Chiswick is one of the few remaining breweries in London, on a site where beer has been brewed since the Civil War, over 350 years ago. The original brewery, situated in the gardens of Bedford House on Chiswick Mall, thrived until the early part of the 19th century, when financial problems forced the owners, Douglas & Henry Thompson and Philip Wood, to seek a partner. John Fuller of Neston Park (Wiltshire) was approached and in 1829 he joined the enterprise. However, the partnership proved difficult and was dissolved, leaving Fuller as the sole owner. It soon became apparent that it was impossible for one man with no brewing experience to run a brewery alone, so in 1845 John Fuller's son, John Bird Fuller, was joined by Henry Smith from the Romford Brewery of Ind & Smith and his brother-in-law, Head Brewer John Turner, thereby forming Fuller Smith & Turner, as it's still known today.

Since then the Griffin Brewery has gone from strength to strength: in 1909 the Beehive Brewery in Brentford was acquired, along with its 34 pubs. In 1929 – a century after the first Fuller had come to Chiswick – a limited company was formed. Today, the descendants of the first partners are still heavily involved in the running of the company. In 2005, Fuller's acquired Gales of Horndean (Hampshire) adding 111 pubs (taking the total to over 360) plus a great range of beers.

Brewery tours begin at the Griffin Brewery tap, The Mawson Arms, and incorporate all parts of the brewing process, from the arrival of the raw materials to the packaging of the beer on the cask racking line. The tour ends with a full tasting session of Fuller's beers, including London Pride. Visitors can also book lunch at The Mawson Arms (☎ 020-994 2936). There's also a shop were you can buy Fuller's beers plus a selection of wines, spirits and champagnes, and a wide range of memorabilia.

> **Over the years Fuller's has established a reputation for running great pubs and brewing outstanding beers, including London Pride, ESB and 1845, all of which have won numerous awards. In fact, three of Fuller's beers – London Pride, ESB and Chiswick Bitter – have been named Champion Beer of Britain, a feat unmatched by any other brewery.**

A fascinating look behind the scenes of a working brewery – and not just for CAMRA members and beer drinkers!

❝ *The ale drinker's dream day out* **❞**

AT A GLANCE

Address: 399 High Street, Brentford, TW8 0DU (☎ 020-8560 8108, 🖥 www.musicalmuseum.co.uk).

Opening hours: Tue-Sun, 11am to 5.30pm, including most Bank Holidays. Closed on Mondays. Guided tours on Tue, 2.30pm, Fri, 11.30am and Sat-Sun, 2.30pm. Group tours by appointment.

Cost: Adults £8, concessions £6.50, children under 16 free when accompanied by an adult.

Transport: Kew Bridge rail station.

MUSICAL MUSEUM

*T*he Musical Museum is unique and contains one of the world's largest collections of automated musical instruments. It was founded in 1963 by the late Frank Holland MBE (1910-89), who was passionate in his belief that self-playing musical instruments should be preserved and not lost to future generations. Holland was a pioneer in this field and firmly believed that collections of musical instruments should be heard as well as seen. His collection eventually consumed all the space in his flat and in 1963 was moved to a redundant church, St George's in Brentford, where it remained until 2008 before moving to the new purpose-built Museum you see today (with a café overlooking the river).

> **The concert hall offers a range of musical entertainment, spanning organ recitals, concerts, cabaret, classical music and light opera, with performers from throughout the UK and overseas (see website for information).**

Today, it's hard to imagine a world without iPods, let alone one with no CDs, Walkmans, ghetto blasters, jukeboxes or stereos, where music can accompany you wherever you go and is accessible at the touch of a button. However, less than 100 years ago most people had never even heard an orchestra, concert pianist or opera singer, and the only way to enjoy recorded music was through an automatic musical machine, such as a wind-up musical box or a self-playing piano.

From the tiny clockwork musical box (first made in the late 18th century) to the self-playing 'Mighty Wurlitzer' concert organ, the collection embraces an impressive and comprehensive array of sophisticated reproducing pianos, pianolas, cranky barrel organs, orchestrions, orchestrelles, residence organs and violin players. The Museum is also home to the world's largest collection (30,000!) of historic musical rolls and an extensive archive of related material. The ground floor galleries display instruments once found in the large houses of the wealthy and in more humble dwellings and cafés, while the street setting reproduces shop windows with displays of musical toys and street instruments, where you can experience the actions and sounds of self-playing instruments.

Upstairs is a concert hall seating 230, complete with a stage and, of course, an orchestra pit from which the Wurlitzer organ console (formerly resident at the Regal Cinema, Kingston) rises to entertain you, just as it did in the cinema in the 1930s.

A unique collection and musical experience for all the family.

66 *A magical musical mystery tour* **99**

Address: **Royal Botanic Gardens, Kew, TW9 3AB** (☎ **020-8332 5655,** 🖥 **www.kew.org/collections/art-images/marianne-north**).

Opening hours: **Daily, 9.30am to between 3.45pm (winter) and 5.30pm (summer); see website for exact times.**

Cost: **Adults £14.50, concessions £12.50, children (under 17) free when accompanied by an adult. Includes admission to most Royal Botanic Gardens' attractions.**

Transport: **Kew Gardens tube station.**

Marianne North

MARIANNE NORTH GALLERY

*T*he beautifully restored and refurbished Marianne North Gallery at Kew Gardens is an experience not to be missed. The Gallery opened in 1882 and is the only permanent solo exhibition by a female artist in Britain.

Marianne North (1830-1890) – naturalist and botanical artist – was a remarkable Victorian woman who travelled the globe to satisfy her passion for recording the world's flora with her paint brush. Although she had no formal training in illustration and was rather unconventional in her methods, North had a natural artistic talent and was very prolific. In 1871, at the age of 40, she began her astonishing series of trips around the world. She was inspired by earlier travels with her father, Frederick North MP, and the exotic plant collections she saw at Kew. Her political connections served her well, providing her with letters of introduction to ambassadors, viceroys, rajahs, governors and ministers throughout the world. In the UK, North also had many supporters, including Edward Lear, Charles Darwin and Sir Joseph Hooker, then Director of Kew.

Between 1871 and 1885, North visited America, Canada, Jamaica, Brazil, Tenerife, Japan, Singapore, Sarawak, Java, Sri Lanka, India, Australia, New Zealand, South Africa, the Seychelles and Chile. Often she would stay away for long periods. In India she visited a number of regions over a period of almost 18 months, while in Brazil she spent 13 months travelling into the interior, making long and arduous journeys across rough terrain during which she completed over 100 paintings. Today her paintings from her travels provide an important historical record.

> In 2008-09, Kew began restoring the Marianne North Gallery, with a £1.8m Heritage Lottery Fund grant and support from donors. The paintings were also restored and conserved.

After exhibiting her paintings in a London gallery in 1879, North had the idea of showing them at Kew. She wrote to Sir Joseph Hooker offering to build a gallery if he would agree to display her life's work in it. The Gallery was designed by James Ferguson, the architectural historian, in a mixture of classical and colonial styles. After a visit to Australia and New Zealand, North spent a year arranging her paintings inside the building, which opened to the public in 1882. The Gallery contains 833 paintings – depicting over 900 plant species – all completed in 13 years of world travel.

An enchanting 'snapshot in time' of the 19th-century natural world.

❝ The lifetime's work of a great naturalist and botanical artist ❞

Address: **Vine Road, SW13 0NE** (💻 **www.richmond.gov.uk > parks and open spaces, http://barnescommon.org.uk**).

Opening hours: **Unrestricted access.**

Cost: **Free.**

Transport: **Barnes rail station.**

BARNES COMMON &
OLD BARNES CEMETERY

*B*arnes Common is a peaceful area of over 100 acres (50ha) of open grassland, trees and woodland, and one of the largest areas of unenclosed common land close to the centre of London. Designated a Local Nature Reserve, it has been owned by the church since the Middle Ages and today is managed by the borough of Richmond-upon-Thames.

Barnes Common was, until 1589, used jointly by the people of Barnes and Putney, when a dispute arose and the people of Barnes refused to allow those of Putney access! Until being drained in around 1880, the common was mainly marshland and almost entirely treeless. Today the common is primarily woodland, coppice and heathland, with some open areas of grass where cricket and soccer are played. The common is home to a wealth of flora (particularly grasses) and fauna, though there are surprisingly few mammals due to its open nature. In the centre of the common is an island of houses at Mill Hill, the site of a former windmill; the original miller's house still exists and is part of Mill Hill Lodge.

The Old Barnes Cemetery is situated within Barnes Common, adjacent to the boundary with Rocks Lane Recreation Ground; it was established in 1854 on 2 acres (0.8ha) of land as an additional burial ground for Barnes parish churchyard. A number of distinguished Victorians are buried here and a wealth of monuments and statues erected to their memory; at the centre of the cemetery is a large memorial to the Hedgman family, who were local benefactors.

> On the edge of the common, on Queen's Ride, is a memorial to the rock star Mark Bolan, who was killed in a car crash here in 1977.

The cemetery closed in the '50s and in 1966 was acquired by the borough council with the intention of turning it into a lawn cemetery – a grass-covered area where graves are marked with commemorative plaques rather than standing memorials. The council demolished the chapel and lodge and removed the boundary railings to prepare it for its new role, but then abandoned their plans and the cemetery. Today it's one of London's forgotten cemeteries, overgrown with trees and shrubs, with many of the monuments vandalised and statues decapitated. It's a sorry sight, though it's also an atmospheric and evocative place with an air of seclusion.

A magnificent green space and poignant cemetery make for a great day out.

❝ *A green oasis with a 'lost' cemetery* **❞**

AT A GLANCE

Address: 1-3 Parson's Green, SW6 4UL (☎ 020-7736 2115,
🖥 www.whitehorsesw6.com).

Opening hours: Sun-Wed, 9.30am to 11.30pm, Thu-Sat, 9.30am to
midnight. Booking recommended for the restaurant.

Cost: Free (apart from a drink or meal).

Transport: Parsons Green tube station.

THE WHITE HORSE

*T*he White Horse is a lovely (huge) historic pub in Fulham overlooking Parsons Green – and a magnet for beer lovers. A coaching inn has existed on the site since at least 1688, although the first recorded mention was in the *Spectator* in August 1712 in relation to the popular annual Parson's Green Fair, where ale tapping (when a tap is inserted into an ale cask) was an eagerly awaited event.

The current White Horse is a haven of Victorian elegance, with a pleasing blend of traditional polished mahogany and wall panels, wood and flagstone floors, wide windows, open fires and contemporary lighting. The main space is a single drinking area around three sides of a vast horseshoe bar with a dining room in the old coach house at the back. Chesterfield-style sofas surround huge tables, ideal for families and groups, though the umbrella-covered outdoor tables bordering the green are the most coveted (weather permitting). Upstairs there's an attractive area for private hire, in what was previously the pub's billiard and dining rooms.

Widely considered to be one of the best beer pubs in the UK, the White Horse maintains a large number of exceptional cask ales, imported keg beers (from Belgium to the US) and a unique selection of bottled beers and ales, including many rare and vintage examples of world classics. There are eight cask ales on offer at the mahogany bar, including Harvey's Sussex Best, Adnams Broadside and Oakham JHB, plus guests. The White Horse also offers over 135 bottled beers, including many from the US, Belgium and the UK, plus a few for which it's London's only stockist.

The White Horse also has a great menu – not serious gastro but modern, home-made British pub grub with a regional European influence. Not cheap but good value in this neck of the woods, plus a selection of inexpensive, tasty bar snacks. There are also roasts on Sundays and BBQs in the garden when the weather permits.

An elegant, comfortable pub with great beer, food and a welcoming atmosphere – what more could you ask for?

> The pub hosts four annual beer festivals: its own local beer festival over the May Bank Holiday, an American Beer Festival around Independence Day in July, a Belgian Beer Festival in August and an Old Ale Festival in November. It also runs a number of smaller events during the year.

 Thoroughbred wins the beer stakes by a distance

BATTERSEA PARK

*B*attersea Park is a delightful 200-acre (83ha) public park – opened in 1858 – situated on the south bank of the River Thames opposite Chelsea. Rarely has an inner city park had so much variety, hidden secrets and simple enjoyment – it's considered by many to be the most interesting of all London's major parks, though it's often neglected.

Before 1846 the area was known as Battersea fields (once a popular spot for duelling) and was a mixture of marshland reclaimed from the Thames and land formerly used for market gardens. Separated from the river by a narrow raised causeway, the fields consisted of low, but fertile, marshes intersected by streams and ditches where the chief crops were carrots, melons, lavender and the famous 'Battersea Bunches' of asparagus.

In 1845, championed by the local vicar and Thomas Cubitt, the builder and developer, whose yards were located across the river in the still marshy area of Pimlico, an application was made to Parliament to form a Royal Park, and the act was passed in 1846. Original designs for the park were laid out by Sir James Pennethorne (1801-1871), though the result varied somewhat from his vision. The park's success depended entirely on the completion of the new Chelsea Bridge – opened in 1858 – which allowed access from north of the Thames.

The park has an interesting history, including housing the fun fair and gardens of the Festival of Britain in the '50s. Today it's home to a small children's zoo, a boating lake, a bandstand and several all-weather outdoor sporting facilities, including tennis courts, a running track and soccer pitches. The park is also the site of the London Peace Pagoda, erected in 1985, while historic and attractive gardens are found in all corners, including the Old English Garden, the Sub-Tropical Garden and the Russell Page Garden. The park contains a wide variety of specimen trees and, not surprisingly, attracts a wealth of wildlife. It's also home to assorted sculptures and an art gallery – the Pump House Gallery (🖥 http://pumphousegallery.org.uk) – plus a number of eating places, including the excellent Italian café, La Gondola al Parco, by the lake.

> On 21st March 1829, the Duke of Wellington and the Earl of Winchilsea met on Battersea fields to settle a matter of honour, although neither actually attempted to shoot the other, and Winchilsea later made a grovelling apology.

The park underwent an £11m refurbishment in 2002-4.

66 *London's most diverse park?* **99**

Address: 38 West Hill, SW18 1RX (☎ **020-8871 1144,** 🖳 **www.demorgan.org.uk).**

Opening hours: Tue-Fri, 1-5pm, Sat, 11am to 5pm.

Cost: Adults £4, children free.

Transport: East Putney tube station.

DE MORGAN CENTRE

*T*he splendid 'De Morgan Centre for the Study of 19th-Century Art and Society' houses the world's largest collection of the work of William De Morgan (1839-1917) – the most important ceramic artist of the Arts and Crafts Movement – and his wife, the painter Evelyn De Morgan (1855-1919). William is credited with the rediscovery of the art of lustre (his work was heavily influenced by the Islamic tiles he saw at the South Kensington – now the Victoria & Albert Museum), while Evelyn was a successful and prolific artist and symbolist painter, whose style was notable for its rich use of colour, allegory, and her emphasis on strong female protagonists.

In 1859, De Morgan was admitted to the Royal Academy School and studied alongside Frederick Walker and Simeon Solomon. In 1863, he was introduced by Henry Holiday to the painter Edward Burne Jones and designer and polymath William Morris. As Morris hadn't been very successful with ceramics, De Morgan took over the tile production side of his business and soon began designing his own tiles. He collaborated with William Morris for many years.

William and Evelyn married in 1887 and, in addition to their art, became involved in many of the leading issues of the day, including prison reform, pacifism, the Suffragette movement and spiritualism – all documented in the Centre.

The Centre's collection was assembled by Evelyn De Morgan's sister, Mrs Wilhelmina Stirling, who wrote several books under the name AMW Sterling, including the De Morgans' biography. She inherited some pieces from the De Morgans and actively sought out other works to add to the collection, which she assembled at her

> **One of De Morgan's earliest commissions was working on the Arab Hall at Leighton House (Kensington), now a museum.**

home, Old Battersea House in London. Following her death in 1965 she bequeathed the collection to be looked after in trust for perpetuity, which gave rise to the De Morgan Foundation Charity in 1967. Parts of the collection have been displayed at a number of locations with associations with William De Morgan, but since 2002 it's home has been the former West Hill Reference Library in Wandsworth, which dates from 1887 and also houses the Wandsworth Museum (🖥 www.wandsworthmuseum.co.uk).

Recently refurbished, the Centre's collection includes ceramics (vases, tiles and panels), oil paintings, drawings and lustre-ware. The Centre also has a wide-ranging programme of temporary exhibitions by contemporary designers (see website).

❝ *Shrine to a remarkable Victorian couple* **❞**

Address: Crane Park, Whitton, TW2 (☎ **020-8891 2334,** 🖥 **www.wildlondon.org.uk).**

Opening hours: **Unrestricted access.**

Cost: **Free.**

Transport: **Whitton rail station.**

CRANE PARK ISLAND NATURE RESERVE

*C*rane Park Island Nature Reserve – one of 60 managed by the London Wildlife Trust – is a linear park situated on the north bank of the River Crane, from Meadway in Twickenham to Hanworth Road in the west. The island was created to contain a mill-pool of water to use to drive mill machinery, remains of which can still be seen (including wheel pits and machine bases), along with various mill streams. The River Crane has had various names, including the 'Powder Mill River' after its most important industry, the Hounslow Gunpowder Works. Situated at the western end of the park, it opened around 1766 and flourished until the early 20th century.

Before the reign of Henry VIII, most gunpowder was imported, but by the mid-16th century gunpowder mills had been established on Hounslow Heath. The mills passed through various owners until 1820, when Messrs Curtis and Harvey purchased them; they expanded the number and capacity of the mills and improved the water supply, developing a site of over 99 acres (40ha). The mills were reputed to have produced the finest black gunpowder in Europe.

After the closure of the gunpowder works in 1926, the new owner sold part of the site for housing and part to Twickenham Council, which created a public park that opened in 1935. The site still contains important industrial archaeological remains, including the Shot Tower (Grade II listed) built in 1828, which is to become a nature study and visitor centre. In 1990, Crane Park Island was designated a Local Nature Reserve.

Nowadays the island is a rich mosaic of woodland, scrub, meadow, reedbed and river bank, which is home to a rich variety of wildlife, from darting dragonflies to secretive foxes, stately herons to noisy marsh frogs. Even the rare water vole makes its home in the earth banks of the river and reedbed. Unfortunately the river was the scene of a major pollution incident in October 2011, although much work has been done to restore the water quality and the reserve's wildlife, and by the time you read this it will be well on its way to recovery.

> **The gunpowder works was a highly dangerous place to work and there were no less than five explosions during its operation, many fatal. The large mounds that can still be seen throughout Crane Park were built to help absorb the impact of explosions.**

❝ *A peaceful haven with an explosive past* **❞**

Address: Rugby House, Twickenham Stadium, 200 Whitton Road, Twickenham TW2 7BA (☎ 0871-222 2120, 🖥 www.rfu.com/museum).

Opening hours: Museum – Tue-Sat and (usually) Bank Holidays, 10am to 5pm, Sun, 11am to 5pm. Tours – Tue-Sat, 10.30am, noon, 1.30pm and 3pm, Sun, 1 and 3pm. Closed on Mon, most Public Holidays and match days (see website).

Cost: Museum – adults £7, concessions and children (under 16) £5, under 5s free. Tours & Museum – adults £15, concessions and children (under 16) £9, family (2 adults, up to 3 children) £45.

Transport: Twickenham rail station.

Webb Ellis (World Cup) Trophy

Calcutta Cup Trophy

WORLD RUGBY MUSEUM

*T*he World Rugby Museum at Twickenham Stadium (usually know simply as Twickenham or Twickers) is the ultimate visitor experience for rugby enthusiasts. Twickenham is the home of English rugby and the game's governing body – the Rugby Football Union (RFU) – whose museum houses the finest collection of rugby memorabilia in the world. It opened in 1996 and takes visitors through the history of the sport from its origins to the present day; more than simply a collection of interesting artefacts, the Museum is 'an inspirational journey through the history of the ultimate team game'.

> The stadium has been through a number of redevelopments over the years, with the stands being continually replaced; the new South Stand was opened in 2006 and increased the stadium's capacity to 82,000.

The stadium was formerly used to grow cabbages – it's still affectionately known as the 'Cabbage Patch' – and saw its first match (between Harlequins and Richmond) on 2nd October 1909: it celebrated its centenary in the 2009/2010 season. It's the second-largest stadium in the UK after Wembley Stadium and the fifth-largest in Europe, and hosts England's home test (international) matches, as well as the Middlesex Sevens, the Aviva Premiership final, the LV Cup and Heineken Cup matches. Although the ground is usually only used for rugby union, it has also hosted the Rugby League Challenge Cup final and other events, including many pop concerts.

Since the birth of the RFU in 1871, a wealth of rugby memorabilia has been accumulated, including dusty minute books, faded letters, early match programmes and tickets for memorable games. More recently the collection has developed to include historical and contemporary photographs, videos, artworks, equipment and other miscellaneous objects – a total of some 10,000. The World Rugby Museum relates the history of international rugby and contains objects from all over the globe. Over the course of a century, the collection grew to such an extent that in 1972 the RFU decided to open a museum, although it didn't come to fruition until the East Stand was redeveloped in the '90s and opened on 16th March 1996.

Stadium Tours (see opposite) are also available, which take you behind the scenes to visit the most exciting and prestigious parts of the stadium, including the royal box, hospitality suites, medical room, players' tunnel and a breathtaking view of the arena from the top of the stand.

A dream day out for rugby fans.

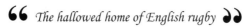

66 *The hallowed home of English rugby* **99**

Address: 40 Sandycoombe Road, Twickenham, TW1 2LR
(🖥 www.turnerintwickenham.org.uk and www.turnershouse.co.uk,
✉ turnerintwickenham@gmail.com).

Opening hours: **First Saturday of the month, 10am to 1pm, April to October 2012, and by arrangement for groups at other times.**

Cost: **£4.**

Transport: **St Margaret's rail station and bus. Street parking is limited and there is no parking on site.**

JMW Turner

The Fighting Temeraire'

SANDYCOMBE LODGE

*S*andycombe Lodge is a lovely Regency villa, the former home of Britain's greatest landscape artist, JMW (Joseph Mallord William) Turner (1775-1851). Supported by his father – a barber and wig maker – at the age of 14 Turner studied at the Royal Academy and by the age of 20 had established his own studio. In 1785, his sister Mary was taken seriously ill and died in 1786, after which his mother's mental health began to deteriorate; she died in a mental institution in 1804. The tragedies drew Turner and his father closer together and they shared a home for many years until his father's death in 1829. Turner never married but had two children by Sarah Danby in 1801 and 1811. In 1802, at the age of 27, Turner became a member of the Royal Academy.

In 1807, Turner purchased a plot of land near the Thames at Twickenham, then a fashionable riverside town. Here he built a villa – Solus Lodge, changing its name after a year to Sandycombe Lodge – to his own design with advice from his friend Sir John Soane, the leading architect of the day. It's a rare example of a house designed and built by a great artist for his own use; examples of sketches and ideas for the house can be found in Turner's notebooks. The external appearance of the house has been altered by the addition of second floors to the original side wings but the interior layout remains, and provides an insight into the character of its owner, being modest and unassuming.

Turner created a large pond covered in waterlilies in the grounds and kept a small boat moored nearby. He sold the house in 1826. The artist's original garden has long since gone, but miraculously the house has survived to this day. In the 1940s it was purchased by the late Professor Harold Livermore (and his wife Ann), who lived here until his death in 2010, when he bequeathed the house to the nation, together with a collection of material about the artist.

Sandycombe Lodge is currently in a 'pre-conservation' state, and Turner's House Trust is preparing to seek major funding for its conservation, after which it will be open on a regular basis. The Friends of Turner's House run various events to support the Trust.

> **The combination of important artistic associations and an unusual architectural history, make this modest villa a building of great importance.**

 Former home of Britain's greatest landscape artist

WHITE LODGE MUSEUM & BALLET RESOURCE CENTRE

*W*hite Lodge in Richmond Park is a fine example of the Neoclassical English Palladian style of architecture. Formerly a royal residence, today it houses the Royal Ballet Lower School for students aged 11-16, and the White Lodge Museum and Ballet Resource Centre.

The house was designed by Roger Morris (1701-54) as a hunting lodge for George II, shortly after his accession to the throne in 1727. Originally called Stone Lodge, it was renamed New Lodge soon after completion to differentiate it from neighbouring 'Brown Lodge'. Queen Caroline, consort of George II, stayed at the Lodge frequently and on her death in 1737 it passed to Robert Walpole, the first Prime Minister of Great Britain. After his death it came to Queen Caroline's daughter, Princess Amelia, in 1751, who caused public outrage by closing the entire park to the public (overturned in 1758). The name White Lodge first appeared in the 18th century after Princess Amelia added two white wings to the main Lodge.

There followed a succession of distinguished occupants including various Prime Ministers; Queen Victoria's aunt, the Princess Mary, Duchess of Gloucester and Edinburgh; the Prince of Wales (the future Edward VII); and assorted other members of the Royal Family, including the Duchess of York, who gave birth to her first child, the future Edward VIII there. In 1932, the rather gloomy, run-down mansion was transformed into a charming home for Prince Albert (future George VI) and Elizabeth and their two daughters, Princess Elizabeth and Princess Margaret.

In 1955, the Sadler's Wells Ballet School was given the use of White Lodge on a permanent basis, later being granted a Royal Charter and becoming the Royal Ballet School in 1956, one of the world's leading ballet schools. The Lodge has recently undergone a huge £22m redevelopment, including a new dining hall, state of the art dance and academic facilities, and new boarding facilities for up to 125 students and resident staff.

The White Lodge Museum and Ballet Resource Centre is the first dedicated ballet museum in the UK. Visitors can learn about the daily life of students at The Royal Ballet School, the history and development of classical ballet, and the appealing story of White Lodge itself.

> **Displays feature material from the Royal Ballet School collections, including Margot Fonteyn's ballet shoes, the death mask of Anna Pavlova and school reports of famous alumni.**

❝ *A home fit for future kings – and prima donnas* **❞**

Address: Richmond Park, Richmond TW10 (☎ 020-8948 3209, 🖥 www.royalparks.org.uk/parks/richmond_park/isabella_plantation.cfm).

Opening hours: From 7am (summer) or 7.30am (winter) to dusk (see website for times).

Cost: Free.

Transport: Richmond tube or rail station or the 85 bus from Putney tube station or by car to Broomfield Hill car park.

ISABELLA PLANTATION, RICHMOND PARK

*T*he Isabella Plantation in Richmond Park is a 42-acre (17ha) ornamental woodland garden – south of Pen Ponds – packed with exotic plants and designed to be interesting all year round. The name is thought to derive from the old English word 'isabel', in use from the 15th century, meaning 'greyish-yellow' – the colour of the soil in this part of the park. In the 17th century the area was known as The Sleyt, a name usually used for boggy ground or an open space between woods or banks, but by 1771 it was called the Isabella Slade. In 1831, Lord Sidmouth, the park deputy ranger, renamed it the Isabella Plantation; he fenced it in to protect the plants from the park's deer and planted oak, beech and sweet chestnut trees.

Today's garden of clearings, ponds and streams was established from the '50s onwards and is largely the work of George Thomson, the park superintendent from 1951-1971. Along with his head gardener, Wally Miller, he removed *Rhododendron ponticum* from large areas and replaced it with other rhododendron species. They established evergreen Kurume Azaleas around the Still Pond and planted other exotic shrub and tree species. The gardens have two ponds, the Still Pond and Peg's Pond, and a small stream flows through it, colonised by ferns, water plantains and brook lime. The Bog Garden was refurbished in 2000.

> **The Plantation has 15 known varieties of deciduous azalea, and houses the national collection of 50 Kurume Azaleas – introduced to the west in around 1920 by the plant collector Ernest Wilson – as well as 50 different species of rhododendron and 120 hybrids.**

Today, the Plantation is a popular part of Richmond Park – at least among those in the know! It contains different species that flower in different seasons, making it a garden for all seasons. In spring there are camellias, magnolias, daffodils and bluebells, while the azaleas and rhododendrons flower in late April. These are followed by Japanese irises and day lilies in summer and then by Guelder rose, rowan and spindle trees in the autumn, when the Acer trees are a riot of colour. During the winter months there are early camellias and rhododendron, as well as mahonia, winter-flowering heathers and stinking hellebore.

The Isabella Plantation is home to an abundance of wildlife and a joy at any time of the year.

❝ *A magical garden for all seasons* **❞**

Address: 67 Kingston Vale, Kingston-upon-Thames, SW15 3RN (☎ 020-8417 5515, 🖥 www.dorichhousemuseum.org.uk and www.dorichhouse.com).

Opening hours: Monthly open days (see website), 11am to 5pm, with guided tours at 11.30am and 2.30pm. Private curator's tours and school visits are also arranged.

Cost: Admission: £4, concessions £3, children under 16 free. Private tours (min. 10 people) £9 per head.

Transport: Kingston or Putney rail station then 85 bus, or by car.

Dora Gordine

DORICH HOUSE MUSEUM

*D*orich House was the studio, gallery and home of the sculptor Dora Gordine (1895-1991) and her husband the Hon. Richard Hare (1907-1966), a Professor of Russian Literature. Built in 1936 and restored by Kingston University in 1994, Dorich House is a fine example of Art Deco design, its severe exterior concealing the warmth of the interiors where Richard and Dora worked and lived. The couple left the house and its collections in trust for the education and enjoyment of the British public, and the newly restored building was opened in 1996 and became a museum in 2004.

Dora Gordine was hailed in 1938 as 'possibly the finest woman sculptor in the world' and she remained a major presence in European sculpture until the late '60s. Trained in Tallinn and Paris during the 1920s, Gordine achieved critical acclaim in 1926 with the bronze *Head of a Chinese Philosopher* (on display at Dorich House) exhibited at the Salon des Tuileries in Paris. She settled in Kingston in 1936 and remained at Dorich House until her death in 1991.

Richard Gilbert Hare was the second son of the 4th Earl of Listowel. Educated at Oxford, the Sorbonne and Berlin University, he developed a lifelong interest in the study and collection of Russian art and culture. Following a brief career in the Foreign Office, he spent the war working for the Anglo-Soviet Relations Division of the Ministry of Information, before becoming a Professor of Russian Literature at the School of Slavonic and East European Studies, University of London. He died suddenly from a heart attack in 1966.

The Museum houses the world's largest collection of Gordine's bronzes and plaster sculptures, as well as many of her paintings and drawings, spanning her early years in Paris in the 1920s to her last works created at Dorich House in the '60s and '70s. Hare's Russian art collection includes icons, paintings, ceramics, glassware, metalwork, folk art and furniture, dating from the early 18th century to the early 20th century. All are displayed in the unique surroundings of this studio home, described as 'one of Kingston's hidden treasures'.

A masterful treasure trove of a collection, worthy of a trip to the suburbs.

> **The two studios, gallery and top floor apartment were designed by Gordine in 1935-6; you may recognise her stylish and artistic interiors, which have been used as sets for films, videos and TV programmes.**

66 *A delightful house and stunning collection* **99**

WIMBLEDON LAWN TENNIS MUSEUM

*T*he Wimbledon Lawn Tennis Museum is the captivating museum of the All England Lawn Tennis Club (AELTC), otherwise known simply as Wimbledon. The Wimbledon tournament (or Championships) is the oldest tennis competition in the world – also considered by many to be the most prestigious – held at the AELTC since July 1877. It's one of the world's four major Grand Slam tennis tournaments, the other three being the Australian Open, French Open and US Open. Wimbledon is the only slam still played on grass, the game's original surface, which gave the game of lawn tennis its name. The tournament takes place over two weeks in late June and early July, culminating with the ladies' and men's singles' finals, scheduled respectively for the second Saturday and Sunday. Each year, five major events are contested, plus four junior events and three invitational events.

> **The total area of the grounds (including car parks) covers over 42 acres (17ha), with 19 grass courts (including the Centre Court and No.1 Court), six American Clay courts and five indoor courts. In the adjoining Aorangi Park there are a further 22 grass courts for practice before and during the championships, and two green acrylic courts.**

Opened in 1977, Wimbledon Lawn Tennis Museum is the largest tennis museum in the world with some 15,000 objects dating back to 1555! The current Museum opened in 2006 and is now a high-tech spectacular with many hands-on exhibits. Wimbledon's rich history is recorded on paper, captured in photos and on film, and presented through objects, memorabilia and interactive displays.

The game's evolution is traced from a garden party pastime to a multi-million dollar professional sport played world-wide, with interactive displays, touch screens, films and audio guides in nine languages. Memorabilia from many famous players from Victorian times to the present day are included in several different exhibits, which change seasonally. Highlights include the championship trophies; a tour by a John McEnroe 'ghost' of normally off-limit areas; a 200° cinema capturing the 'Science of Tennis'; film and video footage of the most memorable and exciting tournament matches; treasures from the first Championship to the most recent, including donations from players; and 'CentreCourt360', which allows you to sample the atmosphere of Centre Court. Guided tours are also available which take visitors behind the scenes at the club.

There's also a shop and café – a great day out for tennis fans.

 The hallowed turf of tennis heaven

AT A GLANCE

Address: **Common, Streatham High Road, SW16/Rookery, Covington Way, SW16 3BX (☎ 020-7926 9000, 💻 www.lambeth.gov.uk > parks and green spaces).**

Opening hours: **Common – unrestricted access; Rookery – daily, 7.30am to sunset.**

Cost: **Free.**

Transport: **Streatham rail station, bus or car.**

STREATHAM COMMON & THE ROOKERY

*S*treatham Common is a large open space at the southern tip of Lambeth, containing areas of woodland, grassland, wild flower meadows and The Rookery (see below), a small and enchanting formal garden. The common has a rich history stretching back to the Norman Conquest and the *Domesday Book*, and boasts spectacular views across south London and to the North Downs of Surrey. It was originally owned by the Crown and then by the Church Commissioners, and has been used and recognised as a common for centuries. In 1883 it was taken over by the Metropolitan Board of Works and an Act of Parliament ensured its protection as a public open space in perpetuity. It's now managed by the borough of Lambeth.

Streatham Rookery is an attractive, formally landscaped area with an ornamental pond, flower and herbaceous beds, and a rock garden with streams, surrounded by Streatham Common. The Rookery is situated in an area formerly known as Streatham Spa, where in the 18th century people would drink water from local springs for their medicinal and healing properties. The Streatham Spa and formal gardens used to be in the grounds of a large house called The Rookery. When the popularity of the spa declined, local residents successfully campaigned to buy the Rookery and save it and the surrounding woodland as a public open space. The Rookery became a public garden and formally opened on 23rd July 1913. Because of its heritage and unique character, the garden is on English Heritage's Register of Historic Parks and Gardens.

> The common includes a café, children's playground and paddling pool, and is also used for fairs and other events, including a kite festival. It's a popular place for walking, running, cycling and other sports, as well as being an important stop on the Capital Ring, a long-distance circular walking route around Greater London.

The modern Rookery contains an ornamental pond, flower and herbaceous beds, and a rock garden with streams. It's also noted for its old cedar trees and the White Garden, designed in the same style as the one at Sissinghurst Castle (Kent). With areas of woodland important for biodiversity and environmental education, it bristles with birdsong and wildlife. The garden also has a café, while in summer the lawns become an open air theatre.

The common and gardens are delightful places to spend a relaxing few hours.

 A great open space with a divine formal garden

AT A GLANCE

Address: **The Vestry Hall Annex, London Road, Mitcham, CR4 3UD** (☎ **020-8648 0127**, 🖥 **www.wandle.org**)

Opening hours: **Wed, 1-4pm, and the first Sunday of the month, 2-5pm.**

Cost: **Adults 50p, Children and concessions 20p.**

Transport: **Mitcham Junction rail station or Tramlink to Mitcham, or bus routes 118, 127, 200, 201 and 280.**

Morden Hall Park Snuff Mill'

William Morris textile design

Goat's Bridge

WANDLE INDUSTRIAL MUSEUM

*T*he Wandle Industrial Museum is a unique and remarkable museum established in 1983 to preserve and interpret the heritage and history of the industries and people of the Wandle Valley. The fast-flowing River Wandle has been used by people living along its banks since prehistoric times, first as a source of water and fish, and later for power to drive water wheels. It isn't navigable, so wouldn't have been used for transport. There's no definitive evidence of when the Wandle was first used as a power source for corn mills, but there were certainly mills along its banks in Anglo-Saxon times (13 mills were recorded in the *Domesday Book*). Today, the Wandle flows through the boroughs of Croydon, Merton, Sutton and Wandsworth.

In its heyday in the 18th and 19th centuries there were around 50 working mills on the Wandle, which at the time was the most industrialised river in the world. The coming of the Industrial Revolution meant that many of the mills added steam power, but a number of waterwheels survived into the 20th century. The Museum also traces the history of Britain's first public railway, the Surrey Iron Railway, a horse-drawn railway that provided an important transport link for the industries of the River Wandle.

Among the many businesses that used the river's power were William Morris's and Liberty's silk printing works at Merton, Connolly, the leather makers, and Young's Brewery, plus the lavender, snuff and dye industries. Connolly Leather produced the best leather in the world, used in Spitfire aircraft and luxury liners, and is still to be found in the Chambers of The Houses of Parliament and in Rolls Royce, Jaguar and Ferrari cars.

> Until its closure in 2006, Young's Ram Brewery in Wandsworth was Britain's oldest continuous brewing site, with a history dating back to the 1550s.

The most famous names associated with the Wandle are William Morris and Arthur Liberty. Morris chose Merton because it was then open fields and he liked the historical connections with Nelson and Merton Priory. The site also had various suitable buildings and a watermill that allowed the printed silk to be washed in the river. Further up river was Liberty's printer (Littler), where silk hand block printing (and later screen printing) was carried out for its shop on Regent Street. Silk printing continued at Merton until the late '70s

An outstanding industrial museum, well worth a visit.

❝ *A gem of a local museum* ❞

AT A GLANCE

Address: Honeywood Walk, Carshalton, SM5 3NX (☎ 020-8770 4297, 🖳 www.friendsofhoneywood.co.uk and www.sutton.gov.uk/index.aspx?articleid=1253).

Opening hours: Wed-Fri, 11am to 5pm, Sat-Sun, 10am to 5pm. Closed Mon-Tue.

Cost: Free.

Transport: Carshalton rail station.

HONEYWOOD MUSEUM

*H*oneywood Museum (Grade II listed) is Sutton borough's heritage centre and local history museum, occupying a lovely 17th-century building on the banks of Carshalton's scenic ponds.

The core of Honeywood dates from the 17th century but the building has had many later additions, including major extensions in 1896 and 1903. The house is rich in period detail, much of which has recently been restored to the 1903 colour scheme. The earliest surviving part of the house (17th century) is a small chalk and flint chequer-work building which is incorporated into the centre of the current house. The deeds to Honeywood show that in 1779 there were two houses standing side by side at the west end of the ponds. The existing building was the northernmost of the two, which in the mid-19th century was called 'Wandle Cottage', while the other was called 'Honeywood'.

In 1883 the freeholds of both properties were acquired by London merchant John Pattinson Kirk (d 1913), probably as a country retreat. He demolished the original Honeywood

> **Today, Honeywood's collection contains over 6,000 items – mainly from the 19th and 20th centuries – representing the history of local communities.**

around 1883-4 and transferred the name to Wandle Cottage, which has been called Honeywood ever since. In 1903, Kirk added a large Edwardian wing to the south end of Honeywood, which was pebble-dashed and decorated in mock Tudor style. The ground floor of the extension contained a magnificent billiards room and drawing room, while the first floor had extra bedrooms and a nursery.

Kirk was around 67 in 1903, therefore it's likely that Honeywood was being turned into a family home for his adopted daughter Lily Kirk Edwards and her husband, Henry. Lily outlived her husband and in 1939 sold the house to Carshalton Urban District Council, which used it for social and community purposes.

During 1989-90 it was converted into a Heritage Centre, which opened in 1990. In 1999-2000 the interior was repainted in the 1903 decorative scheme and in 2011-12 the Museum underwent a major refurbishment. It now has new exhibition rooms in the north corridor and on the ground floor, including a scullery, a WWII room and an Edwardian childhood room. The Museum also has a shop, café and garden, plus an art gallery with changing exhibitions and a programme of special events throughout the year.

❝ *A lovely house and museum in a picturesque location* **❞**

AT A GLANCE

Address: Church Hill, Harefield, UB9 6DU (☏ 01895-825960, 🖳 www.stmarys-harefield.com).

Opening hours: No regular opening hours, but arrangements can be made to visit most mornings. See website for service times.

Cost: Free (but donations are welcome).

Transport: Car is best, though there are regular bus (nos 331 and U9) links with Uxbridge, Denham, Ruislip and Northwood.

ST MARY'S HAREFIELD

*S*t Mary's Harefield is the parish church of Harefield and the town's oldest building. A church is thought to have stood on the site before the Norman conquest, though the oldest parts of the existing church date from the 12th century. A priest is first mentioned in the manor of Harefield in the *Domesday Book* (1086). In the late 12th century the advowson (right to appoint a priest) was given to the Knights Hospitallers, but after the Dissolution (and the Knights' destruction) the Newdigate family became Lords of the Manor and patrons of the church. The church remained a 'private peculiar' (outside of the jurisdiction of the Bishop) until 1847, becoming a parish church in 1898.

Unusual features include the raised chancel, the three-deck pulpit and the gallery above the north aisle. The building still retains some medieval features, but has been much altered and restored in almost every century. In the 1100s, there was a chancel and a nave, traces of which remain in the west wall of the current nave; the present chancel was built in the 1200s. In the 1300s, the current nave was built and the front two bays of the south aisle added as a chapel, known as the Brackenbury Chapel. In the 1500s, the current north aisle and Breakspear Chapel were built and the tower added, which houses six bells, the earliest dating from 1629. In the 1700s, the chancel arch was widened and the chancel roof and east window given the style you see today. In the 1840s, the south aisle was extended to its present length, which required the re-siting of many monuments, and the heraldic glass probably dates from this time.

In the churchyard is a Commonwealth War Graves Commission cemetery, where 111 Australian soldiers and a nursing sister are buried. They died at the No. 1 Australian Auxiliary Hospital – set up in Harefield House in 1915 – most after succumbing to wounds sustained during the disastrous Gallipoli campaign.

An extraordinary building with a long and extraordinary history – well worth a visit.

> **The most remarkable feature of the church – for which it's most famous – is its wealth of monuments, including mediaeval brasses, hatchments and sepulchral monuments, to the Newdigate, Ashby and other families. The most notable of the sepulchral monuments is probably that to Alice Spencer, Countess of Derby (1559-1637) – a relative of Diana Princess of Wales – in the southeast corner of the chancel.**

❝ *A 12th-century jewel of a church* ❞

AT A GLANCE

Address: Ruislip, Hillingdon, HA4 7XR (☎ 01895-250635, 🖥 www.ruislipwoodstrust.org.uk).

Opening hours: **Unrestricted access.**

Cost: **Free.**

Transport: **Ruislip tube station, M13 or 331 bus or by car.**

RUISLIP WOODS

*R*uislip Woods is an area of rare ancient woodland in Hillingdon surrounding Ruislip Lido lake; extending to 726 acres (294ha), in May 1997 it was designated the first National Nature Reserve in an urban area of England. The reserve comprises four woods: Park Wood, Mad Bess Wood and Copse Wood in Ruislip, and Bayhurst Wood in Harefield. Poor's Field and Tartleton's Lake in Ruislip are also part of the reserve.

Following the Norman conquest of England in 1066, Ernulf de Hesdin was given the manor of Ruislip, including the woods, which he passed to Bec Abbey in 1087. During the Abbey's ownership, timber from the woods was used in the construction of the Tower of London in 1339, Windsor Castle in 1344, the Palace of Westminster in 1346 and the manor of the Black Prince in Kennington – plus numerous important ships. Locally, the Great Barn on the Manor Farm site was constructed of oak from the woods. King's College, Cambridge became lords of the manor in 1451 and owned the woods until 1931, when Park Wood was sold to the local authority. The remaining woods were purchased from other owners and Ruislip Woods was formed.

The woods are rich in rare flora and flora including many ancient forest trees such as English oak, sessile oak, hornbeam, beech, silver birch, the wild service tree, aspen, rowan, field maple, crack willow, wild cherry, hazel and holly. Wild flowers are also found in abundance and include common knapweed, harebell, rosebay willowherb,

> **The woods are the remains of dense forests that covered the county of Middlesex from prehistoric times, which were gradually cleared for farming and housing. Evidence of Bronze Age settlements has been found within the woods during archaeological excavations.**

heather, bluebells, wood anemone, yellow archangel, snowdrops and honeysuckle. Among the many species' of birds that inhabit or visit the woods are mute swan, Canada goose, magpie, robin, green woodpecker, jay, nuthatch, lesser spotted woodpecker, greater spotted woodpecker, cuckoo, sparrow hawk, tree creeper, tawny owl, willow tit and woodcock. Resident mammals include badger, fox, hedgehog, stoat, weasel, mink, grey squirrel, plus several species of bats.

Today the woods offer a quiet haven for recreation, including walking, running, cycling and horse riding, while Ruislip Lido – a 60-acre (24ha) lake with sandy beaches and a narrow gauge railway around it – is situated on the edge of the woods.

66 *A national treasure of ancient woodland* ****

Address: Ravenor Farm, 29 Oldfield Lane, Greenford, UB6 9LD (☎ 020-8575 6644, 💻 www.london-motorcycle-museum.org).

Opening hours: Sat-Sun and Bank Holidays, 10am to 4.30pm. Pre-booked school visits Mon-Thu, 10am to 3pm.

Cost: Adults £5, concessions £2.50, children (5 to 14) £1, under 5s free.

Transport: Greenford tube station or South Greenford rail station.

LONDON MOTORCYCLE MUSEUM

*T*he London Motorcycle Museum (LMM) is London's only motorcycle museum focusing on Britain's long and distinguished biking history and heritage. The Museum contains some 150 machines and other exhibits on permanent display. Between 1960 and 1973, the Museum's founder Bill Crosby (b 1932) hoarded many choice bikes and one day was approached out of the blue by a friend asking if he would like to display them, following which Bill's bikes were moved to Syon Park where they were displayed alongside a collection of vintage cars. This worked well for a few years until the premises closed in February 1979. The collection then had a number of temporary venues in Derbyshire, until finding its present home in 1997.

The ever-growing collection (see website for an inventory) includes a 1902 Ormonde (a past participant in the Pioneer Run) and a 1903 Clyde (with a SIMS magneto). There's also a number of unique prototypes and 'media stars' and a wealth of iconic British

> **The Museum's bikes have appeared in *Eastenders, Dad's Army* and *George and Mildred.***

machines, including racers and road bikes from ABC to Zenith, plus the Crosby collection of Triumphs including the last Triumph T140 out of the Meriden gates in 1983 and a 1991 Norton rotary in Paramedic livery. Among the ever-changing exhibits are a 1930s Coventry Eagle 1,000cc Flying 8, a 1911 Rudge TT, a 1907 Brown Precision, an ohc BSA Rocket 3, the Triumph P1 prototype Trident (owned by the Trident & Rocket 3 Owners Club), an immaculate 1959 Norton Dommie 99, an equally perfect 1959 Velocette Venom, a 1975 Triumph Tiger 100 Grand Prix, a 1966 BSA Lightning works production racer, and several other rarities and prototypes from biking's golden era when roads were less congested.

The LMM isn't just a great static display and each year their bikes appear in shows and exhibitions across the country and abroad; these have included the TR30C's Beezumph rally, Beaulieu Motorcycle World, Hampshire Police and Cheshire Police open days, Paris's Bike Show and 'The Art of Motorcycle' in Rio de Janeiro, plus countless other events, gatherings and meets. Bikes also regularly appear at community events, county shows and carnivals, as well as the Museum's own special events and ride ins.

A great day out for bikers and an engrossing showcase of British engineering at its best.

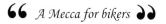

66 *A Mecca for bikers* **99**

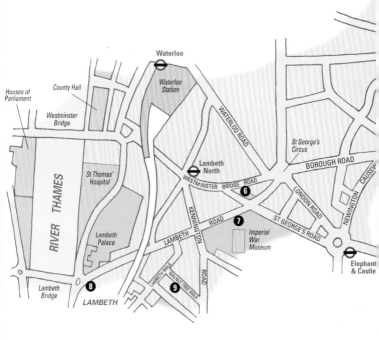

CHAPTER 8

SOUTHEAST LONDON

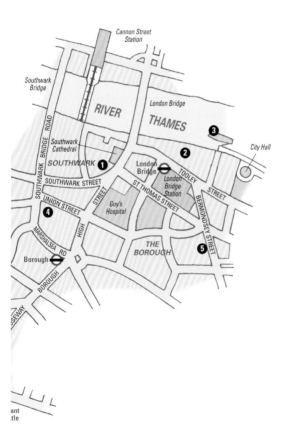

Cannon Street
Station

Southwark
Bridge

RIVER

THAMES

London Bridge

SOUTHWARK
BRIDGE ROAD

Southwark
Cathedral

SOUTHWARK ❶

SOUTHWARK STREET

London
Bridge

❷

❸

City Hall

UNION STREET

HIGH STREET

ST THOMAS STREET

London
Bridge
Station

TOOLEY STREET

BERMONDSEY STREET

❹

Guy's
Hospital

MARSHALSEA RD

THE
BOROUGH

❺

Borough

BOROUGH

SEWAY

ant
tle

N.B. See next page for more maps

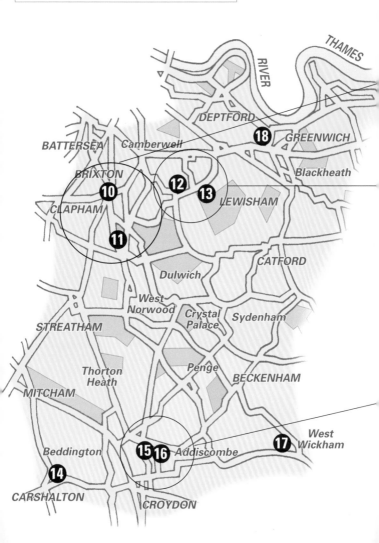

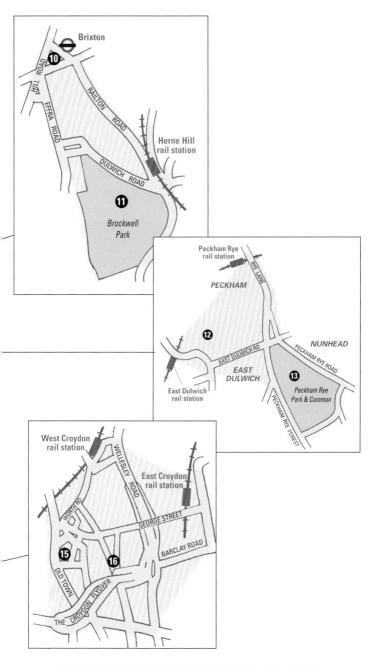

N.B. See individual pages for detailed maps for nos 14, 17 & 18

Address: **9 Stoney Street, SE1 9AA** (☎ **020-7407 2495,**
🖥 **www.markettaverns.co.uk/the_market_porter.html).**

Opening hours: **Mon-Fri, 6-8.30am and 11am to 11pm; Sat, noon to**
11pm; Sun, noon to 10.30pm.

Cost: **Free (apart from a drink).**

Transport: **London Bridge tube station.**

THE MARKET PORTER

*T*he Market Porter is a handsome traditional pub in an attractive setting, opposite Borough Market in Southwark – hence the name – on a site where there has been a pub since 1638. Many of the pub's customers work at the market, which is why the pub opens under special licence from 6-8.30am for hearty breakfasts. The Porter is also a honeypot for real ale enthusiasts, with possibly the best selection in London and beers changing up to nine times a day!

Situated on a corner, the Porter looks impressive, especially when its hanging flower baskets are in bloom. Inside there are several bars, each varying in character, but all timber-rich and cosy, be it panelling or beams, rustic wooden floors or barrel ends. On entering the handsome horseshoe-shaped bar decorated with pump clips, you're confronted with around a dozen handpumps offering real ales from throughout Britain – a daunting choice. However, there's a high turnover – around 50 beers rotate over a week – so the great beer you had last week may not be on offer when you return. The regular is Harvey's Sussex Best, with some obscure beers, seasonal brews and old favourites making up the rest.

> **The Market Porter was transformed into the 'Third Hand Book Emporium' in the film *Harry Potter and the Prisoner of Azkaban*, and was located next to 'The Leaky Cauldron'.**

The bar is sparsely furnished – to provide more standing room for drinkers – although there's an extension at the back with tables and chairs. There's no outdoor seating area but customers spill onto the street, particularly when the weather's fine. Upstairs there's an attractive restaurant serving lunches and evening meals, The Porter isn't renowned for its food, although it offers hearty English pub grub, including beer battered cod and chips, Cumberland sausage and mash, and steak, Harvey's ale & mushroom pie, with roasts on Sundays – there's also a bar menu offering sandwiches and paninis.

The pub is invariably packed to the gunwales, so isn't a venue for a quiet drink (except perhaps in the restaurant) or comfort, though it may be possible on a wet day in mid-afternoon when the market is shut…

The Market Porter is a fine place with a mixed crowd and a real pub atmosphere. It's well worth a visit, particularly if you combine it with a trip to the foodie heaven of Borough Market (Thu-Sat) next door.

❝ *A delightful pub with a fantastic range of beers* ❞

Address: **Tooley Street, SE1 (☎ 020-7403 3583).**

Opening hours: **Unrestricted access.**

Cost: **Free.**

Transport: **London Bridge tube station or London Bridge City Pier.**

HAY'S GALLERIA

*H*ay's Galleria (Grade II listed) is a riverside leisure and shopping complex in Southwark on the south bank of the Thames – a striking blend of historic and modern architecture – which opened in 1987 as part of the 'London Bridge City' development. It's named after its original owner, the merchant Alexander Hay, who acquired the property – then a brewhouse – in 1651. In around 1840, John Humphrey Jr acquired a lease on the property and commissioned William Cubitt (father-in-law to two of his sons) to convert it into a 'wharf'. It was renamed Hay's Wharf in 1856.

During the 19th century the wharf was the largest in the Port of London and the chief destination for tea clippers such as the *Cutty Sark*. At its height, 80 per cent of the dry produce imported into London passed through the wharf, which led to it being dubbed the 'larder of London'. Hay's Wharf also pioneered cold storage, receiving New Zealand butter as early as 1867. The wharf was rebuilt following the Great Fire of Tooley Street in 1861, and continued in use for almost a century. It was badly damaged during the Blitz in WWII and trade declined drastically after the war, when the surrounding area became increasingly economically depressed.

In the late '80s, with the increasing urban regeneration of the Thames Corridor and nearby London Docklands, the main dock was filled in, and both the wharf and the tea and produce warehouses surrounding it were restored. The entire space was then enclosed within a vast glass and steel barrel-vaulted roof – reminiscent of the magnificent Victorian railway termini – thus creating the Galleria.

In its new role as a leisure and shopping centre, the wharf offers a range of eating places including Café Rouge, Côte Brasserie and The Fish Restaurant at Balls Brothers (with a pétanque pitch). There's also an excellent pub with a riverside terrace, The Horniman at Hay's, named after one of the main tea-producing companies associated with the trade here.

The Galleria's unique atmosphere is enhanced by a varied programme of special events, including lunchtime concerts.

> The centrepiece of the Galleria is an acclaimed 60ft (18.3m) kinetic bronze sculpture of a ship, *The Navigators*, by David Kemp, unveiled in 1987 to commemorate the Galleria's shipping heritage. The sculpture weighs 14 tonnes and is a bizarre and captivating symphony of moving parts, water jets and fountains.

 A striking blend of old and new in perfect harmony

Address: **The Queen's Walk, SE1 2JH** (☎ **020-7940 6300,**
🖥 **www.iwm.org.uk/visits/hms-belfast).**

Opening hours: **Daily, 10am to 6pm. Closed 24-26th December.**

Cost: **Free.**

Transport: **London Bridge tube station.**

HMS BELFAST

*H*MS *Belfast* is a remarkable museum ship – originally a Royal Navy light cruiser (one of ten Town-class cruisers built) – permanently moored on the Thames and operated by the Imperial War Museum.

Construction of *Belfast*, named after the capital city of Northern Ireland where it was built, began in December 1936. She was launched on St Patricks Day, 17th March 1938 and commissioned in early August 1939 shortly before the outbreak of WWII. *Belfast* was initially part of the British naval blockade against Germany, but in November 1939, she struck a mine and spent almost three years undergoing repairs. Returning to action in November 1942 with improved firepower, radar equipment and armour, *Belfast* was the largest and most powerful cruiser in the Royal Navy.

In June 1944, *Belfast* took part in Operation Overlord supporting the Normandy landings and a year later was redeployed to the Far East to join the British Pacific Fleet, just as WWII was coming to a close. She saw further action in 1950-52 during the Korean War.

> **Belfast saw action escorting Arctic convoys to the Soviet Union during 1943 and in December 1943 played an important role in the Battle of North Cape, assisting in the destruction of the German battleship Scharnhorst.**

Belfast underwent extensive modernisation between 1956 and 1959, and a number of further overseas commissions followed before she was placed in reserve in 1963. In 1967, efforts were initiated to avert *Belfast*'s scrapping and preserve her as a museum ship. Initial efforts by the Imperial War Museum, the National Maritime Museum and the Ministry of Defence were unsuccessful, prompting the formation of the private HMS Belfast Trust which finally succeeded in saving the ship in July 1971. The *Belfast* was moored on the Thames near Tower Bridge and opened to the public in October 1971, becoming a branch of the Imperial War Museum in 1978.

When *Belfast* was first opened to the public, visitors were limited to the upper decks and forward superstructure, but nine decks are now open to the public. Access to the ship is via a walkway which connects the quarterdeck with the pedestrianised footpath on the south bank of the Thames. A visit to HMS *Belfast* consists of three broad sections: 'life on board', 'inner workings' and 'life at war' (see website).

A rare opportunity to visit a preserved WWII war ship. Last, but not least, the *Belfast* also has a café.

❝ *Experience life on a battle cruiser!* **❞**

Address: **50 Redcross Way, SE1 1HA** (☎ **020-7403 3393**, 🖥 **www. londongardensonline.org.uk/gardens-online-record.asp?id=sou074 and www.bost.org.uk).**

Opening hours: **Daily, 7.30am to sunset.**

Cost: **Free.**

Transport: **Borough tube station.**

Octavia Hill

RED CROSS GARDEN

*R*ed Cross Garden is a delightful small garden (just one-third of an acre) that formed part of Octavia Hill's pioneering social housing scheme in Southwark, consisting of two small rows of Tudor, revivalist-style cottages and a community hall (now privately owned), designed by Elijah Hoole. The Garden predated the buildings and was designed by Miss Emmeline Sieveking of the Kyrle Society in 1887 and officially opened in 1888.

An energetic social reformer, particularly for the provision of well-designed affordable housing and attendant community facilities, Octavia Hill was also passionate about the need for public open spaces. She was closely involved in the Kyrle Society,

> **Upon the death of Octavia Hill (1838-1912) the public mourning comparable only to that for Florence Nightingale.**

whose Open Space Committee played an important role in saving recreational open space in London from building development, and also in creating new public open spaces. This work led directly to the establishment of the National Trust, first mooted in 1885, of which Hill was a co-founder. She was involved in the creation of parks such as Vauxhall and Brockwell, and participated in many campaigns, including those that led to saving Queen's Wood, Parliament Hill Fields, West Wickham Common, Archbishop's Park and Hilly Fields.

Red Cross Garden was created to provide 'an open air sitting room for the tired inhabitants of Southwark' and had an elaborate layout of curved lawns, flower beds and serpentine paths, an ornamental pond with a fountain, a bandstand and a covered children's play area. There were once two mosaics in the Garden, of which only one, 'The Sower', remains, restored in 1956 and again in 2005.

During WWII the railings were removed for the war effort and the caretaker dismissed, and by 1948 the layout of the Garden had disappeared. It still appears treeless in a photograph of 1965, although some trees were subsequently planted. In 2005, the Bankside Open Spaces Trust (🖳 www.bost.org.uk.), with Heritage Lottery funding and support from local people and Southwark Council, restored the Garden to its former glory, complete with pond, bridge, fountain, flower beds, winding paths, lawn and benches. The Green Flag award-winning Garden reopened in 2005, and was officially opened by HRH The Princess Royal on 1st June 2006.

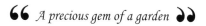

66 *A precious gem of a garden* **99**

AT A GLANCE

Address: 62-66 Bermondsey Street, SE1 3UD (☎ 020-7403 2800, 🖥 www.londonglassblowing.co.uk).

Opening hours: Mon-Sat, 10am to 6pm. Classes (full day) are also offered – see website for information.

Cost: Free.

Transport: Borough or London Bridge tube station.

Peter Layton

LONDON GLASSBLOWING STUDIO & GALLERY

*T*he London Glassblowing Studio & Gallery was established by Peter Layton in 1976 (in an old factory on the Thames at Rotherhithe), and was among the first hot-glass studios in Europe. Now situated (since 2009) on vibrant Bermondsey Street, opposite Zandra Rhodes' Fashion and Textile Museum, the gallery offers a light, spacious area for the display of contemporary glass.

Peter Layton is one of the world's most famous and respected glassblowers who has done much to promote glassmaking as an art form. He has influenced and nurtured several of the UK's leading glassmakers and inspired many more internationally. At the age of 75, Layton remains active and is regarded as the 'grand old man of glass'. Some glassmakers create technically brilliant pieces and follow a precise pattern, while others prefer to create more abstract works that are looser and evolve during the creative process. Layton's work falls firmly into the latter category – he's noted for his strong use of colour, organic forms and the sculptural quality of his larger pieces.

London Glassblowing is one of Europe's leading glassmaking workshops, renowned for its particular flair in the use of colour, form and texture. Layton operates his studio like a collective, where glassblowers are free to use the kilns to create their own work and develop their skills, as well as work on pieces that help to pay the vast energy bills. He has always put creativity before commercial needs, which is why his Gallery is an Aladdin's cave of unique and surprisingly affordable works of glass art, each signed by the artist. Much of the richly coloured glass art on sale is Layton's own work, which can also be found in museums, galleries and exhibitions across the UK, Europe and the US. The Studio also accepts commissions.

London Glassblowing offers introductory classes in glassblowing under the guidance of a qualified glassmaker, which are designed to teach the basic techniques. The emphasis is on providing a hands-on experience and includes gathering the molten glass, blowing, shaping and forming.

Visitors experience the heat and magic of an ancient craft, while watching molten glass evolve into something of beauty and value. The Studio has a schedule of exhibitions throughout the year (see website for information).

> **You can see the stunning results of Layton's work in his book, *Peter Layton and Friends: Celebrating London Glassblowing.***

 The magical world of glassblowing in all its glory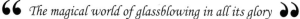

Address: Cathedral House, Westminster Bridge Road, SE1 7HY (☎ 020-7928 5256, 🖥 www.southwark-rc-cathedral.org.uk)

Opening hours: Daily, 9am to 6pm. See website for service times.

Cost: Free (but donations are welcome).

Transport: Lambeth North tube station.

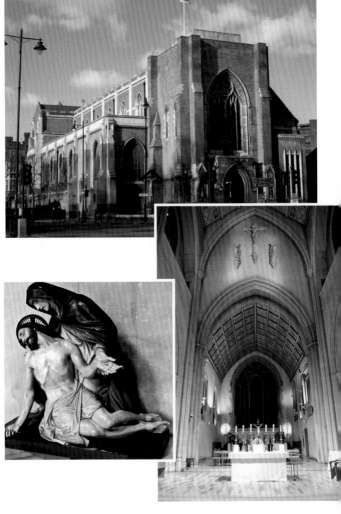

ST GEORGE'S CATHEDRAL

*S*t George's Cathedral is a majestic Roman Catholic cathedral in the borough of Southwark. Opened in 1848, in 1850 it became the first Roman Catholic church raised to cathedral status since the English Reformation in the 16th century. It was designed in the Gothic Revival style by Augustus Pugin (1812-1852) – famous for his work with Charles Barry on the Houses of Parliament – who was also the first person to be married in the Cathedral on 10th August 1848.

Like so many London buildings, particularly churches, St George's has had a chequered history. Despite its later Victorian restoration by the Scottish architect F. A. Walters and terrible damage during WWII, much of Pugin's grand design has survived (though it wasn't nearly as grand as his original design). The post-WWII restoration by Romilly Craze (1892-1974) preserved the sheer scale and impact of the building as well as some of its details, including the beautiful Blessed Sacrament chapel, the nearby Knill Chantry (designed by Pugin's son Edward), the Thomas Doyle monument, the altar frontispiece, the aisle walls and some original pillars.

> **It's sad and ironic that Pugin should have spent some of his last days in the building opposite the church, the Bethlem Royal Hospital (Bedlam) – see page 309.**

The cathedral was reopened after restoration in 1958 and has played host to many notable visitors, including Pope John Paul II (1982) – who's depicted in one of the cathedral's many fine stained-glass windows – and the Dalai Lama (1998). The year 2011 saw the partial restoration of the 1958 John Compton organ and the installation in the chancel of the George Pace Choir Stalls, a gift from (Anglican) St Alban's Cathedral.

St George's has a fine musical tradition, with a variety of musical styles represented at the different masses, from family hymns and congregational style worship at the 10am mass, to instrumental and contemporary music from across the world at the 6pm mass. The superb acoustics attract many orchestras and choirs to perform in the nave, and the Whitehall Orchestra and Trinity College of Music are frequent visitors. The cathedral also has an established choral tradition with a resident choir of men and boys who sing at the 11.30am solemn mass each Sunday and on major feast days. The choir's repertoire encompasses Gregorian Chant, Tudor polyphony, Renaissance, Baroque, classical and romantic masses, and motets.

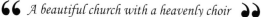 *A beautiful church with a heavenly choir*

Address: **Geraldine Mary Harmsworth Park, St George's Road, SE1 6ER** (💻 **www.tibet-foundation.org/art_culture/tibetan_peace_garden**).

Opening hours: **Summer, 8am to 9.30pm; winter, 8am to 4.30pm.**

Cost: **Free.**

Transport: **Lambeth North or Elephant & Castle tube station.**

His Holiness the Dalai Lama

TIBETAN PEACE GARDEN

*T*he Tibetan Peace Garden – full name 'Tibetan Garden of Contemplation and Peace' or *Samten Kyil* – is a beautiful, tranquil garden situated in Geraldine Mary Harmsworth Park in Southwark. Hamish Horsley was the designer and sculptor of the Peace Garden, ably assisted by a team of skilled professionals. The Garden is a simple, poignant plea for peace, incongruously sited in the shadow of the Imperial War Museum – which very effectively records the history of modern warfare. The Garden was commissioned by the Tibet Foundation and opened and consecrated in 1999 by His Holiness the Dalai Lama; it honours one of his principal teachings: the need to create understanding between different cultures and to establish places of peace and harmony in the world.

The Garden also serves to create a greater awareness of Buddhist culture. At its heart is the Kalachakra Mandala, which is associated with world peace; here for the first time cast in bronze, it forms the central focus of the garden. Contemporary western sculptures – set on the north, south, east and west axis – represent the four elements of air, fire, earth and water (the open arena represents the fifth element, space). Around the Mandala are eight meditation seats representing the noble eightfold path: right view, thought, speech, action, livelihood, effort, mindfulness and concentration.

Near the Garden's entrance is the Language Pillar, containing a peace message for the new Millennium – in Tibetan, English, Chinese and Hindi – from His Holiness the Dalai Lama. The pillar design is based on the Sho Pillar, a 9th-century treaty stone in Lhasa acknowledging the rights of both Tibet and China to coexist in peace. The three carved steps at the top of the pillar represent peace, understanding and love.

The inner gardens are planted with herbs and plants from Tibet and the Himalayan region, while the pergola is covered with climbing plants, including jasmine, honeysuckle and scented roses. The surrounding area is landscaped and planted with trees in a collaboration between the borough of Southwark and the local community.

A spiritual, uplifting garden where visitors can enjoy a few moments of peace and reflection.

> The Garden stands as a monument to the courage of the Tibetan people and their patient commitment to the path of non-violence and peace. It also reminds us that Tibet's culture is a treasure of our common heritage and how vital it is that it be kept alive.

 A symbol of peace in a troubled world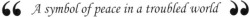

AT A GLANCE

Address: **1 Lambeth High Street, SE1 7JN (☎ 020-7572 2210,
🖥 www.rpharms.com/about-pharmacy/our-museum.asp).**

Opening hours: **Mon-Fri, 9am to 5pm for ground floor displays
(no booking necessary). Closed Bank Holidays. Tours (1½ to 2 hours
– pre-booking required), Mon-Thu, 1pm.**

Cost: **Free for ground floor displays; tour fee is £50 for ten people.**

Transport: **Lambeth North or Waterloo tube station.**

ROYAL PHARMACEUTICAL SOCIETY MUSEUM

*T*he Royal Pharmaceutical Society (RPS) Museum is an absorbing museum founded in 1842 as a scientific collection of *materia medica* for use by pharmacy students in the society's school of pharmacy. The museum moved to its current site in Lambeth (along with the rest of the Pharmaceutical Society) in 1976.

The Pharmaceutical Society of Great Britain was founded on April 15th 1841 by a group of leading London chemists and druggists, although the dispensing of drugs and medicines wasn't regulated until 1868, before which anyone could operate as a chemist or druggist. The society received its Royal Charter from Queen Victoria in 1843.

The RPS Museum provides a wide range of services and activities for everyone interested in pharmacy. It contains a unique collection of around 45,000 objects covering all aspects of British pharmacy history, including traditional dispensing equipment; drug storage containers (including fine 'Lambeth delftware' jars from the 17th and 18th centuries); proprietary 'brand name' medicines dating from the 18th century to the present day; bronze mortars; medical caricatures; and a photo archive.

The ground floor area contains cased displays on themes of 'The Evolving Pharmacy' and 'Lambeth's Pharmacy Past', to 'Pharmacy and Nature' and 'Making Medicines'. Visitors can also discover how pharmacies have changed over the centuries and compare today's experiences with how people trained to

> The pharmacy profession can be traced back at least as far as the Sumerian civilisation in 4,000BC in what is now modern day Iraq.

be pharmacists in the 1800s. Objects on display range from 18th-century seahorses to current painkillers, and from equipment used to make pills in the 1800s to jars used to hold 16th-century medicinal ingredients.

The 'Developing Treatments' display case focuses on the way that different medical conditions have been treated over time. Each year the RPS examines different conditions from the earliest records to modern times, with the display changing in March to mark National Science and Engineering Week. In 2012, the display explored how controlled substances such as cannabis, coca, cocaine, opium, morphine and heroin have been viewed and used throughout history as pharmaceutical treatments. Visitors should bear in mind that they need to take a tour in order to see most of the remarkable collection.

The Museum has wide-ranging appeal, whether you're a health professional, historian or just interested in the history of healthcare.

66 *Keep taking the pills…* **99**

Address: Walnut Tree Walk, off Kennington Road, SE11 6DN
(☎ 020-7587 1131, 🖳 www.rootsandshoots.org.uk).

Opening hours: Mon-Fri, 10am to 4pm. Also evening and weekend
events (see website or telephone for information).

Cost: Free.

Transport: Lambeth North tube station.

ROOTS & SHOOTS GARDEN

*T*he Roots and Shoots Garden (RSG) – full name 'Roots and Shoots Wildlife Garden and Study Centre' – is an outstanding, award-winning centre in Kennington, created by Linda Philips to provide vocational training for urban youngsters. The Garden was established in 1982 by the Lady Margaret Hall Settlement – a charity working in North Lambeth since 1897 – for young people mainly from Lambeth and Southwark. Up to twenty 16-19 year-olds with moderate learning disabilities spend a year in the Garden acquiring the necessary skills and self-confidence to find and retain employment.

The project was given a derelict 1-acre (0.4ha) site by Lambeth Council, which now contains an eco-training centre, plant nursery, shop, wildlife study centre and wild garden, providing environmental education for schools and the community. Diverse habitats have been developed in the Garden to increase and promote the biodiversity of insect, plant and bird life. Surrounded by high buildings, the site is a lush inner-city oasis in which plants from warm temperate and Mediterranean climates flourish.

An eco building – clad in wood with sustainable energy and other environmental features – is the hub of Roots and Shoots' activities; completed in 2005, it was officially opened in 2007 by HRH The Prince of Wales. It has a large photovoltaic roof (for solar energy), which generates around 50 per cent of the garden's electricity needs, solar water heating, rainwater collection for the WCs and to water plants, and built-in insect and bird boxes in the cladding. It also houses the training rooms, office and reception, plus a hall and meeting rooms.

> The Garden is also the base for the London Beekeepers' Association (💻 www.lbka.org.uk), who hold meetings and courses here; its honey – some of the best in London – is sold in the RSG shop.

The RSG has won a number of awards, including the 'Sustainable City Award' (2010) for its work on biodiversity and education for local communities; the London Spade Award 2011 from the Metropolitan Public Gardens Association for excellence in the provision of horticultural and environmental education; and the Man and the Biosphere Urban Wildlife Award (2011) for excellence. The last mentioned is awarded by the UK Committee of the UNESCO programme on Man and the Biosphere, to recognise the work of organisations that promote biodiversity and interactions between people and the environment.

The Roots and Shoots Garden is an inspiration to all – every community should have one.

 An exceptional and inspiring award-winning garden

Address: Electric Avenue, Pope's Road and Brixton Station Road SW9 (☎ 020-7926 2530, 🖥 http://brixtonmarket.net and www.friendsofbrixtonmarket.org).

Opening hours: Street trading, Mon-Sat, 8am to 6pm (3pm Wed); Arcades, Mon-Wed, 8am to 6pm, Thu-Sat, 8am to 10pm, Sun, 10am to 5pm; Shops, daily, 8am to 7pm.

Cost: Free.

Transport: Brixton tube station.

BRIXTON MARKET

*B*rixton Market is a actually a number of markets, comprising a vibrant street market and covered market areas in the nearby arcades: Reliance Arcade, Market Row and Granville Arcade (the last recently rebranded as 'Brixton Village' – packed with culinary treats). Nowadays, the market has expanded to cover several areas of Brixton, including Brixton Station Road.

The Market began life on Atlantic Road in the 1870s and subsequently spread to Brixton Road, which had a wide pathway. It became a popular attraction with working class shoppers, who were entertained by street musicians. Electric Avenue (made famous by Eddy Grant with his eponymous 1983 hit song), now part of the street Market, was built in the 1880s and was one of the first streets in London to have electric light. Glazed iron canopies covered the footpath, although these were badly damaged during WWII and removed in the '80s.

The Market comprises three areas (recently Grade II listed); the open-air Market Row (1928), which contains Electric Avenue – and two covered arcades – Reliance Arcade (1924) and Granville Arcade (1937), now renamed 'Brixton Village'. The three market arcades form an extensive network of stalls and are rare survivors, recently joined by a themed market or event each Saturday on Brixton Station Road, which also hosts a Sunday farmers' market (10am to 2pm).

After the huge wave of immigration in the '50s, the Market became an important focal point for the black community. It sells a wide range of foods and goods, but is best known for its African and Caribbean produce, including specialties such as flying fish, breadfruit and all manner of weird looking fresh meats, reflecting the diverse community of Brixton and the surrounding areas. The Market has a heaving, bustling atmosphere that you won't find elsewhere in London; whereas many markets are interesting to wander around and browse the wares on offer, Brixton Market is a real market offering a wide choice of world produce at modest prices with minimum frills. The Atlantic Road part of the market offers more in the way of clothes, leather goods, household linen and children's toys, rather than food.

> **Brixton Market has a unique character, which distinguishes it from other London markets and shopping areas: a combination of history, interesting architecture, the variety of goods on sale and the cultural mix of Brixton, generally acknowledged as the symbolic 'soul of black Britain'.**

 London's most vibrant and colourful market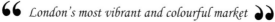

Address: **Norwood Road, SE24 (☎ 020-7926 9000, ⌨ www.lambeth.gov. uk > parks, www.brockwellpark.com and http://madforbrockwellpark. com).**

Opening hours: **Daily, 7.30am to sunset (see website for exact closing times).**

Cost: **Free.**

Transport: **Brixton tube station or Herne Hill rail station.**

BROCKWELL PARK

*B*rockwell Park (125-acre/51ha) – created in 1892 – is one of south London's best and most diverse public parks, offering something for everyone. Its centrepiece is the late Georgian Brockwell Hall (Grade II* listed), designed by D. R. Roper in a style loosely termed 'free Grecian'. It was built between 1811-1813 for John Blades, a wealthy Ludgate Hill glass merchant, who also created Brockwell Hall Park Estate. The perimeter of today's park reflects the boundary of the original estate.

On the death of John Blades in 1829, the Hall and Estate passed by marriage to the Blackburn family who lived here until 1888, when they were acquired by the London County Council (LCC) as a public park. The purchase followed a campaign led by Thomas Lynn Bristowe, the first MP for Norwood, who was instrumental in raising funds from public, church, charity and private subscription. Ironically, the man who did so much to create the public park died of a heart attack on the steps of Brockwell Hall shortly after taking part in the opening ceremony. In 1901 the LCC acquired a further 43 acres (17ha) of land north of the original park.

> **The park is the venue for various community events, including the Lambeth Country Show in September, an impressive Guy Fawkes' firework display, open air theatre and concerts.**

Brockwell Hall has recently been restored, following extensive fire damage in February 1990, and now presents visitors with a view that's close to the original Georgian concept of a country house set in a park estate. Since 1892, the ground floor of the Hall has served as a café – the building and surrounding paths afford panoramic views of London.

The park incorporates a wealth of facilities and green areas, including ornamental ponds, wetlands, a wild meadow, open grassland, community greenhouses, formal flower beds, a tranquil walled rose garden (the former kitchen garden of the Hall) with benches and a charming 19th-century clock tower. Sports facilities include tennis courts, a bowling green, a purpose-built BMX track, basketball, football, cricket, tennis courts and the magnificent Brockwell Lido (Grade II listed – see ⌨ www.brockwelllido.com), opened in July 1937 and recently restored to its former glory (with a gym). The park also has a children's play area, a paddling pool, a miniature railway, plus a café, toilets, picnic areas and shelters.

 A magnificent jewel of a local park

Address: 28 Marsden Road, SE15 4EE (☎ 020-7252 9186, 🖥 www.wildlondon.org.uk).

Opening hours: Tue-Thu and Sun, 10.30am to 4:30pm.

Cost: Free.

Transport: East Dulwich rail station or car.

CENTRE FOR WILDLIFE GARDENING

*T*he Centre for Wildlife Gardening is an idyllic spot in Peckham developed in the late '80s and run by London Wildlife Trust. The Trust manages over 40 London-wide reserves and is the only charity dedicated solely to protecting the capital's wildlife and wild spaces. It campaigns to save important wildlife habitats, engaging London's diverse communities through access to nature reserves, volunteering programmes and education work.

The Centre for Wildlife Gardening was previously a council depot, but has developed beyond all recognition over the past 20 years and is now home to an award-winning visitors' centre demonstrating innovative environmental building techniques. The Centre offers practical advice to city gardeners and is the perfect place to learn new skills and obtain ideas and inspiration. It has a demonstration wildlife garden with a range of inspiring mini habitats showing how you can help wildlife however much space you have available, including the mini-beast village, summer meadow, woodland copse, stag beetle sanctuary, wildlife pond, bog garden and flowery chalk bank. There's also a wildflower nursery and some well used community raised beds. Species you may spot include frogs and newts, grasshoppers and stag beetles, foxes and a wide variety of songbirds. Children are also well catered for with a small toddlers' sand-pit area, a nature trail and picnic facilities. The plant nursery supplies British wildflowers, herbs, cottage-garden plants and pond plants, as well as native trees, shrubs and climbers in season. It also sells delicious 'Peckham' honey from its hives.

> **The Wildlife Trusts (🖥 www. wildlifetrusts.org) is the UK's largest voluntary organisation dedicated to conserving the country's wildlife habitats and species, whether they be in the countryside, in cities or at sea.**

The Centre organises school visits with hands-on outdoor learning experiences linked to the National Curriculum, and works with the Southwark Adult Learning Service as a delivery partner for family learning, particularly with regard to adults with learning disabilities. It also offers a wide range of talks and workshops in the visitors' centre. The Centre welcomes volunteers to take part in practical gardening activities such as general garden maintenance, the potting up and planting out of plants, pond maintenance, clearance of invasive plants, and the creation of log piles to provide habitats for insects and reptiles. The Centre for Wildlife Gardening won a Green Flag Community Award in 2011.

A favourite place for families, gardeners and wildlife enthusiasts.

 Man and nature in perfect harmony 🎵🎵

PECKHAM RYE PARK & COMMON

*P*eckham Rye Park & Common comprise one of the most beautiful green spaces in south London, totalling 113 acres (45.7ha). Managed by Southwark Council, they consist of the historic Peckham Rye Common (64 acres) to the north and Victorian Peckham Rye Park (49 acres) to the south. Peckham Rye has a long history and is recorded as being cultivated before the Norman Conquest in the 11th century; 'Pecheham', which may have been 'Peche's Home', was referred to in the *Domesday Book* (1086), when it was owned by Bishop Odo of Bayeux. By around the 14th century the area was known as Peckham Rye, which originally only referred to the River Peck, 'rye' meaning watercourse in Old English. Peckham Rye Common was for centuries used as a deer park, though local people had common rights.

When the Lord of the Manor of Camberwell Friern proposed to develop the land in 1868, Peckham Rye Common was purchased by Camberwell Vestry to ensure that it remained a public open space. The land that comprises Peckham Rye Park was in turn purchased by

> **Peckham Rye also has an Arboretum, a lake, a nature garden, an adventure play area and a café, while sports facilities include soccer pitches, a skate park, a bowling green and an outdoor gym with state-of-the-art equipment.**

the Metropolitan Board of Works in 1882, and in 1890 the adjacent Homestall Farm was bought, and Peckham Rye Park was created and opened in 1894. The park had an artificial lake with island and bankside walks, rock and water gardens, an American garden, a Japanese garden and an ornamental old English Garden, later renamed the 'Sexby Garden' after Colonel J. J. Sexby, the LCC's first Chief Officer of Parks. The park was redeveloped in 1936 and the paths re-laid with York stone paving.

As with many London parks, Peckham Rye was rundown and neglected after WWII and wasn't restored to its former splendour until 2004-5 with funding from the Heritage Lottery Fund and Southwark Council. The formal Sexby Garden remains at its centre, containing a wide variety of plants and shrubs, rose pergolas, fountains and benches. The park also contains a Japanese garden featuring a series of stream fed ponds, with Japanese plants and shrubs, and a Japanese bridge and shelter. The park has been awarded Green Flag status annually since 2007.

 Beautiful green spaces in south London

Address: Wallington, SM6 (☎ 020-8770 5000/4781 (manor tours), 🖳 www.sutton.gov.uk/index.aspx?articleid=3869 and www.friendsofbeddingtonpark.co.uk).

Opening hours: Park has unrestricted access; Carew Manor is open for tours of the great hall and dovecote (booking necessary) on certain days (see website).

Cost: Free. Manor tours, £4.50.

Transport: Hackbridge rail station or car.

Sir Nicholas Carew

BEDDINGTON PARK & CAREW MANOR

*B*eddington Park was originally part of the deer park attached to Carew Manor (Grade I listed), which was once a major country house. The *Domesday Book* (1086) mentions two Beddington estates, which were united by Nicholas Carew to form Carew Manor in 1381. The family reached its zenith in the Tudor period, when the park occupied almost all the land between today's Mitcham Common, Beddington Lane, Croydon Road and London Road. Sir Nicholas Carew was one of Henry III's young favourites and a member of Henry's Privy Chamber.

The Manor of Beddington remained in the Carew family until Sir Nicholas Carew was executed for treason in March 1539. His lands were seized and returned to the Crown but his son, Sir Francis Carew, was later restored to his inheritance by Mary I. The home was rebuilt in its present form in around 1709 and another Nicholas Carew added two extra wings. Unfortunately, a fire shortly after destroyed much of the interior. By the mid-18th century the fortunes of the Carew family had declined and most of the northern part of the park had been converted into fields. The manor was home to the Royal Female Orphanage Asylum from 1762 until 1968 and now contains council offices and Carew Manor School.

At the beginning of the 18th century, a long canal-like lake was created in front of Carew Manor, with avenues of trees along either side. The southern part survived as a deer park until the Carew estate was sold in 1859. Shortly after, the park was acquired by Canon Alexander Henry Bridges, the wealthy rector of Beddington, who filled in the long lake and replaced the avenue of trees along it. He carried out a great deal of planting and most of the older trees in the park date from this time.

Carew Manor's banqueting hall survives from the original house and boasts a splendid hammerbeam roof. The house also contains a collection of fine period furniture, antiques and works of art. Part of the orangery built by Sir Francis Carew, claimed to be the first in England, also survives, along with an early 18th-century dovecote (Grade II* listed).

> In about 1591, Sir Walter Raleigh secretly, and without royal permission, married Elizabeth Throckmorton of Carew Manor, one of Elizabeth I's maids of honour, for which he was imprisoned in the Tower of London.

 A splendid park and 14th-century manor house

Address: Old Palace Road, Croydon CR0 1AX (☎ 01883-742969, 🖳 www.friendsofoldpalace.org).

Opening hours: Only open for tours (2 hrs) on certain days – see website for information. Bookings are unnecessary except for groups of ten or more. Also open (free) during Open House London weekend (see 🖳 www.londonopenhouse.org).

Cost: Adults £7 (includes tea and cake), concessions £6, children aged under 16, £3.

Transport: Tramlink to Church Street or train to East or West Croydon station.

CROYDON (OLD) PALACE

*C*roydon Palace – now known as the Old Palace – is a spectacular surviving 15th-century palace that was the summer residence of the Archbishops of Canterbury for over 500 years. Nowadays the buildings comprise part of the Old Palace School, an independent girls' school of the Whitgift Foundation.

The manor of Croydon was connected with the Archbishop of Canterbury from at least the late Saxon period, and records of buildings date back to before 960. The palace as it now exists is a group of largely 15th- and 16th-century buildings. The 15th-century Great Hall – thought to have been installed by Archbishop Stafford (d 1452) – has a late 14th-century, two-storey porch and a vaulted ceiling to the lower chamber. The hall interior has a rich 16th-century timber roof and windows with interesting features such as the late Gothic interior porch. The hall was partially remodelled in the 17th century by Archbishops Laud and Juxon, who also rebuilt the chapel.

West of the hall are the state apartments, including the first-floor guard room, now the school library. The room is ascribed to Archbishop Arundel (Archbishop 1396-1414), and has an arch-braced roof with carved stone supports and an oriel window. Other rooms have later panelling and fireplaces. The chapel contains fine 17th-century stalls and an elaborate corner gallery; the altar rails are now in the guard room. The exterior of the whole palace is stone or red brick, with early stone windows or Georgian sash windows.

The relationship between Croydon and the Archbishops was of great importance, several of whom were local benefactors. Six are buried in Croydon Minster, neighbouring the Palace: John Whitgift, Edmund Grindal, Gilbert Sheldon, William Wake, John Potter and Thomas Herring.

By the late 18th century, Croydon Palace had become dilapidated and uncomfortable and the local area was squalid. An Act of Parliament enabled it to be sold and Addington Palace (on the outskirts of Croydon) to be purchased in 1807, which became the new Episcopal summer residence for much of the rest of the 19th century.

> **Archbishop Whitgift, who first called it a 'palace', liked Croydon for "the sweetness of the place". However, not everyone admired Croydon Palace; Henry III found the low-lying site "rheumatick", a place where he could not stay "without sickness", while Sir Francis Bacon thought it "an obscure and darke place" surrounded by its dense woodland.**

 A rare, surviving 15th-century Archbishop's palace

Address: **Level 1, Croydon Clocktower, Katharine Street, Croydon, CR9 1ET** (☎ **020-8253 1022**, 🖥 **www.museumofcroydon.com**).

Opening hours: **Mon-Sat, 11am to 5pm, including most Bank Holidays (but check).**

Cost: **Free.**

Transport: **East Croydon rail station and Tramlink to George Street.**

MUSEUM OF CROYDON

*T*he Museum of Croydon is an appealing local museum situated within the Croydon Clocktower arts facility. The Museum opened in 2006 and showcases historical and stylish artefacts associated with the borough of Croydon. The majestic Croydon Clocktower (Grade II listed) is part of the original town hall and library complex, built in 1892-96.

The Museum comprises an eclectic collection, including the Croydon art collection containing over 2,000 paintings, prints and drawings. Depictions of local scenes and landmarks are stored alongside prints by Henry Moore and Bridget Riley and paintings by Bengali poet Rabindranath Tagore. The social history collection includes items used by Croydon residents from around 1800 to the present day.

The Museum also houses pottery and glass from late 19th- and 20th-century excavations on the site of Croydon Saxon cemetery, plus a collection of historical objects designed to be handled by visitors, used in education sessions to help people learn about life in the past. It also has an oral history collection, containing some 500 interviews with people who lived and worked in Croydon.

> **The Museum includes the story of black composer Samuel Coleridge-Taylor (1875-1912), who lived most of his short and tragically curtailed life in Croydon.**

The Museum's highlight is the stunning Riesco Collection of Chinese Ceramics, donated to the people of Croydon by local businessman Raymond Riesco. The whole collection – numbering some 230 items dating from the pre-Tang period to the Qing dynasty (2,500 BC to the 18th century) – is on permanent display in the Riesco Gallery. It includes around 180 porcelain items, 30 pieces of Chinese stoneware and 20 earthenware items, consisting mostly of high quality vessels, such as wine and tea cups and snuff bottles, and figures including grave goods and religious statues, mostly made for the Chinese (rather than the export) market.

The priceless collection features beautiful colours and fabulous decoration, including blue and white porcelain, famille verte, famille rose, Chinese Imari and celadon. Star items include an 1,800-year-old earthenware water pot made to look like a toad and radiant yellow pieces which belonged to the Chinese Emperor. There are regular temporary exhibitions in the Riesco gallery on the themes of ceramics and Chinese culture, many of which showcase outreach, community and education projects inspired by the collection.

The Museum of Croydon is an educational and fun place to spend a few hours. There's also a café and bar.

 Discover a stunning Chinese ceramics collection

Address: **Monks Orchard Road, Beckenham, BR3 3BX (☏ 020-3228 4227, 🖥 www.bethlemheritage.org.uk).**

Opening hours: **Mon-Fri, 9.30am to 4.30pm (archive by appointment) and selected Saturdays. Confirm before visiting as the museum was being re-housed in late 2012. Closed Bank Holidays and other (NHS) statutory holidays, plus 24th December to 2nd January.**

Cost: **Free.**

Transport: **Eden Park or West Wickham rail station.**

BETHLEM ROYAL HOSPITAL MUSEUM

*T*he Bethlem Royal Hospital Museum is the fascinating museum of the ancient Bethlem Royal Hospital – a psychiatric hospital variously known as St Mary Bethlehem, Bethlem Hospital, Bethlehem Hospital and Bedlam – now located in Beckenham. Although no longer based at its original location, Bethlem Royal Hospital is recognised as the world's first and oldest institution to specialise in mental illnesses.

Bethlem has been a part of London since 1247, first as a priory for the sisters and brethren of the Order of the Star of Bethlehem, from where the building took its name. Its first site was in Bishopsgate, where Liverpool Street station now stands. In 1337 it became a hospital which admitted some mentally ill patients from 1357, but it didn't become a dedicated psychiatric hospital until later.

> **In the 18th century people used to go to 'Bedlam' to stare at the lunatics. For a penny one could peer into their cells, view the freaks of the 'show of Bethlehem' and laugh at their antics.**

Early 16th-century maps show Bethlem, next to Bishopsgate, as a courtyard with a few stone buildings, a church and a garden. Conditions were consistently dreadful, with care amounting to little more than restraint, and the hospital became infamous for the brutal ill-treatment meted out to the mentally ill. In 1675, Bethlem moved to a magnificent new Baroque building in Moorfields designed by Robert Hooke, which provided better facilities and more spacious accommodation.

Eighteenth-century Bethlem was famously portrayed in a scene from William Hogarth's *A Rake's Progress* (1735), the story of a rich merchant's son whose immoral living causes him to end up in Bethlem. In 1815, the hospital moved to St George's Fields, Southwark, to buildings designed by James Lewis (part of which is now the Imperial War Museum). Bethlem moved to its present site in 1930.

Since 1970, there has been a Museum at Bethlem Royal Hospital that records the lives and experiences, and celebrates the achievements, of those with mental health problems. It includes items from the hospital's art collection, which specialises in work by artists who suffered from mental health problems, including former Bethlem patients William Kurelek, Richard Dadd, Vaslav Nijinsky and Louis Wain. Other notable exhibits include a pair of statues by Caius Gabriel Cibber, known as *Raving and Melancholy Madness*, from the gates of 17th-century Bethlem Hospital, 18th- and 19th-century furniture and alms boxes, restraint devices and archive documents dating back to the 16th century.

 A unique and beguiling small museum

Address: Mary Ann Gardens, SE8 3DP (☎ 020-8692 7449).

Opening hours: **Contact church for visiting and services times.**

Cost: **Free (but donations are welcome).**

Transport: **Deptford or New Cross rail station.**

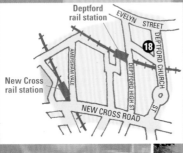

ST PAUL'S, DEPTFORD

*S*t Paul's, Deptford (Grade I listed) is an exuberant 18th-century church and one of London's finest Baroque parish churches, designed by Thomas Archer (1668-1743) – the architect of St John's Smith Square – and built between 1712 and 1730. It was one of 50 churches that were planned by the New Church Commissioners, though only 12 were actually constructed. A pupil of Sir John Vanbrugh, Archer adopted a robust classical style inspired by Baroque churches in Rome. The plan form, in the shape of a Greek cross, is based on an ideal church plan prepared by Vanbrugh.

The church is built of Portland stone and is almost square, raised on a crypt that is mostly above ground, thus requiring a flight of stairs to enter. The most unusual feature of the building is the circular tower with a steeple, around which is wrapped a semi-circular portico (believed to be copied from St Maria della Pace in Rome) of four giant Tuscan columns. The body of the church is approximately square in plan, with two additional side entrances in the middle of the walls, each approached by a grand staircase. The east wall has a projecting apse.

The interior is spectacular and theatrical, with two side aisles each separated by two giant Corinthian columns, which continue as attached columns on the other walls. There are side galleries supported by the giant columns, with an organ gallery above the entrance. The east window is in the form of a Venetian window following the curve of the apse, the latter being divided by small Tuscan columns. Four private pews. like Royal boxes, protrude from each corner on columns.

> **Architectural expert Nikolaus Pevsner said that St Paul's "came closer to Borromini and the Roman Baroque than any other English church of this date", an opinion echoed by Simon Jenkins (*England's Thousand Best Churches*) when he said, "it's the kind of building foreigners can never credit to the English".**

By the early '90s, the church and churchyard had fallen into disrepair and the north and south staircases to the podium were partially buried. In 1997, the Heritage Lottery Fund awarded the largest grant ever given to a parish church (just over £3m), which enabled the church to be restored. It was re-dedicated in a special service led by the Bishop of London on 1st October 2004.

 A pearl in the heart of Deptford

London Sketchbook

ISBN: 978-1-907339-37-0

Jim Watson

London Sketchbook is a unique guide to the most celebrated landmarks of one of the world's major cities. In ten easy walks it takes you on a fascinating journey around the most famous of London's huge variety of vistas, with identification of the panoramic views and relevant historical background along the way.

Jim Watson's illustration technique is traditional line and wash, but his approach is that of a curious neighbour, seeking out the scenes which give each area its individual character – while keeping a keen eye open for the quirky and unusual.

INDEX

Where to Live in London

ISBN: 978-1-907339-13-4

David Hampshire & Graeme Chesters

Essential reading for newcomers planning to live in London, containing detailed surveys of all 33 boroughs including property prices and rental costs, schools, health services, shopping, social services, crime rates, public transport, parking, leisure facilities, local taxes, places of worship and much more. Interest in living in London and investing in property in London has never been higher, both from Britons and foreigners.

£15.95

Living and Working in London

ISBN: 978-1-907339-31-8

Graeme Chesters & David Hampshire

Living and Working in London, is essential reading for anyone planning to live or work in London and the most up-to-date source of practical information available about everyday life. It's guaranteed to hasten your introduction to the British way of life, and, most importantly, will save you time, trouble and money! The best-selling and most comprehensive book about living and working in London since it was first published in 1999, containing up to twice as much information as some similar books.

£14.95

PHOTO

Flickr

Pages 14 (top), 18 (main), 24 (bottom), 26 (top, bottom right), 28 (bottom left), 30, 32 (all), 34 (all), 36 (top, bottom), 40 (centre, bottom left), 50 (all), 54 (all), 56 (right), 66 (top), 70 (all), 74 (all), 76 (bottom two), 78 (main), 80 (bottom right), 82 (bottom two), 84 (small), 86 (all), 88 (top, bottom right), 90 (top two, bottom left), 92 (all), 94 (all), 100 (all), 102 (all), 104 (all), 108 (bottom left), 110 (main, centre & bottom left), 114 (all), 116 (top right, bottom left), 120 (all), 122 (bottom), 124 (top left and right, bottom left), 130 (top), 132 (centre & bottom), 134 (bottom), 136 (bottom two), 142 (bottom left & right), 144 (top & bottom right), 146 (top), 148 (top), 150 (all), 152 (bottom left), 154 (all), 162 (top two), 164 (bottom two), 166 (bottom right), 172 (centre), 174 (bottom left), 176 (top), 178 (main), 180 (bottom), 184 (all), 186 (bottom left & right), 192 (all), 200 (top), 202 (all), 204 (top), 206 (top), 208 (top & bottom left), 212 (all), 218 (middle), 220 (all), 224 (bottom), 230 (bottom left & right), 234 (centre), 236 (main), 238 (top right & bottom), 242 (main, bottom left & right), 246 (bottom), 254 (top & bottom), 260 (top & bottom), 262 (top & bottom right), 266 (all), 268 (bottom), 270 (bottom), 276 (bottom), 278 (bottom), 280 (bottom), 282 (top), 286 (all), 288 (bottom left), 296 (all), 298 (bottom right), 300 (bottom left), 302 (top right), 306 (bottom), 310 (all)

Wikipedia

Pages 14 (bottom), 16 (centre), 26 (bottom left), 38 (all), 42 (top), 48 (top right, bottom left), 52 (bottom right), 56 (main), 82 (top), 88 (bottom left), 90 (bottom right), 106 (main), 126 (top right), 138 (top), 164 (top), 172 (bottom), 174 (top), 176 (bottom left), 180 (top), 208 (top right), 216 (all), 240 (top), 250 (centre), 254 (main), 268 (centre), 278 (top), 280 (top), 282 (bottom left & right), 302 (top left),

Miscellaneous

Pages 1 © English Heritage, 10 © Chester Tugwell, 16 (top, bottom) © BDA, 18 (bottom) © 121buildings.com, 20 (all) © The Photographers' Gallery, 22 (all) © HOSB, 24 (top) © broadwayworld.com, 28 (main, bottom right) © Two Temple Place, 36 (centre) © marthafleming.net, 40 (top) © garshol.priv. no, 42 (bottom) © ticketsinventory.com, 44 (top) © islingtontribune.com, 44 (bottom) © gallery.nen.gov.uk, 46 (top) © sternbergclarke.co.uk, (top right) © avocadosweet.com, (bottom left) © loveartscotland.com, (bottom right) © dorotheasharp.blogspot.com, 48 (top left) © ibtimes.com, (bottom right) © lostsplendor.tumblr.com, 52 (main) © www.britainonview.com, (left) © london-attractions.info, 56 (left) © Methodist Central Hall, 58 (top) © elsalondon. org, (bottom left) © cliftonchambers.co.nz, (bottom right) © kindersleystudio. co.uk, 60 (top right) © patrickbaty.co.uk, (centre) © venues-london.co.uk, (bottom) © englishconcertsingers.co.uk, 62 (all) © Serpentine Gallery, 64 (top) © e-architect.co.uk, (bottom) © nationwidevehiclecontracts.co.uk, 66 (top left) © artfund.org, (bottom) © london-traveltips.com, 72 (all) © Barbican Centre, 76 (top) © joannadobson.wordpress.com, 78 (top left) © City of London Police Museum, (top right) © thelondonphile.com, 80 (top and bottom left) © Drapers' Hall, 84 (main) © philipparandles.blogspot.com, 96 © Watermen's Hall, 106 (top right) © wildlifeandlandscapes.blogspot.com, (top left) © Natural History Museum, 106 (top two, bottom right) © Institut Français, 110 (top left) © victorianweb.org, 112 (all) © Royal Court Theatre, 116 (top left, bottom right)

CREDITS

London's Secret Walks
Explore the City's Hidden Places

ISBN: 978-1-907339-51-6, 320 pages

Graeme Chesters

A walking guide with a difference, that takes you off the beaten tourist track to explore the city's secret and enigmatic side, and discover its lesser-known (but no less fascinating) sights. Discover the city's hidden ancient buildings, secret gardens, beautiful and poignant sculptures and monuments, bizarre street art and trivia, ancient pubs, historic shops, and much, much more.

Contains 25 walks from Putney to Spitalfields, Paddington to Borough, Kensington to Clerkenwell, taking in most of central London. **Printed in colour.**

£11.95

London's Secrets:
Museums & Galleries

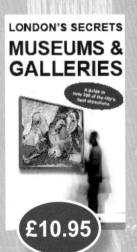

ISBN: 978-907339-96-7, 320 pages

Robbi Atilgan & David Hampshire

London is a treasure trove for museum fans and art lovers and one of the world's great art and cultural centres, with more popular museums and galleries than any other world city. The art scene is a lot like the city itself – diverse, vast, vibrant and in a constant state of flux – a cornucopia of traditional and cutting-edge, majestic and mundane, world-class and run-of-the-mill, bizarre and brilliant. From old masters to street art and everything in between, London has it all in spades – not just great national collections but a wealth of smaller 'secret' museums and galleries. And best of all, most of them offer free entry!

So, whether you're an art lover, a culture vulture, a history buff or just looking for something to entertain the family during the school holidays, you're sure to find inspiration in London. All you need is a comfortable pair of shoes, an open mind – and this book! **Printed in colour.**

£10.95